The Police:

Six Sociological Essays

The Police:

Six Sociological Essays

Edited by

David J. Bordua

Associate Professor of Sociology
University of Illinois

John Wiley & Sons, Inc. New York · London · Sydney

This book is part of a group of publications on organizations and professions prepared in conjunction with the work of the Center for Social Organization Studies, University of Chicago, under the direction of Morris Janowitz. One book is entitled *The New Military: Changing Patterns of Organization*, 1965; the second volume deals with *The Nursing Profession: Five Sociological Essays*, 1966, edited by Fred Davis. Another book on *Innovation in Mass Education* is in preparation by David Street, University of Chicago.

10 9 8 7 6

Library of Congress Catalog Card Number: 66-29624

Printed in the United States of America

ISBN 0 471 08891 9

List of Contributors

DAVID J. BORDUA is Associate Professor of Sociology, University of Illinois. He has published on juvenile delinquency, authoritarianism, mobility aspirations of high school students, and police command and control processes. He is currently studying police control of juveniles.

JOHN H. McNAMARA is Director of Research and Evaluation, Economic Opportunity Commission of Santa Clara County, San Jose, California. He has published papers on alcoholism, urban contact patterns and scalogram analysis. He is currently conducting research on poverty.

IRVING PILIAVIN is Associate Professor, School of Social Welfare; Associate Research Analyst, Survey Research Center and Research Associate, Center for the Study of Law and Society, University of California at Berkeley. He has published on delinquency causation, police-juvenile encounters, and organizational conflict in correctional institutions. He is currently initiating studies of the behavior of witnesses to crimes.

ALBERT J. REISS, JR. is Professor and Chairman, Department of Sociology and Director of the Center for Research on Social Organization, University of Michigan. His many books and articles include works on urban sociology, occupational status, deviant behavior, police command and control processes, and research methodology. He is currently engaged in studies of the organization and operation of large municipal police systems.

ALLAN SILVER is Assistant Professor of Sociology, Columbia University. He is coauthor (with R. T. McKenzie) of a forthcoming book on working-class Conservatism in urban England. He is currently working on studies of elite perspectives toward military repression and legislative reform in nineteenth-century England and (with Jack Ladinsky) of popular democracy and judicial independence in Wisconsin.

JEROME H. SKOLNICK is Associate Research Sociologist, Center for the Study of Law and Society, University of California at Berkeley. He has published on the sociology of law, the consequences of legal stigma, and the sociological theory of parole. He is the author of a sociological analysis of municipal police operations, *Justice Without Trial: Law Enforcement in Democratic Society*, 1966.

CARL WERTHMAN is Assistant Professor of Sociology and Research Associate at the Center for the Study of Law and Society, University of California at Berkeley. He has written on juvenile delinquency and housing and is the author of a forthcoming book on delinquent gangs. He is currently studying the relations of social planning and social class.

JAMES Q. WILSON is Associate Professor of Government at Harvard. From 1963 to 1966 he was the Director of the Joint Center for Urban Studies of M.I.T. and Harvard. Professor Wilson is the author of *Negro Politics: The Search for Leadership*, 1960; *The Amateur Democrat: Club Politics in Three Cities*, 1962; (with Edward C. Banfield) *City Politics*, 1963; and editor, *Urban Renewal: The Record and the Controversy*, 1966. He has written numerous articles on urban affairs, minority groups, the police, and political parties.

J. RICHARD WOODWORTH is a graduate student and National Institute of Mental Health Fellow, University of California at Berkeley. He has written on the social control of sexual behavior and the role relationships of prosecuting attorneys. He is currently doing research relating moral consensus, agency sharing of dossiers, and law enforcement.

Preface

As the initial chapter by Allen Silver indicates, the establishment of the modern uniformed police constituted a recognition that coercive social control could not remain in the hands of nonspecialists; a recognition that the maintenance of social integration required an organizational deployment of coercion which defined all citizens as worthy of protection; a recognition that the maintenance of order required the substitution of law for politics and the substitution of the daily efforts of police for the occasional and overreactive use of military force. Thus victims and offenders would not be ranged against each other as estranged enemies but as common members of a civic community. Development of modern police has necessitated innovations in organization and in legal control of police. Such innovations continue, and it is these continuing changes in police practice and organizational structure, as adaptations to changes in the urban community and to changes in legal control of both populace and police, that constitute the focus of the second chapter by Albert J. Reiss, Jr., and David J. Bordua.

Chief among the contemporary developments in the urban community to which the police must adapt is the rising demand of the Negro population for the fruits of legal equality and civil dignity. This means in the terms of the Reiss and Bordua chapter that the police decreasingly respect the private dispute settling arrangements among some lower-class Negroes. Crime is so prevalent in some Negro ghettos as to constitute a significant and deep-rooted subculture. The price of civic inclusion, here as everywhere, is a forced modification of subcultural practice in the interest of more uniform legal protection. Correlatively while the police, activating existing law, respond to the demand for better police protection, the Negro population demands better protection from the police. Equal protection by the state and equal protection from the state must go hand in hand.

In this context the investigation by Carl Werthman and Irving Piliavin of contacts between police and Negro gang boys in a large western city indicates that the goals of effective law enforcement and effective respect for the citizenry are, as always, difficult to achieve. They are especially difficult when segments of the populace that are partly excluded from the civic community organize themselves specifically as antagonists to the police and sustain their morale by such antagonism.

The difficulty presented by the trend toward progressive civic inclusion of Negroes is not the only development treated in these chapters that has implications for the future. The greater efficiency and organizational sophistication of the police is part of a general bureaucratization of social service and social control in an ever more complex and urbanized society. The chapter by J. Richard Woodworth and Jerome Skolnick warns of some possible consequences of this increasing organizational and interorganizational sophistication. With efficient welfare and police services which work more closely together American society must confront the fact that inefficiency and lack of cooperation can no longer be relied upon to soften the impact of legal regulation.

It is particularly appropriate that Woodworth and Skolnick raise this problem in connection with the enforcement of one of the more ambiguous areas of law. The description of the handling of statutory rape complaints indicates that for all the modernization of police practice which has occurred in the last few decades, much of the business of the police is still to serve as the general cleanup squad for a society whose zeal for creating laws is not always matched with the same willingness to accept their implications.

Police organization has changed unevenly, but markedly, in American municipalities. One way of describing this change has been to use the term professionalization. Police professionalization means many things. One is an increasing effectiveness of internal control, management and deployment with use of skilled management and computer systems specialists, often civilians. Another is a greater emphasis on both pre-employment education and in-service training, often of university level. But professionalization also means a transformation of the organizational base for occupational honor, a transformation which sometimes occurs in the form of crisis-produced reform. The chapter by James Q. Wilson indicates that professionalization may deal with the key problem of police perception of public disrespect by decreasing the relevance of public opinion and heightening the capacity of police organization itself to be a source of police self-respect.

Professionalization of the police heightens the significance not only of the substantive law but also of the law governing the police themselves. Monitoring the legality of police behavior has traditionally been a function of the courts in the United States and recent decisions of the United States Supreme Court regarding search and seizure, interrogation, and right to counsel may foreshadow even greater change in this area of law.

More significant perhaps than these court decisions is an increasing recognition in legal and other circles that traditional court regulation of the police through reversal of convictions or refusal to convict may be inadequate. With the highly fragmented police system of the United States, the seemingly simple matter of transmitting new court rulings in a form usable by departments and individual officers is a difficult job. New developments in training and regulating the police include suggestions for provision of better legal training services, foundation grants to improve police administration, and federal grants-in-aid under provisions of the Law Enforcement Assistance Act.[1]

It is not likely that these changes alone will produce everywhere in the United States the standards of police efficiency and legality that prevail in the best departments. Local political and social forces, however, can interact with the professional standards of local departments to produce high quality even under otherwise adverse conditions. This fact is dramatically illustrated in the public statement of the chief of police of Greenville, Mississippi, during the "long hot summer" of civil rights agitation in 1964 when other departments in the state were displaying something less than legality and restraint.[2]

> The issue with us is not which race assaults the other, but rather the idea of professional law enforcement. We intend to enforce the laws of the state and city as written without regard to one's station in life. This is the only way that peace and order can be obtained and continued.

All these conditions—professional, organizational, communal, legal—ultimately affect the ways in which police departments recruit

[1] For a thorough discussion of these new developments see Wayne R. La Fave, "Improving Police Performance through the Exclusionary Rule—Part I: Current Police and Local Court Practices," *Missouri Law Review*, Vol. 30, (1965), pp. 391–458. Also the same author's paper, "Improving Police Performance Through the Exclusionary Rule—Part II: Defining the Norms and Training the Police," *Missouri Law Review*, Vol. 30, (1965), pp. 566–610.

[2] Chief William C. Burnley is quoted in James W. Silver, *Mississippi; The Closed Society* (enlarged edition), Harvest Books, Harcourt, Brace and World, New York, 1966, p. 357 fn.

and train new officers and the ways in which new men learn to perform the complex role of policemen. The chapter by John H. McNamara focuses on the uncertainties of the police role and the processes of recruitment and training which determine the degree of fit between the men, their training, and the demands of the job. It seems especially appropriate that the volume should include a chapter on the New York City Police Department, since it was there that the modern municipal police system began in the United States.

Recent controversy in New York and elsewhere over proposed civilian review boards, greater minority group representation among police and the propriety of police membership in the John Birch Society perhaps indicates that, having partly conquered the politics of patronage and corruption, the police may now face a new politics of racial progress on the one hand and ideological penetration on the other.[3]

As this volume goes to press the nation is reacting to the riots in Negro ghettos of many cities during the Summer of 1966. Widespread use of National Guard troops demonstrated that the American municipal police, though increasingly skilled at riot control, are not basically designed as a military force to suppress armed disorder. The summer's events further demonstrate that effective police work of a more routine nature can be severely hampered when the police become the focus of major social conflict. With the cry of "black power" being countered by talk of a rising "white backlash" the role of the police becomes ever more difficult. Firmness and fairness on the part of the police will be needed in addition to an improved capacity to provide better law enforcement while simultaneously reducing avoidable provocation.

The larger society moreover has an even greater responsibility to remove the underlying sources of unrest so that the police role can be reduced to its proper scope. The police will be under great pressure to become antagonists from the one side and hired oppressors from the other. The ideal of professional law enforcement will be imperiled if social support for evenhandedness and legality disappears. It seems more than ever that the professional commitments of police at all levels will be a valuable resource during what may be a considerable period of racial antagonism.

The chapters in this volume reflect a growing and more sympathetic interest in the police among sociologists and other scholars. Recent

[3] Thomas R. Brooks, "The Finest Could Be Finer," *The New York Times Magazine,* April 3, 1966, p. 281; J. P. McFadden, "Who Will Protect the Police," *National Review,* April 5, 1966, p. 311.

works by social scientists and others, along with a selection of older publications, are listed in the Selected Bibliography, which concludes the volume. Scholarly interest combined with new Federal Government research support through the Office of Law Enforcement Assistance and the continued activity of other public agencies and private foundations should mean a large increase in research and writing on the police in the near future.

This rather new willingness to study police problems and organization should enable sociologists to improve their understanding of social order and social change. It should also enable them to contribute in some measure to the solution of the difficult problems that will continue to confront American communities and their police.

David J. Bordua

November 1966
Urbana, Illinois

Acknowledgements

The editor of a volume such as this owes most to the authors themselves. I would like to take this opportunity to express my appreciation for their patience as well as their more visible contributions. In addition I would like to thank Morris Janowitz for his continuing encouragement and assistance. Mrs. Jane Gottschalk rendered valuable aid with the job of editing the manuscripts, as did Thomas Smith in helping to compile the Bibliography. Finally I would like to thank the Center For Advanced Study In the Behavioral Sciences where I was a Fellow when work on the volume was begun.

David J. Bordua

Contents

The Demand for Order in Civil Society: A Review of Some Themes in the History of Urban Crime, Police, and Riot*

Allan Silver

CRIMINALS AND THE "DANGEROUS CLASSES"

Crime and violence in the life of city dwellers have long evoked complaints which have a quite contemporary tone. Peaceful and propertied people in eighteenth-century London, for example, confronted a level of daily danger to which they and their spokesmen reacted indignantly. It was in such terms that Daniel Defoe dedicated a pamphlet on crime to the Lord Mayor of London:

> The Whole City, My Lord, is alarm'd and uneasy; Wickedness has got such a Head, and the Robbers and Insolence of the Night are such, that the Citizens are no longer secure within their own Walls, or safe even in passing their Streets, but are robbed, insulted and abused, even at their own Doors. . . . The Citizens . . . are oppressed by Rapin and Violence; Hell seems to have let loose Troops of human D——ls upon them; and such Mischiefs are done within the Bounds of your Government as never were practised here before (at least not to such a degree) and which, if suffered to go on, will call for Armies, not Magistrates, to suppress.[1]

* I want to thank Daniel Bell, Burton Fisher, Robert Fogelson, Morris Janowitz, and Jack Ladinsky for their comments on an earlier version. I am indebted to the Russell Sage Foundation's Program in Law and Sociology at the University of Wisconsin for the leisure and stimulus to consider, among other matters, the issues discussed in this paper.

[1] *An Effectual Scheme for the Immediate Prevention of Street Robberies and Suppressing of all other Disorders of the Night; with a Brief History of the Night-houses and an Appendix Relating to those Sons of Hell call'd Incendiaries* (London, 1730).

In the body of his pamphlet, Defoe describes a situation of pervasive insecurity, stressing the mounting and unprecedented extent of criminal attack. The idea of crime wave is already quite explicit:

> Violence and Plunder is no longer confin'd to the Highways. . . . The Streets of the City are now the Places of Danger; men are knock'd down and robb'd, nay, sometimes murther'd at their own Doors, and in passing and repassing but from House to House, or from Shop to Shop. Stagecoaches are robb'd in High-Holbourn, White-Chappel, Pall-Mall, Soho and at almost all the Avenues of the City. Hackney-Coaches and Gentlemen's Coaches are stopt in Cheapside, St. Paul's Church-yard, the Strand, and other the most crowded streets, and that even while the People in Throngs are passing and repassing . . . 'Tis hard that in a well-govern'd City . . . it should be said that her Inhabitants are not now safe. . . .[2]

We may note in passing that equally contemporary themes richly abound in magazines that urban Americans read six decades ago. To cite but two examples:

> Individual crimes have increased in number and malignity. In addition to this . . . a wave of general criminality has spread over the whole nation. . . . The times are far from hard, and prosperity for several years has been wide-spread in all classes. Large sums are in unaccustomed hands, bar-rooms are swarming, pool-rooms, policy shops and gambling houses are full, the races are played, licentiousness increases, the classes who "roll in wealth" set intoxicating examples of luxury and recklessness, and crime has become rampant.[3]

In that period, it was, of course, commonplace also to ascribe the fundamental causes of mass criminality to large-scale immigration:

> In the poorer quarters of our great cities may be found huddled together the Italian bandit and the bloodthirsty Spaniard, the bad man from Sicily, the Hungarian, the Croatian and the Pole, the Chinaman and the Negro, the cockney Englishman, the Russian and the Jew, with all the centuries of hereditary hate back of them. They continually cross each others' path. It is no wonder that altercations occur and blood is shed. . . .

[2] *Ibid.*, pp. 10–11.

[3] James M. Buckley, "The Present Epidemic of Crime," *The Century Magazine*, (November 1903), p. 150.

> We claim to be a rich and prosperous city and yet we cannot afford to employ enough policemen to keep thieves and burglars out of our houses and thugs and robbers from knocking us on the head as we walk along our own streets. . . . The bald, bare, horrible fact is that the conditions existing in Chicago today are the most criminal and damnable of any large city on the face of the earth.[4]

Thus the current rhetoric of concern about crime and violence draws on established motifs of both older and newer vintage: an indignant sense of pervasive insecurity; a mounting current of crime and violence as a result of both unaccustomed prosperity and prolonged poverty; the bad example of the self-indulgent wealthy; the violent proclivities of immigrants and other newcomers; and the ironic contrast between the greatness of the metropolis and the continued spread of crime.

But at times there was a somewhat different attitude toward urban crime and violence. In the London and Paris of the late eighteenth and the early nineteenth centuries, people often saw themselves as threatened by agglomerations of the criminal, vicious, and violent—the rapidly multiplying poor of cities whose size had no precedent in Western history. It was much more than a question of annoyance, indignation, or personal insecurity; the social order itself was threatened by an entity whose characteristic name reflects the fears of the time—the "dangerous classes." The phrase occurs repeatedly. Thus, an anonymous essayist of 1844 writes of the situation in urban England, where "destitution, profligacy, sensuality and crime, advance with unheard-of-rapidity in the manufacturing districts, and the dangerous classes there massed together combine every three or four years in some general strike or alarming insurrection which, while it lasts, excites universal terrors. . . . ,"[5] But even where the term is not explicitly invoked, the image persists—one of an unmanageable, volatile, and convulsively criminal class at the base of society.[6]

[4] James Edgar Brown, "The Increase of Crime in the United States," *The Independent* (April 11, 1907), pp. 832–33.

[5] "Causes of the Increase of Crime", *Blackwood's Magazine* (July 1844), p. 2. The phrase appears in another work published four years later, *The Communist Manifesto*—where, however, it is instantly interpreted in terms of the "lumpenproletariat" idea.

[6] Honoré Antoine Frégier, *Les Classes Dangereuses de la Population dans les Grandes Villes* (Paris, 1840) is a work often cited by contemporaries. A relevant modern work on Paris is Louis Chevalier's *Classes Laborieuses et Classes Dangereuses à Paris pendant la Première Moitié du XIX Siècle* (Paris, 1958).

This imagery is only in part the product of class antagonisms in early industrial society; rather, the working classes were included in an older and continuing concern with criminality.[7] Urban administrators regarded the swelling numbers of the poor as unmanageable. Indeed, the image of the "dangerous classes," as distinct from that of pervasive criminality, seems to have flourished especially during periods of very rapid population growth, reflecting the migration of the numerous poor, without employment skills or a history of urban life. During this period, the labor force of the metropolis was still not primarily industrial.[8] Thus, the events and antagonisms of early industrialism inflamed but did not create the image of the "dangerous classes." It referred primarily to the unattached and unemployed. An advocate of police reform in London, writing in 1821, defined the problem in these terms:

> The most superficial observer of the external and visible appearance of this town, must soon be convinced, that there is a large mass of unproductive population living upon it, without occupation or ostensible means of subsistence; and, it is notorious that hundreds and thousands go forth from day to day trusting alone to charity or rapine; and differing little from the barbarous hordes which traverse an uncivilized land. . . . The principle of [their] action is the same; their life is predatory; it is equally a war against society, and the object is alike to gratify desire by stratagem or force.[9]

In the Paris of that time, he writes, "le proliferation des classes dangereuses était . . . l'un des faits majeurs de l'existence quotienne de la capitale, l'un des grands problèmes de l'administration urbaine, l'une des principales préoccupations des tous, l'une des formes les plus incontestables de l'angoisse sociale." The city was one "où le crime a une importance et une signification que nous ne comprenons guère. . ." (pp. iii–iv).

[7] Influential books expressing this concern were Henry Fielding's *Enquiry into the Causes of the Late Increase of Robbers* (1751) and Patrick Colquhoun's *Treatise on the Police of the Metropolis* (1796). According to Chevalier (*op. cit.*, pp. 451–68), the Parisian bourgeoisie made little distinction between the "industrious" and the "dangerous" poor.

[8] According to the census, the population of London tripled in the first half of the nineteenth century. On its occupational composition, see the *Census of Great Britain in 1851* (London, 1854), p. 182, *passim.*

[9] George Mainwaring, *Observations on the Present State of the Police of the Metropolis* (London, 1821), pp. 4–5. The anonymous essayist of 1844, quoted above on the connection between the dangerous classes and the "manufacturing districts," went on to write: "In examining the classes of society from which the greater part of the crime comes, it will be found that at least three-fourths, probably nine-tenths, comes from the very lowest and most destitute. . . . If

As class tensions involving the threat of riot and revolutionary violence subsided in London, the older concern with diffuse criminality rather than the "dangerous classes" reemerged. Thus, Henry Mayhew's immense reportage on London's criminals, vagabonds, and casually employed, published in 1861, was suffused variously by moralism, indignation, pity, compassion, horror, and mere curiosity—but not by the sense of dread that had earlier afflicted those confronted by the dangerous classes.[10] Indeed, contemporary writing in midcentury London exhibits a sense of relief and victory over the forces of mass violence. Contrasting the present with the past, a writer in 1856 observed that "the only quarter in which any formidable riot could take place would be eastward, in the neighborhood of the docks, where there are at least twelve thousand sailors in the river or on shore, ready for a spree, fearless and powerful, and acting with an undoubted esprit de corps. These, if associated with the seven or eight thousand dock labourers and lightermen, would certainly produce a force difficult to cope with."[11] Such a prospect clearly was judged as a great improvement.

To judge from contemporary accounts, New York did not experience a comparable sense of relief or improvement. Indeed, it appears that by 1872 New York was already being compared unfavorably to London with respect to crime and violence:

> . . . If the vice and pauperism of New York are not so steeped in the blood of the populace [as in London and other European

---

we examine who it is that compose this dismal substratum, this hideous *black band of society,* we shall find that it is not made up of any one class more than another—not of factory workers more than labourers, carters or miners—but it is formed by an aggregate of the most unfortunate or improvident of *all classes. . . ." Blackwood's Magazine* (July 1844), p. 12 (italics in original).

[10] This was the fourth and final volume of *London Labour and the London Poor,* separately titled *Those That Will Not Work.*

[11] *London Quarterly Review* (July 1856), p. 94. Many observers, though still concerned with criminality, acknowledge a change for the better at this time. Remarking that accounts of the earlier situation in London "seem like tales of another country," a writer in 1852 went on to detail improvements: "No member of Parliament would now venture to say that it was dangerous to walk in the streets of London by day or night. . . . Bad as the dens of infamy in London still are, they are not to be compared with those older places of hideous profligacy. . . . In the most disorderly part of the town, such as St. Giles, Covent Garden, and Holborn, the streets every Sunday morning exhibited the most outrageous scenes of fighting, drunkenness and depravity. . . . Crimes, too, are greatly diminished in atrocity. The large gangs of desperate robbers, thirteen or fourteen in number, now no longer exist. . . ." *Edinburgh Review* (July 1858), p. 12–3.

> cities] they are even more dangerous. . . . They rob a bank, when English thieves pick pockets; they murder, where European prolétaires cudgel or fight with fists; in a riot they begin what seems about to be the sacking of a city, where English rioters merely batter policemen or smash lamps. . . .[12]

For this observer, whose book is largely concerned with relief and other remedial programs among New York's poor, the dangerous classes are very much a part of the city—which, after all, had only a decade earlier suffered the great Draft Riot of 1863:

> There are thousands upon thousands in New York who have no assignable home, and "flit" from attic to attic, and cellar to cellar; there are other thousands more or less connected with criminal enterprises; and still other tens of thousands, poor, hard-pressed. . . . Let but Law lift its hand from them for a season, or let the civilizing influences of American life fail to reach them, and, if the opportunity afforded, we should see an explosion from this class which might leave the city in ashes and blood.[13]

Such rhetoric is not, as we have seen, an inevitable expression of concern with criminality, riot, and violence—even when these were of an order unthinkable in daily urban life today.[14]

What are some of the factors that underlie relationships between urban criminality and disorder and the significance ascribed to them by the peaceful and propertied classes? An adequate answer to this question would need to consider important aspects of economic, political, and urban history, the labor movement, and demography. For our purposes, however, we will focus on two aspects of the situation that until recently have been neglected: the significance of the police and the culture of riotous protest.

THE POLICED SOCIETY

Some modern nations have been police states; all, however, are policed societies. Practical men have never underestimated, though

[12] Charles L. Brace, *The Dangerous Classes of New York* (New York, 1872), p. 26.

[13] *Ibid.*, p. 29.

[14] Thus, Defoe saw the intolerable conditions of his time as a result of the arrogance and bad influence of a rapidly increasing group of prostitutes and their "bullies"; and his solution was to disperse them by raids (*op. cit.*, pp. 26–32).

they have often distorted, the importance of the police. Sociological theory in the "social control" tradition, however, has usually slighted the police in favor of normative or voluntary processes.[15] The significance of the police, for our purposes, can best be understood as they appeared to a generation for whom modern police were an unprecedented innovation—Englishmen in the middle third of the nineteenth century.

The London police, created in 1829, were from the beginning a bureaucratic organization of professionals.[16] One of their tasks was to prevent crime by regularly patrolling beats, operating under strict rules which permitted individual discretion. The police also had a mission against the "dangerous classes" and political agitation in the form of mobs or riots. On all fronts they were so successful that initial and strong objections to them rapidly diminished; from being a considerable novelty, they quickly became a part of "British tradition."

[15] In the book which more than six decades ago named and founded this tradition, E. A. Ross was crisply aware of the expanding role of police: "In the field of physical coercion, there is an increase in the number of lictors, bailiffs, police, and soldiers told off to catch, prod, beat, and hold fast recalcitrants, and they are brought under a stricter discipline. They are more specialized for their work, and an *esprit de corps* is carefully cultivated among them." *Social Control* (New York, 1901), pp. 398–9. Furthermore, Ross was quite tough-minded about the cause of this development: "All this does not happen by simple fiat of the social will. Certain groups of persons—the executive, cabinet, the central government, the party machine, the higher clergy, the educational hierarchy, 'authorities' of every kind in short—are always striving for more power. When the need of a more stringent control makes itself felt, they find the barriers to their self-aggrandizement unexpectedly giving way before them. Formerly they were held in check, while now they find encroachment strangely easy" (*Ibid.*). Neither kind of emphasis survived the subsequent failure of works in social control to treat the characteristics of the policed society in a comprehensive way or to see organized and legitimate coercion as intrinsic to social control. (Representative treatises are L. L. Bernard, *Social Control,* New York, 1939, and Richard T. LaPiere, *A Theory of Social Control,* New York, 1954.) Ross himself distinguished between the normative processes of "public opinion"—uniquely flexible, preventive, and ubiquitous—and the coercive effects of "law"—which were clumsy, retrospective, and remote (*op. cit.*, pp. 89–105). Important and influential as this distinction is, it tends to obscure—as we shall see—some of the distinctive features of policed society. Recent attempts to incorporate civil violence in the framework of social theory are included in *Internal War,* Harry Eckstein, ed. (New York, 1964), especially the essays by Eckstein, Parsons, and Feldman.

[16] Useful accounts of British police history are the writings of Charles Reith, especially *The Police Idea* (1938), *British Police and the Democratic Ideal* (1943), *The Blind Eye of History* (1952), and *A New Study of Police History* (1956). See also F. C. Mather, *Public Order in the Age of the Chartists* (Manchester, 1959). Like most contributors to the English literature on "public order," these writers—especially Reith—work from palpably conservative assumptions.

The policed society is unique in that central power exercises potentially violent supervision over the population by bureaucratic means widely diffused throughout civil society in small and discretionary operations that are capable of rapid concentration. All of these characteristics struck contemporary observers as remarkable. Fear of mob or riot diminished when early police showed that fluid organization can overcome numbers:

> There seems to be no fear a London mob will ever prove a serious thing in the face of our present corps of policemen. A repetition of the Lord George Gorden riots would be an impossibility. Those who shudder at the idea of an outbreak in the metropolis containing two millions and a half of people and at least fifty thousand of the "dangerous classes" forget that the capital is so wide that its different sections are totally unknown to each other. A mob in London is wholly without cohesion, and the individuals composing it have but few feelings, thoughts or pursuits in common. They would immediately break up before the determined attack of a band of well-trained men who know and have confidence in each other.[17]

Another writer put the same point in more impersonal terms:

> As each police constable being alone might easily be overpowered, and as the men of each section, or even division, might be inferior in numbers to some aggregation of roughs or criminals collected in a given spot, it is arranged that . . . reserves of force can be gathered . . . and concentrated upon the disquieted area, and as the commissioners command the whole district, and the force is organized and united, while roughs act in small areas, and have diverse and selfish interests, the peace of London may be held secure against violence.[18]

The peaceful and propertied classes appreciated two other advantages of the modern police: they relieved ordinary respectable citizens of the obligation or necessity to discharge police functions, especially

[17] "The Police and the Thieves", *London Quarterly Review* (July 1856), p. 93.
[18] "The Metropolitan Police System", *Westminister Review* (January 1873), p. 16. An early historian of the New York Draft Riot of 1863 was similarly impressed by the decisive contribution of the telegraphic system in linking police stations within the city to each other and to those in Brooklyn. He devoted considerable space to the mob's attacks on the telegraphic system, citing the defense of its equipment and personnel as a key phase in the struggle for control of the streets. See J. T. Headley, *The Great Riots of New York* (New York, 1873).

during emergencies; and they also made less likely a resort to the military for the purposes of internal peace-keeping. Both involved changes in the relationship of these classes to the criminal or disorderly.

In unpoliced society, police functions were often carried out—if at all—by citizens rotating in local offices (sheriffs, constables, magistrates) or acting as members of militia, posses, Yeomanry corps, or watch and ward committees.[19] Not only was this system inefficient but it also directly exposed the propertied classes to attack. Agrarian men of property were frequently willing to undertake these tasks. Thus the Yeomanry, a cavalry force whose characteristic tactic was the sabre charge, was largely composed of small landowners[20] who were especially zealous in police duty against mobs and riots and especially disliked by working people.[21] For these reasons, the Yeomanry were particularly popular among the landowning classes as a means of defense. Praising them in the course of a parliamentary debate in 1817, for example, a member observed that "the people would in many instances be debarred from violence by seeing those arrayed against them to whom they were accustomed to look up to as their masters."[22]

But this machinery exposed the Yeomanry, once an emergency had passed, to direct attack in the course of daily life.[23] It also enabled private persons sometimes to modify police missions to suit their own proclivities and convenience. Thus, during the extensive agricultural uprisings of 1830 in southern England, fifty men of the village of Holt enrolled as special constables and "declared their willingness to turn out to protect all property except threshing machines; they did not wish to show disrespect to their poorer neighbors."[24] Yet threshing machines were the very form of property then under attack.

[19] A good summary is in F. C. Mather, *Public Order in the Age of the Chartists,* pp. 75–95.

[20] John Fortesque, *A History of the British Army* (London, 1923) Vol. XI, p. 43). Since the yeomanry were required to supply their own horses and equipment, their status as agrarian men of property was largely assured. See K. Chorley, *Armies and the Art of Revolution* (London, 1943), p. 167.

[21] J. L. and B. Hammond, *The Town Labourer* (London, 1928), p. 89. Also, F. C. Mather, *op. cit.,* p. 148. Yeomanry, for example, precipitated the "Peterloo" massacre.

[22] Quoted in Reith, *The Police Idea,* p. 191.

[23] For example, many resigned when they received threatening letters after Peterloo. See Ione Leigh, *Castlereagh* (London, 1951), p. 127.

[24] J. R. M. Butler, *The Passing of the Great Reform Bill* (London, 1914), p. 132.

The urban and industrial propertied classes, however, were much less eager to take up the tasks of self-defense as volunteer or co-opted police. Landowning military officers attempting to encourage self-defense among commercial or industrial capitalists met with much reluctance. Replying in 1819 to advice from Wellington, the army commander in the newly industrializing north of England replied in exasperated terms:

> I have always fought against the dispersal of my force in trivial detachments; it is quite impossible to defeat the disaffected if they rise, and at the same time to protect any town from plunder; that resistance should be made by the inhabitants. . . . But I am sorry to say the general remark from the manufacturers is that government is bound to protect them and their property.[25]

We are dealing here not merely with the classic confrontation of an agrarian military tradition and a pacific commercial and industrial one; what also emerges is a specific demand for the bureaucratization of police functions. Not only did the manufacturing classes wish to avoid personal danger and inconvenience while protecting their property, but they also saw that—contrary to the social rationale underlying the yeomanry—the use of social and economic superiors as police exacerbated rather than mollified class violence.[26] This emerges clearly in the testimony of one Thomas Ashton, "the owner of considerable property in manufactures, and the employer of about 1500 persons," before the Royal Commission of 1839 concerned with extending the professional police from London to the provinces.[27] Among other reforms, Ashton favored the use of personnel from outside a locality affected by violence and for a reason other than the reluctance of local personnel to act against their neighbors:

> On such urgent occasions, I think it extremely desirable that a stipendiary magistrate should be sent into the district and entrusted with the administration of the law. A great majority

[25] Despatch of General Byng quoted in Reith, *The Police Idea,* p. 202.

[26] "Respectable tradesmen cannot, without detriment to themselves, be so engaged as constables . . ." (George Mainwaring, *Observations on the Police . . .*, p. 46).

[27] *First Report of the Commissioners Appointed as to the Best Means of Establishing an Efficient Constabulary Force in the Counties of England and Wales* (London, 1839), pp. 158–9.

of the more serious disturbances originate in disputes between master and servant. The local magistracy is chiefly composed of the resident landowners and manufacturers, and the irritation of the workmen against their employers is greatly increased when they find the person, with whom the disputes have arisen openly supported by, and giving directions to, the military, and subsequently punishing them for breaches of the peace, which would never have been committed unless such disputes had occurred. Ought the employer to be placed in such a situation? Is it likely that animosities would be allayed or peace maintained by it? What safety has the proprietor of machinery?

This reasoning was accepted by the commissioners in their report, which was largely written by the Benthamite reformer Edwin Chadwick:

In several instances where there was an effective resistance given to the rioters, we have been informed that the animosities created or increased, and rendered permanent by arming master against servant, neighbour against neighbour, by triumph on one side and failure on the other, were even more deplorable than the outrages actually committed. . . . The necessity for such painful and demoralizing conflicts between connected persons should be avoided by providing a trained and independent force for action in such emergencies. . . . The constitutional authority of the supreme executive is then emphatically asserted. In reply to recent inquiries made of local authorities in the manufacturing districts, why they took no steps for the repression of riotous or alleged treasonable proceedings within their districts, why so long a career of criminal incitements was permitted, the prevelant answer has been, that such proceedings were understood to be exclusively within the province of government.[28]

Thus, at a time when the agrarian rich often sought to multiply and reconstruct the traditional means of self-defense against violent uprising and attack, those who sprang from the newer sources of wealth turned toward a bureaucratic police system that insulated them from popular violence, drew attack and animosity upon itself,

[28] *Ibid.*, p. 205.

and seemed to separate the assertion of "constitutional" authority from that of social and economic dominance.[29]

Other means than a bureaucratic police—especially the army itself—were available for this purpose. But although the army played a crucial role during crises or situations with revolutionary potential, it was ill-equipped to meet the enduring needs of a policed society.[30] It was largely officered by an agrarian class which sometimes did not distinguish itself for zeal in protecting the property of manufacturers.[31] More fundamentally, however, it was difficult for the army to act continuously in small dispersed units in civilian society, although it might do so on an emergency basis. More characteristic of the army was an alternation between no intervention and the most drastic procedures—the latter representing a declaration of internal war with lingering consequences of hate and resentment.[32] The police were designed to penetrate civil society in a way impossible for military formations and by doing so to prevent crime and violence and to detect and apprehend criminals.[33] Early descriptions by contemporaries describe both sorts of police action, taken today as routine, as novel and startling.[34]

The police penetration of civil society, however, lay not only in its narrow application to crime and violence. In a broader sense, it represented the penetration and continual presence of central politi-

[29] "I hope to get up a troop of Yeomanry at Cheltenham," wrote Lord Ellenborough during the critical year of 1832, "but this requires delicate management. . . . Yeomanry however we must have, or we shall be beaten." A. Aspinall, *Three Early Nineteenth Century Diaries* (London, 1952), p. 275.

[30] See the accounts in F. C. Mather, *Public Order in the Age of the Chartists*, pp. 153–81, and Joseph Hamburger, *James Mill and the Art of Revolution* (New Haven, 1963), pp. 203–14.

[31] See, for example, Frank Darvell, *Popular Disturbances and Public Order in Regency England* (Oxford, 1934), pp. 80–1, 267–8.

[32] All these points of superiority of police over army were explicit among those who advocated or created the early professional police. See for example, the *First Report of The Commissioners . . . , op. cit.*, pp. 159–61; George Mainwaring, *Observations on the Present State of the Police . . .* , p. 69; Charles Reith, *British Police and the Democratic Ideal*, pp. 9–30; and *Edinburgh Review* (July 1852), p. 6.

[33] Great stress was initially laid on the "preventive principle," at the time a new principle in internal peace-keeping. See Reith. *ibid.*, pp. 18–23, and the same author's *A New Study of Police History*,, pp. 221–4. For the view of a contemporary advocate of police, see Mainwaring, *op. cit.*, pp. 9–10.

[34] Note, for example, the obvious astonishment that underlies an account of the tracing of a burglar, who had robbed a house in central London, to an obscure hiding place in the East End ("The Police System of London," *Edinburgh Review*, July 1852, pp. 8–10).

cal authority throughout daily life. In an important defense of characteristically modern social arrangements, Edward Shils has argued that close integration of the social and geographic periphery is a unique achievement of "mass society." In his view

> mass society is not the most peaceful or "orderly" society that has ever existed; but it is the most consensual. The maintenance of public peace through apathy and coercion in a structure of extremely discontinuous interaction is a rather different thing from its maintenance through consensus in a structure of more continuous interaction between center and periphery. . . .[35]

But in Shils' account the integration of the periphery emerges entirely as a moral or normative process:

> The mass of the population is no longer merely an object which the elite takes into account as a reservoir of military and labor power or as a possible or actual source of public disorder. . . . Most of the population . . . stand in closer moral affinity and in a more frequent, even though mediated, interaction with the center than has ever been the case. . . . The greater proximity to the center—to the institutions which constitute it and the views which are embodied in it. There is, accordingly, a greater feeling within the mass of being a part of the same substance of which one is oneself formed.

That the modern nation represents an unprecedented extension of the organizational and moral community is undoubted. But the wholly normative language in which this account is cast risks eliding the simultaneous extension of the police throughout the "periphery" both as the agent of legitimate coercion and as a personification of the values of the "center." Far from being a latter-day consequence of organizing the police for purely coercive tasks, this was explicit in early police doctrine and much remarked upon by early observers. Their accounts stress the capacity of bureaucratic organization to make the values of the "center" palpable in daily life by means of detached persons operating on organizationally defined missions.

> Amid the bustle of Piccadilly or the roar of Oxford Street, P.C.X. 59 stalks along, an institution rather than a man. We seem to have no more hold of his personality than we could

[35] "The Theory of Mass Society," *Diogenes* (1962) pp. 53–4 (for this and succeeding quotations).

> possibly get of his coat buttoned up to the throttling-point. Go, however, to the section-house . . . and you no longer see policemen, but men. . . . They are positively laughing with each other![36]

And they also stress the power of the police over mass disorder, which stems not only from superior organization and the rational application of force but also from its presence as the official representative of the moral order in daily life:

> The baton may be a very ineffective weapon of offence, but it is backed by the combined power of the Crown, the Government, and the Constituencies. Armed with it alone, the constable will usually be found ready, in obediance to orders, to face any mob, or brave any danger. The mob quails before the simple baton of the police officer, and flies before it, well knowing the moral as well as physical force of the Nation whose will, as embodied in law, it represents. And take any man from that mob, place a baton in his hand and a blue coat on his back, put him forward as the representative of the law, and he too will be found equally ready to face the mob from which he was taken, and exhibit the same steadfastness and courage in defense of constituted order.[37]

In this setting, early police doctrine and observers agreed from the beginning that it was necessary to rely on the moral assent of the general population; even the earliest policemen were elaborately instructed in the demeanor and behavior required to evoke, establish, and sustain that assent.[38] This was more than a mere technical convenience. The replacement of intermittant military intervention in a largely unpoliced society by continuous professional bureaucratic policing meant that the benefits of police organization—continual pervasive moral display and lower long-term costs of official coercion for the state and propertied classes—absolutely required the moral cooperation of civil society.

Thus, the extension of moral consensus and of the police as an instrument of legitimate coercion go hand in hand. Along with other ramifying bureaucratic agencies of the center, the police link daily life to central authority. The police, however, rely not only on a technique of graduated, discretionary, and ubiquitous coercion but

[36] "The Police and the Thieves," *London Quarterly Review* (July 1856), p. 93.
[37] "The Police of London," *London Quarterly Review* (July 1870), p. 48.
[38] Charles Reith, *A New Study of Police History,* pp. 140–2.

also on a new and unprecedentedly extensive form of moral consensus. The center is able to supervise daily life more closely and continuously than ever before; but police organization also requires pervasive moral assent if it is to achieve the goals peculiar to its technique. In earlier times, as we have seen, voluntaristic and nonbureaucratic police permitted the sabotage of official coercion by allowing participating classes to make their services conditional. In a policed society (as distinct from a police state), a hostage is also given to fortune: the fundamental assent, not of the classes who comprise volunteer or nonprofessional quasi-police, but of the general population. Without at least a minimal level of such assent, coercive functions become costly in exactly the ways that those who created the policed society in England sought to avoid. In this sense, then, the extension of the moral community and of the police are aspects of the same historical development.

CULTURES OF RIOTOUS PROTEST

The themes of mass criminality and of political riot and mob protest have long been intertwined. In a notable and recent contribution George Rudé has been especially concerned to refute the classic view—associated with such nineteenth-century conservatives as Burke, Taine, and Le Bon—that political crowds, mobs, and riots are essentially criminal in character.[39] According to Rudé's analysis, demonstrating crowds and mobs in the latter half of the eighteenth an the first half of the nineteenth century were characteristically composed not of pauperized, unemployed and disorganized "rabble" but of locally resident, respectable, and employed people.[40] It is not surprising that privileged classes attempt to define popular protest as criminal—that is, fundamentally and unconditionally illegitimate. But this rhetoric and the very real fears of privileged and propertied people facing recurrent popular agitation in an unpoliced age, must not lead us to overlook the evidence for another aspect of this older relationship between elite and agitational population: riots and mobs, however much they were feared and detested, were also often means of protest that articulately communicated the desires of the population to a responsive, if not sympathetic, elite.[41]

[39] *The Crowd in History, 1730–1848* (New York, 1964), pp. 7–8, 199–204.
[40] *Ibid.*, p. 47–65.

[41] Expressions of this fear are vivid and aboundingly frequent. "At this time," wrote the Tory poet Southey in 1812, "nothing but the Army preserves us from the most dreadful of all calamities, an insurrection of the poor against

This is a major feature of Eric Hobsbawm's analysis of the pre-industrial "city mob."[42] While stressing that such mobs were a "pre-political phenomenon" and often reacted directly to fluctuations in wages and food prices, Hobsbawm also emphasizes, in effect, the normative character of such riots:

> . . . There was the claim to be considered. The classical mob did not merely riot as a protest, but because it expected to achieve something by its riot. It assumed that the authorities would be sensitive to its movements, and probably also that they would make some immediate concession; for the "mob" was not simply a casual collection of people united for some *ad hoc* purpose, but in a recognized sense, a permanent entity, even though rarely permanently organized as such.[43]

---

the rich, and how long the Army may be depended upon is a question which I scarcely dare ask myself" (Elie Halevy, *A History of the English People*, New York, 1912, Vol. I. p. 292). Seven years later a peer discussing the political situation observed: "We are daily assailed with undisguised menace, and are little removed from the expectation of open violence. . ." (*Substance of the Speech of the Rt. Hon. Lord Grenville in the House of Lords, November 19, 1820*, London, p. 23). A year later in a memorandum to Liverpool, Wellington, then Prime Minister—urging the creation of a police force—wrote: "I feel the greatest anxiety respecting the state of the military in London. . . . Very recently strong symptoms of discontent appeared in one battalion of the guards. . . . There are reports without number in circulation respecting all the Guards. . . . Thus, in one of the most critical moments that ever occurred in this country, we and the public have reason to doubt the fidelity of the troops, the only security we have, not only against revolution but for the lives and property of every individual in this country who has anything to lose. . ." (Quoted in Reith, *The Police Idea*, p. 213). Robert Peel, fearing for his family's safety at their country estate, left London during the crisis of 1831 and asked a friend to send weapons. "I have this day got you fourteen carbines, bayonets, and accoutrements," the friend replied. "How will you have them sent to you? I have only desired a cask of ball cartridges to be put in the case" (Tresham Lever, *The Life and Times of Sir Robert Peel*, New York, 1942, p. 144). A general description of the situation is given in Reith, *Police Principles and the Problem of War*, pp. 46–8. In his revisionist account, *James Mill and the Art of Revolution*, Joseph Hamburger maintains that this standard portrait of elite mentality is exaggerated and that it does not apply to the Whig reformers in the period before 1832, who were more concerned with long-range than with imminent crises (see pp. 33–47).

[42] *Primitive Rebels: Studies in Archaic Forms of Social Movements* (Manchester, 1959).

[43] *Ibid.*, p. 111.

Insisting with Rudé on the essentially noncriminal character of such riotous protests, Hobsbawm summarizes the system as a whole:

> Provided that the ruler did his duty, the populace was prepared to defend him with enthusiasm. But if he did not, it rioted until he did. This mechanism was perfectly understood by both sides, and caused no political problems beyond a little occasional destruction of property. . . . The threat of perennial rioting kept rulers ready to control prices and distribute work or largesses, or indeed to listen to their faithful commons on other matters. Since the riots were not directed against the social system, public order could remain surprisingly lax by modern standards.[44]

We will briefly illustrate the system as described by Hobsbawm and Rudé with an example from rather late in this period—London in 1831.[45] "Illuminations" were occasions on which those favoring a given cause or person placed lights in their windows; and it often happened that demonstrating crowds went from house to house demanding that those within "illuminate" and smashing their windows or sacking their houses if they did not. The residences thus besieged were usually selected with precision—the ruling class in eighteenth- and early nineteenth-century cities was not anonymous, physically inaccessible, or effectively insulated by a professional and preventive police force. Such a crowd, pressing for electoral reform of the Commons, gathered in April 1831. The following is a contemporary account of its doings, clearly written from an unfriendly point of view:

> . . . The reformers of London endeavoured to get up an illumination on Monday, the 25th; but that having been a failure, they prevailed on the Lord Mayor to announce another for the evening of Wednesday the 27th. On that evening, the illumination was pretty general. . . . The mobs did a great deal of mischief. A numerous rabble proceeded along the Strand, destroying all windows that were not lighted. . . . In St. James' Square they broke the windows in the houses of the Bishop of London,

[44] *Ibid.*, p. 116.
[45] See the summary of this theme in *The Crowd in History,* pp. 254–7. See also the interesting article by R. B. Rose, "Eighteenth Century Price Riots and Public Policy in England," *International Review of Social History* (1961), pp. 277–92, and the more general remarks in this connection by Joseph Hamburger, *op. cit.,* pp. 199–202.

> the Marquis of Cleveland and Lord Grantham. The Bishop of Winchester and Mr. W. W. Wynn, seeing the mob approach, placed candles in their windows, which thus escaped. The mob then proceeded to St. James' street where they broke the windows of Crockford's, Jordan's, the Guards, and other Club houses. They next went to the Duke of Wellington's residence in Piccadilly, and discharged a shower of stones which broke several windows. The Duke's servants fired out of the windows over their heads to frighten them, but without effect. The policemen then informed the mob that the corpse of the Duchess of Wellington was on the premises, which arrested further violence against Apsley House. . . .[46] After the action just described the mob marched off to attack other residences, including that of Robert Peel, the political founder of the police.

At every point the normative character of the mob is clear. In this case their cause was generally popular, and they had the support of the Lord Mayor and many other worthies favoring reform, whereas many mob actions, of course, lacked such sanctions. But "antagonistic cooperation" between the mob and parts of the elite had a long history.[47] Indeed, even prereform electoral politics sometimes required parts of the elite not only to compete for the favor of the people but to expose themselves to rough treatment by electors and nonelectors alike. Thus, a French observer of 1819, watching the customary postelection procession of successful parliamentary candidates, de-

[46] *Annual Register,* 1831, p. 68. Quoted by Reith in *British Police and the Democratic Ideal,* pp. 90–1. Hamburger places this incident squarely in the "tradition of riot" (see *James Mill. . . .* , pp. 139–42).

[47] It is Hamburger's thesis that in the case of the Reform Crisis of 1830–1832, proreform leaders manipulated the threat of the mob, rather than wielding a substantial revolutionary threat. But this sort of manipulation was itself a tradition—for a case that succeeded before the mob ever took to the streets, see Thomas Perry, *Public Opinion, Propaganda and Politics in Eighteenth Century England: a study of the Jew Bill of 1753* (Cambridge, Massachusetts, 1962). So strong was this tradition that Lady Holland, the wife of the great Whig aristocrat prominent in the struggle for reform, could remark disapprovingly on Wellington's reaction to the prospect of mob attack on his house: "Is it not strange that the Duke of Wellington has boarded with very thick planks *all* his windows upstairs to Piccadilly and the Park? . . . The work of *darkness* began on Coronation Day and is now completed. He says, I hear, that it is to protect his plate glass windows from the mob, who will assail him on the Reform Bill! As it cannot be for thrift, it looks like defiance; and the mob will be irritated when they discover his intentions." Earl of Ilchester, ed., *Elizabeth, Lady Holland to Her Son,* (London, 1946), p. 118. (Italics in original.)

scribed a scene which Halevy calls "one long familiar to the English public":

> [They] were immediately pelted with filth, greeted with a shower of black mud. . . . I saw Lord Nugent with one side all black. . . . Lord John Russell attempted with difficulty to wipe off the stinking patches of dirt which continually bespattered his cheeks. . . . Some had their windows broken and their furniture damaged. The houses of Lord Castlereagh and several others met with the same fate. The constables were insufficient to restore order, and the troops had to be called out.[48]

The English elite, then, sometimes lived on rather casual terms with popular volatility so long as the latter did not—as for a time the "dangerous classes" and early working class movements seemed to—challenge the fundamentals of the current system. They did not do so willingly, to be sure, but in a kind of symbiosis in which "consideration" was exchanged for "support." Thus, to see everyday, nonrevolutionary violence or unruliness solely or even largely as an impediment to the emergence of stable democracy is to blur important distinctions between kinds of popular violence and ways in which it may be integrated into a political system. Popular violence which forms part of an articulate system of demands and responses, in which needs and obligations are reasonably clear to each party, may not be at all necessarily "irrational," "criminal," or "pointless"—to use words often applied to riotous protest in contemporary democracies. Indeed, the English case suggests that—granted the many other conditions that lie outside our present scope—such a system may well conduce to the establishment of stable democracy. For although Hobsbawm calls the system "pre-political," it is one in which ordinary people express their will and elites have learned to listen.[49] The exist-

[48] Halevy, *op. cit.*, p. 118.

[49] It is suggestive to compare Hobsbawm's perceptive comment on the situation in parts of Europe which did not experience a comparably gradual development of democratic institutions. Speaking of popular riot and enthusiasm in support of the *status quo*, he remarks: "Legitimate monarchs or institutions like churches may not welcome this. The Emperor Francis I of Austria took a poor view of the revolutionary legitism of his people, observing correctly: 'Now they are patriots for me; but one day they may be patriots against me!' From the point of view of the genuinely conservative institution, the ideal is obediance, not enthusiasm, whatever the nature of the enthusiasm. Not for nothing was 'Ruhe ist die Erste Bürgerpflicht' (Tranquility is the first duty of every citizen) the slogan of every German princeling" (*Primitive Rebels* . . . , p. 119).

ence of the normative culture of mob and riot in many places other than England is enough to show—if the disclaimer need be made at all—that the mere existence of normative riot and violence is not a sufficient condition for the emergence of institutionalized democracy.[50] Yet in an age when institutions did not organize, represent, or press the claims of ordinary people, and in which the streets were therefore a political arena, it is important to distinguish between kinds of popular violence, rather than consider it wholly as an anachronism.

THE DEMAND FOR ORDER IN CONTEMPORARY DEMOCRACY

Such a protodemocratic system of riotous demand and elite response, however, is confined to unpoliced, hierarchical, pre-industrial society. It is not found where entrepreneurs or managers, career bureaucrats, or professional politicians have displaced former ruling groups; where popular volatility may disrupt tightly woven political and market ecologies; and where the state makes its presence felt ubiquitously in the form of police. In the latter situation, the demand for "law and order" becomes what it was not before—a constitutional imperative stemming from an unprecedentedly pervasive consensus and personified and enforced by police. Simultaneously, the standards of daily decorum increasingly restrict occasions for normative violence; thus Georg Sorel observed at the start of this century how marked had been the decline of daily and casual violence during the last, and how crucial a role these new standards played in the emerging policy of the liberal democratic state toward both the working and dangerous classes.[51]

With rising standards of public order has come an increasing intolerance of criminality, violence, and riotous protest. Daniel Bell

[50] See Hobsbawm, *passim*. See also the comprehensive discussion by Charles Tilly, "Reflections on the Revolution of Paris," *Social Problems* (Summer 1964), pp. 99–121, which, among other matters, deals with the literature on these themes in the case of France.

[51] See Chapter 6 of *Reflections on Violence*. On the special sensitivity of modern society to public disorder, see Karl Polyani, *The Great Transformation* (New York, 1944), pp. 186–7: "The market system was more allergic to rioting than any other economic system we know. . . . In the nineteenth century breaches of the peace, if committed by armed crowds, were deemed an incipient rebellion and an acute danger to the state; stocks collapsed and there was no bottom to prices. A shooting affray in the streets of the metropolis might destroy a substantial part of the nominal national capital."

has suggested that a breakdown of spatial barriers between the daily round of urban propertied classes and the criminal or unruly poor has made the former more aware of violence in daily life.[52] We may perhaps envisage three stages in such a sequence: one in which the prosperous or respectable often lived in unimagineable closeness to crime and the threat of riot or mob; a second in which these groups succeeded in insulating themselves—spatially, by regroupment in and outside the centers of cities and organizationally, by the police;[53] and a third in which penetrations of these barriers evoke a response which would be considered exorbitant by the standards of earlier years.

The character of the police as a public bureaucracy may also raise expectations about the level of public peace it is possible to attain. As the instrument of public policy they are easily seen in terms of a naive social instrumentalism—as technicians applying efficient means that are in principle capable of fully realizing their ends. Have not public bureaucracies eliminated plague, solved the enduring problems of urban sanitation, and prevented gross impurities in purchased foods? Why cannot the police similarly "clean up" crime and control violence?[54] In short, the historic and strategic success of the police raises expectations and exposes them to pressures engendered by the idea of a uniformly peaceful civil society.[55]

Not only are expectations of public order higher than before, but the arena to which these expectations refer has expanded. It has

[52] "The Myth of Crime Waves: the actual decline of crime in the United States," in *The End of Ideology* (New York, 1962), pp. 151–74.

[53] "The beats vary considerably in size; in those parts of the town which are open and inhabited by the wealthier classes, an occasional visit from a policeman is sufficient, and he traverses a wide district. But the limits of the beat are diminished, and of course the frequency of the visits increased, in proportion to the character and the density of the population, the throng and pressure of traffic, and concentration of property, and the intricacy of the streets. . . . Nor must it be supposed that this system places the wealthier localities at a disadvantage, for it is an axiom in police that you guard St. James' by watching St. Giles'" ("The Police System of London," *Edinburgh Review,* July 1852, p. 5). St. Giles was one of the most notorious of London's "rookeries."

[54] It is more than accidental that Edwin Chadwick (see p. 26, above) was also a prime mover in the reform of urban sanitation. See his report, *Sanitary Conditions of the Labouring Population in England, 1842* (London, 1843).

[55] See Bell, *op. cit.*, p. 152 on the relationship between better policing and a "higher" crime rate. The artifactual character of this relationship, sometimes hard for contemporaries for whom the police are taken for granted to grasp, was obvious to an observer witnessing the transition to a policed society. See "Causes of the Increase of Crime," *Blackwood's Magazine* (July 1844), p. 5.

done so not only because of the continuing, though obviously very incomplete, extension of a single moral order throughout the national community—a process which takes territoriality rather than the divisions of class, locality, or group as its ideal boundaries. The arena of expectation widens as smaller formations—regions, states, local communities—find it harder to control or influence the moral climate in which they live. The "nationalization" of civil rights, federal involvement in municipal programs like housing, the erosion of the power of localities to control the content of mass media, pressure from judiciaries on informal and quasilegal police practices—all mean that smaller formations come to see themselves as less able to control or influence their moral destiny.[56] Thinking themselves more vulnerable to incursion from the larger society, they extend moral demand and expectations to a wider environment than in the past was thought relevant to daily life.

These trends mesh with others. The imagery of the "dangerous classes" is being reborn in contemporary America. The nascent demand for a pervasively benign environment arises as the urban poor, disorganized, and unemployed—especially Negroes—bear more heavily upon the awareness and daily life of an urban society in which proportionately more people are "respectable" than ever before.[57] Violence, criminality, and riot become defined not only as undesirable but as threatening the very fabric of social life. Police forces come to be seen as they were in the time of their creation—as a sophisticated and convenient form of garrison force against an internal enemy.[58] Lacking a strong tradition of urban violence as a form of

[56] Attempting to account for respectable people's greater awareness of violence in daily life, Bell has also suggested that the emergence of heterogeneous audiences for the mass media, which include groups previously less exposed to violent themes, has heightened awareness of violence even as its occurrence in daily life has declined (*ibid.*, pp. 170–4). Simultaneously, local communities and states are losing their formal powers to control such materials and are relying more often on informal control. (See Richard Randall, *Some Political Theories in Motion Picture Censorship Decisions: Prior Restraint Reconsidered.* Paper delivered at the Midwest Conference of Political Science, Bloomington, Indiana, April 1965.)

[57] Here we follow Shils' argument, *op. cit.*, p. 56.

[58] For the American police this situation may render a chronic problem acute. At the time when the police are more urgently charged than ever before to do society's "dirty work" but also are more stringently supervised by the public, various interest groups and the judiciary, their morale and operating problems are further exacerbated by their failure to embody moral consensus in the eyes of the general community, their "clientele," and themselves as thoroughly as do the British police. For detailed observations about some of these matters,

articulate protest, it is all the easier to define such events as merely criminal.[59] Such definitions work not only on the respectable but also on the riotous poor. Like American society as a whole, the American poor lack a traditional past: on neither side of the boundaries of class and race do the conditions for "articulate riot" exist in generous measure. "Criminal" acts like looting and violent assault are likely to dominate riotous protest, rather than explicitly political gestures. Similarly, the propertied and respectable are ill-prepared to react in terms other than a confrontation with uncontained and shapeless criminality. Articulate riot, however, requires that both rioters and their target or audience jointly define the meaning of riotous acts. The frequency with which recent riots by Negroes in American cities are interpreted officially as "meaningless"[60] contrasts with the ability of the English elite, especially before it was severely threatened from the late eighteenth century on, to interpret the meaning of riotous behavior.

Current concern over violence and riot, then, involves a problem of the political language in which these events are described and interpreted. The problem is likely to sharpen as the official stance, relying in part upon the rhetoric of diagnostic sociology, becomes strained by the urgent pressure of events. The gap between the official diagnostic style and a cultural response that makes little provision for "normative riot" is likely to widen as the urban situation grows even more aggravated. It therefore remains to be seen whether American elites—creative, professional, and political—can or will sustain a diagnostic posture that seeks and interprets the meaning of these events.

It is not to idealize even the optimal "traditional" political society—that of England—with its brutalities, squalidness, and hardness of soul, to point out that it often provided the unorganized poor with

---

especially the last, see Michael Banton, *The Policeman in the Community* (London, 1964), a comparative account of Scottish and American police forces.

[59] Obviously, the rural South would require special treatment. See W. J. Cash, *The Mind of the South* (New York, 1941), *passim*, and H. C. Brearly, "The Pattern of Violence", in W. T. Couch, ed., *Culture in the South* (Chapel Hill, 1934). Our focus, however, is on urban situations. Thus, for example, there is a suggestion in that the few food riots of nineteenth-century New York, in 1837 and 1857, were carried out largely by foreign-born, rather than native, poor. See the chapters on these episodes in J. F. Headley, *The Great Riots of New York* (New York, 1873).

[60] I am indebted to Robert Fogelson's analysis (as yet unpublished) of these riots and of the official responses to them—notably the McCone Commission's report on the Watts riot of August 1965.

a language by which, in the absence of representative institutions or the ability to participate in them, they might articulately address the propertied classes through riot and disorder. And it is not to derogate the American adventure in modernity to suggest that, however richly endowed with representative and responsive institutions, it has not provided such a language for those in its cities who have long been outside their compass—a language whose grammar is shared by speaker and listener, rioter and pillaged, violent and frightened.

Environment and Organization: A Perspective on the Police

Albert J. Reiss, Jr. and David J. Bordua

INTRODUCTION

This chapter presents a general perspective on the metropolitan police as an object of sociological research. The chapter is neither a detailed presentation of formal research hypotheses nor a presentation of research findings. An organizational perspective on the consequences of police relations to the environing system is presented as an orienting image within which more specific theoretical and empirical work can proceed.[1] Several topics are selected to illustrate the general application of the perspective. The facts are gleaned from general observation, research underway, and the literature on the police.

POLICE AND THE ENVIRONING SYSTEM

The municipal police as an organizational system is especially adapted to an analysis that stresses its relations with the organized environment and its boundary transactions and moves from these to consideration of internal differentiation and problems of integration, coordination, and control. All organizations can be so studied, of course, but since Weber the broad fashion among sociologists has been to focus on the internal structure of organizations and on task differentiation as it is manifested within the organization. Unlike many organizations, however, the police have as their fundamental task the creation and maintenance of, and their participation in, external

[1] We attempt to make explicit what is often left implicit in research programs—the generalized "image" out of which more specific work flows. See, for example, Daniel Glaser, "Criminality Theories and Behavioral Images," *American Journal of Sociology,* Vol. 61 (March 1951), pp. 433–44.

relationships. Indeed, the central meaning of police authority itself is its significance as a mechanism for "managing" relationships.

Directing traffic, investigating complaints, interrogation, arresting suspects, controlling mobs and crowds, urging prosecutors to press or drop charges, testifying in court, participating with (or battling, as the case may be) probation officers in juvenile court, presenting budget requests to the city council, pressing a case with the civil service commission, negotiating with civil rights groups, defense attorneys, reporters, irate citizens, business groups, other city services, and other police systems—even such an incomplete list indicates the probable values of a perspective that emphasizes transactions and external relationships. The list also indicates something else of considerable significance. All of these transactions can be and often are antagonistic ones. Because of the complexity of organizational relationships with the environment, apparent even from a partial listing of police activities, we have chosen to concentrate our discussion of the external environment of the police and its internal consequences by selecting a few basic environmental features. These are the nature of the legal system, the nature of violative activity, and civic accountability. They are brought to bear upon a variety of organizational transactions and internal processes, especially on problems of production, strategy and tactics, and command and control.

The basic social mechanisms available to the police all flow from their role in the legal system. Yet, the legal system broadly considered is the source of some of the most severe problems of adaptation faced by the police. Because of this dual involvement with law, much of our early discussion of external relations deals with the police and the legal system. The legal system is not a seamless web of tightly articulated rules and roles, however, but a loose-jointed system held together at many points by microsystems of antagonistic cooperation and discretionary decisions.

Modern metropolitan police exist only in view of the fact that communities are legally organized.[2] The problem of the external parameters of police operation and organization, in its broadest sense, inheres both in the nature of the urban community and in the nature of the legal system. Indeed, the fundamental position of the police may be conceived as mediating between the two. On the one hand, the

[2] Something like police can occur in societies that would ordinarily not be termed legally organized. See Richard D. Schwartz and James C. Miller, "Legal Evolution and Societal Complexity," *American Journal of Sociology,* Vol. LXX (September 1965), pp. 159–69.

police are a fundamental representative of the legal system and a major source of raw material for it. On the other, the police adapt the universalistic demands of law to the structure of the locale by a wide variety of formal and informal devices.

Later we discuss several features of the modern urban community as they impinge on the social structure of law enforcement. In this section we concentrate on some key aspects of the legal system and on the implications of the fact that the governance of communities is done by legal rather than other means. The broad designation "legal system" may be broken into the "legality" component, the "legal content" component, the "legal order" component, and the "government" component.[3]

The value of these distinctions, will perhaps be more apparent if we discuss first the one most familiar—the "legal content" component. By this we mean simply the actual content of laws. The importance for our purposes is that even modern societies differ considerably in the substance of the things they make illegal, and violations under them differ considerably in their impact on police strategy and tactics. A prime example is the well-known tendency of American society to make illegal many service crimes such as gambling.

By the "government" component we mean simply that the legal system is always organized politically into larger or smaller, more or less centralized, units. Even further, powers of government may be separated or combined in various patterns. Thus in the United States the police are organized to parallel the federal structure of local, state, and national government. Although the matter of levels of government has been widely discussed as a central "problem" in police administration, we are not particularly concerned with the matter here, since our focus is on the single community rather than intergovernmental aspects of the context of police operations.[4]

The third aspect of the legal system is the "legal order" component. By this we mean the complex apparatus involved in the administration of justice, especially those aspects with which the police are likely to come into contact routinely, such as the prosecutor and the courts.

[3] Except for the government component, the division follows closely that proposed by Roscoe Pound, who also discusses the confusions centering around the various uses of the terms "law" and "legal." Roscoe Pound, "The Sociology of Law," *Twentieth Century Sociology*, Georges Gurwitch and Wilbert E. Moore, eds., (New York, The Philosophical Library, 1945).

[4] See the somewhat outraged treatment of Donal E. J. MacNamara, "American Police Administration at Mid-Century," *Public Administration Review*, Vol. X (Summer 1950), pp. 181–9.

Because of the unique significance of this aspect of the legal system, we will devote considerable attention to it.

Finally, the "legality" component to which we now give special attention refers only to the procedural aspects of the exercise of legal power.

LEGALITY, POLICE, AND COMMUNITY

In one sense, the police provide the primeval social service—protection of life and property. Unlike some other social services, however, the existence of a public agency largely precludes the performance of the service on a private basis. The very existence of the modern police signifies that in the broadest sense the exchange of property and the infliction of injury may take place only under definite rules. Moreover, disputes arising out of property exchange or personal altercation may be resolved only within definite limits. The body of legal rules that specify the acceptable modes of procedure in the resolution of disputes may collectively be deemed the canons of *legality*. The basic elements of legality—objective definitions of right, "due process," notice, citizen compliance, and official accountability—are primarily aspects of the ways citizens are treated rather than descriptions of specific statutes or judicial rulings. In the Anglo-Saxon tradition, the courts provide the primary definitions of legality in this sense with varying admixtures of legislative action and constitutional undergirding.

A society based upon such procedural and value premises, however, presents two closely intertwined problems. We can anchor the discussion of them by defining them very generally in terms of the subsystem relations involved. The first is the citizen-to-citizen relationship.

Within very broad limits, citizens must generally avail themselves of police services rather than resort to "self-help" in dealing with problems of person or property. The existence of police symbolizes not only that the citizen will be protected from the violator but that the violator will be protected from the citizen. One way the police serve the cause of legality, therefore, is to assure by their presence and performance that a set of rules prevails which make it *unnecessary* for the citizen to be continually prepared to defend himself or his property. We may, in fact, partly define the "maintenance of law and order" as the maintenance of a set of social conditions such that over the society as a whole, the expectation of attack on person or property has a probability below the level at which the citizenry resorts to "self-help." The maintenance of these conditions is always problematic, and in some localities of American society, "law and order" is sustained only with difficulty.

Comparison of the linkage among legality, police, and community in criminal law areas with the corresponding linkage in civil law is of sociological interest. The two great divisions of the law of civil wrongs—torts and contracts—involve much the same concern with the avoidance of "self-help" as a response to injury. Indeed, the traditional distinction in jurisprudence between civil remedies and criminal sanctions, with the former accruing to the injured party and the latter to the "state," obscures similarities between the two areas.

In the area of civil wrongs, especially tort law, the law is reactive rather than proactive, i.e., the legal system does not patrol or search out wrongs and take action but rather leaves to private initiative the invocation of the legal process. Closely related to the reactive stance of civil law is a very broad presumption favoring the private ordering of conduct and even of the resolution of disputes.[5] Thus legal ethics seem clear. The lawyer may not behave like a patrolman and search out tort victims or sufferers from breach of contract to encourage civil suits. Compare this doctrine of legal restraint with the doctrine of "aggressive patrol," which figures so prominently in modern police thinking.

On close examination many of the seemingly stark differences between the organization of civil remedies and the organization of criminal sanctions become less clear-cut. They perhaps can be seen most clearly if we look from the perspective of the private arrangement system itself. The determinants of the decision to call the police, for example, to deal with a neighborhood juvenile, are presumably complex but not totally unlike the decision to sue for damages.[6] A large part of police intervention is initiated by the victim. Moreover, the police have as one of their fundamental responsibilities the determination of when a "victim's" complaint in fact warrants formal action. No crime may have been committed, or if there is one, it may be

[5] For a jurisprudential discussion of the significance of private ordering with a sociological cast, see Henry M. Hart, Jr., and Albert M. Sacks, *The Legal Process: Basic Problems in the Making and Application of Law* (Cambridge, Mass., tentative edition, mimeo, 1958) Chap. 1.

[6] Or, indeed, the decision to be sticky about formal contractual provisions in business dealings. Stewart Macaulay, "Non-contractual Relations in Business: A Preliminary Study," *American Sociological Review*, (February 1963), pp. 55–69.

so minor that department policy dictates only cursory attention. Like the civil lawyer, the policeman also becomes sensitive to subtleties of private vengeance masquerading as public duty.

Beyond these elements of "victims" initiating police activity, police "adjudication" policy, and their upholding of "disinterested" canons of legality, the operating procedures of police bear other similarities to civil procedure. Foremost among these is the tendency of police to let stand, or even to encourage, private settlement of disputes—even where violence may be present or likely. Among the "private arrangements" that the police may protect are their own relationships with categories of violators.

This aspect of policing is discussed in more detail later on, but at this point it is appropriate to indicate that the police in a sense are a service without clients. The police serve the public as a collectivity rather than distributively.[7] Enforcement must be initiated where there is no personal victim or/and complainant. Given the lack of guidelines either from the public as client or from a specific victim or complainant as client, the police can become in effect their own clients. We take this to be one of the fundamental features in the oft mentioned tendency of the police to develop a supermoralistic perspective and to see themselves as engaged in a "private" war on crime. Of basic significance here is that the courts and the police are in a relationship of "antagonistic cooperation" so that the legal order itself can be described only with difficulty as the "client" of the police.

Thus in many ways the respect for private ordering that is formal in civil law is informal in criminal law. Unlike the civil side, a large organized body of officials—the police—intervene between law and practice and may come to participate in such private arrangements themselves. From this perspective it is useful to see the police not as discretionless ministerial officers but as somewhat analogous to the practicing attorney, whose roles as advocate, counselor, and officer of the court are not totally dissimilar (though better legitimated) to the roles played by the policeman.[8]

[7] See the discussion of commonweal organizations in Peter M. Blau and W. Richard Scott, *Formal Organizations* (San Francisco, Chandler Publishing Co., 1962), p. 54.

[8] There is a considerable law review literature on police discretion and what we have termed private arrangements involving the police. Most useful for the sociologist is the work of LaFave. Wayne R. LaFave, *Arrest: The Decision to Take a Suspect Into Custody* (Boston, Little, Brown and Co., 1965). Also, Wayne R. LaFave, "The Police and Nonenforcement of the Law—Part I," *Wis-*

Informal practice allows the police to vary their relationship to the many private dispute settling procedures available; hence, the degree to which formal legality is extended to (or imposed upon) different groups in the population varies considerably.[9] Among the private arrangements that the police may allow to stand is the use of violence among subordinate or peripheral groups in the society. The most outstanding instance until recently has been the willingness of the American police to respect intraracial violence among Negroes, thus implicitly defining the Negro population in a sense as a group "without the law." Correlatively, the police established private arrangements with the Negro violator that included their extrajudicial use of force as a substitute for "due process." Whether such private adjudication is less predictable, less merciful, and less just seems open to dispute, but such arrangements clearly imply that a segment of the population is operationally treated as outside the pale of legality.

The broader problem involved here is, of course, the central one of the conditions under which membership in the *state* supersedes membership in other collectivities as a determinant of both formal and operative rights. Historical developments for at least two centuries have tended to define state membership, that is, citizenship as prevailing over other statuses in determining individual rights. Nevertheless, here as elsewhere there have been many lags between formal declaration and informal practice.[10]

---

consin Law Review, Vol. 1962, No. 1 (January), pp. 104–37 and "The Police and Nonenforcement of the Law—Part II," *Wisconsin Law Review*, Vol. 1962, No. 2 (March), pp. 179–239. See also Joseph Goldstein, "Police Discretion Not to Invoke the Criminal Process: Low-Visibility Decisions in the Administration of Justice," *The Yale Law Journal*, Vol. 69, No. 543 (1960), pp. 543–94, and Edward L. Barrett, Jr., "Police Practices and the Law—From Arrest to Release or Charge," *California Law Review*, Vol. 50, No. 1 (March 1962), pp. 11–55.

[9] Informal practice in the police area may often be highly formalized. Indeed, it may even be written down. Formal, written department policy and procedure may be considered informal with respect to the law. Operating norms at all levels in police organizations may differ from either the law or department written rules. One of the more puzzling aspects of the control of police by the courts is the fact that the courts rarely take judicial notice of written police department rules and decide cases as though the individual policeman were a free agent. See the comparison of court rulings and police manuals in Goldstein, *op. cit.*

[10] T. H. Marshall proposes a historical scheme from which much of the above has been drawn. He argues that the lower classes were first the recipients of civil legal status and then later of welfare or social rights as adjuncts of citizenship. In the United States, at least, one can argue that large segments of the

Up to this point we have tried to establish a general perspective that emphasizes the similarities between civil and criminal legal operations. The key points here are (1) that many features are formal in the civil law are "informal" in the criminal law (2) that the relations between private ordering and public determination are important in both areas (3) that large areas of police operation are closer to the reactive model of civil adjudication than to the generally held proactive model of criminal process (4) that the maintenance of legality as *between citizens* always involves some balance of police willingness either to "respect" or to override private arrangements and (5) that the conditions under which citizens invoke the criminal process may determine the nature and boundaries of subsystem solidarity as well as of police behavior.

We purposely have emphasized the role of the police in securing as well as symbolizing legality as between citizens since this is a relatively neglected aspect of the larger problem. The other face of the legality problem is that of the relations between the citizenry and the police. Since this aspect of the problem has received much more attention, we will make only a few general remarks in the discussion of police in the legal order.

THE POLICE IN THE LEGAL ORDER

Liberal democratic societies stemming from the English tradition formally organize enforcement of the law and the maintenance of order *within* the society in both the military and the police but principally in the police. The extension of the role of law in legality, due process, the exercise of discretion, and enacting justice when accusations or arrests are made is formally organized in the public prosecutor and the courts. This functional separation of powers in which ordinarily the police are expected to enforce the law and the judiciary to determine the outcome of events creates problems for both organizations and appears to account for some aspects of police organization and work.

Although the police are formally organized to enforce the law and maintain public order, it is apparent they are involved at the same time in enacting justice. It is important to note that all three key

---

population had access to unemployment and old age insurance *before* developing any meaningful access to civil legality. This is true even in the formal sense for Negroes in the South, for example. T. H. Marshall, *Citizenship and Social Class* (Cambridge, Cambridge University Press, 1950).

terms—order, legality and justice—are ambiguous terms in any social system. But what philosophers, social scientists, and lawyers have argued over for centuries, the police must do every day. The point requires little documentation. A policeman on duty, for example, when confronted with a situation of law enforcement or threat to public order must make decisions about the evidence and whether the act violates the law. Decisions to hold for investigation, to arrest or release, or to enforce order likewise require the extension of legality. His decision may, and often does, involve him at the same time in dispensing equity. Police, in short, make important decisions that affect outcome. They either do justice or limit the judicial function of courts, particularly by determining the nature of the evidence and who is to be held for adjudication.

Court decisions to dismiss charges are often viewed by the police as a rejection of their decisions. Such decisions may be particularly galling to the officer, since he regards his rules of knowing as more valid than the court's rules of evidence in making a decision. Furthermore, court decisions to dismiss offenders or to return offenders to the community often affect police work, as released offenders frequently create problems for continued law enforcement. The most obvious examples of this kind occur in police work with juveniles, vagrants, and habitual drunks. Police dissatisfaction with rehabilitation workers such as probation officers likewise stems in part from the fact that they have been unable to control disposition of the case; today's probationers are not infrequently tomorrow's work.

Police dissatisfaction with the administration of justice by the courts results in their doing justice, a tendency to settle things outside the courts to be sure that "justice is done." Nowhere is this more apparent than when police are expected to continue law enforcement involving violators that the court sends back to the community. The police then may take the law in their own hands and dispense justice, even if it means using violence. The continuing conflict between the police and the courts over admissibility of evidence, techniques of interrogation, the status of the confession, and the use of force, together with their separate definitions of justice, are likewise consequences of the separation of powers.

Transactions among police officers, public prosecutors, and the judiciary not infrequently have the effect of subverting the goals of law enforcement, since each is in a position to sanction the other's behavior. That individual or collective sanctions do not always achieve the intended goal is clear when the effect of sanctions of one part on another is examined. A single example may serve as an illustration.

Judges often negatively sanction police officers for failing to develop cases that meet court standards. It is not uncommon for a judge to criticize publicly from the bench an officer new to the service with a terse statement that fails to explain the grounds constituting an effective case. This judicial practice leaves the young officer in a quandary that often leads him to turn to the informal police system for advice about responses to judicial practice. Not infrequently this course of action leads to poor police technique and the development of cases where there is no intention to prosecute. Such responses lead to further judicial criticism that department administrators may ultimately perceive as an unwillingness by the court to convict. At this juncture, however, police practice may have deteriorated to the point where the court could not convict, if it would. Negative sanctions by the court and prosecutors thus lead to a deterioration of police practice which subverts judicial goals.

There is no necessary reason why these systems must be related in a cumulative set of negative sanctions. Police, prosecutors, and jurists sometimes take steps to cope with predicaments caused by negative sanctions, evolving practices that moderate these effects. They provide, for example, for prosecutors to advise officers prior to their apperance in court, through to be sure, prosecutors may use officers for their own intended sanctions of judicial behavior. The conflict between police practice and legality stems in part, however, from the fact that American courts traditionally resist giving advisory opinions and from the fact that jurists and prosecutors, as lawyers, do not perceive that they have an educational obligation toward the officers or their clients in the situation.

The legally defined end of a police department is to enforce the law. The measure of success of a police department is presumably some measure of the degree to which it has in fact enforced the law. There are two major ways that success gets defined for departments. The first kind is a measure of aggregate success, whether of a crime rate, arrests, crimes cleared by arrest, convictions, or value of stolen property recovered. The second is the success it has in meeting public demands to solve a particular crime problem as, for example, when a crime outrages the public conscience.

Police are relatively free to define their own criteria of success in crimes known to them, arrests made, and crimes cleared through arrest, despite national attempts to standardize the criteria. They can determine a successful arrest per se and satisfy themselves when a case has been cleared by arrest. They can recover stolen property incident to arrest and clearance, or independent of it, as is often the case for stolen autos. Their productivity record in these areas, however can be compared with that of other cities through the uniform crime reporting system organized through the FBI. The media of communication hold the local police system accountable for its record in this system.

So far as the public is concerned police departments generally have a low success rate in the proportion of crimes cleared through arrest. Only about one in four offenses known to the police is generally cleared by arrest.[11] Clearance through arrest is greater for crimes against persons than crimes against property and for misdemeanors such as vagrancy, drunkenness, and disorderly conduct, though the latter bring few credits in the public ledger. The low success rate in crimes cleared by arrest creates a dilemma for the police administrators in their efforts to maintain a public image of themselves as productive in a market oriented society. It is neither sufficient nor publicly acceptable for American police to justify themselves by their roles as simple representatives of moral or legal order.[12] They are under considerable pressure from local organizations such as the newspapers and crime commissions and from the FBI, who interpret the statistics in relation to their own goals, goals that not infrequently conflict with those of the police department.

The dilemma created by the necessity to maintain a public image of success in the face of aggregative measures of lack of success can readily lead to the manipulation of the statistics to create a favorable public image. Police departments, in fact, build up their *volume* of production largely out of misdemeanors rather than felonies, out of crimes against property rather than against persons, and in these days from juveniles and traffic. Tradition oriented departments often artificially inflate their success rate by getting arrested persons to "cop out" to additional offenses or by charging offenses to an arrested person on the basis of a *modus operandi.*

The separation of enforcement from outcome creates additional dilemmas for the department in defining its success rate. Assuming legal police conduct, it is through convictions only that the penal

[11] Federal Bureau of Investigation, U.S. Department of Justice, *Crime in the United States: Uniform Crime Reports—1965* (Washington, D.C., U.S. Government Printing Office, 1964), Table 8, pp. 97ff. A total clearance rate of 26.3% is reported for seven major crimes. Clearance rates varied from 90.5% for murder to 19.6% for larceny. *Ibid.,* p. 97.

[12] Compare Banton's analysis of the degree to which the police in Scotland justify themselves by simply existing as symbols of order. Michael Banton, *The Policeman in the Community* (New York, Basic Books, 1965).

sanctions presumed efficacious in reducing crimes can be forthcoming. And it is also through conviction only that the police's sense of justice can be vindicated. The conviction rate, however, is subject to police control only within narrow limits. Both prosecutors and courts intervene. The courts do so with the avowed purpose of scrutinizing police conduct, especially when legality as well as violation of the law is defined as an issue. While department arrest figures may define the policeman's success, acquittals in court may define his failures.

These dilemmas in defining success are partially resolved by the development of a complex bargaining process between police and prosecutors, the shifting of departmental resources in directions of maximum payoff from a conviction point of view, the development of a set of attitudes that define the police as alone in the "war on crime," and the elaboration of success measures that do not require validation by the courts.

All major metropolitan departments elaborate measures of success that they can manipulate independent of the prosecutor and the courts. Investigations of organized crime are publicized, though there is relatively little success in conviction in relation to the effort expended. Arrests under public pressure of well-known gangsters or crackdowns on prostitution, gambling, or narcotics peddling have their symbolic public relations value even if it is difficult to secure convictions, and they make undue claim on limited resources. Successful prosecution of the most serious or violent crimes against persons, such as homicide, forcible rape, and aggravated assault, likewise are used for their symbolic value, though they account for only a small volume of all crimes known to the police.[13]

Police concern for clearance of crimes through arrest is not infrequently a response to immediate public pressures that they maintain a safe community as well as to the more general and continuing one that they are an effective and efficient department. The police, for example, may come under fire when a neighborhood is plagued by a series of assaults or strong-arm robberies or when the "public" is offended by any specific crime. Police concern then shifts to clearing up these particular crimes so that they may reduce public pressure by an announcement that the perpetrators have been brought into custody.

[13] Federal Bureau of Investigation, *op. cit.*, p. 47. These three offenses accounted for 8.1% of the total number of index crimes reported for 1965. The index crimes are all major crimes. The annual report of any large city department will show that these "public outcry" offenses are *quantitatively* a much smaller proportion of all crimes known to the police.

Police administrators are confronted with a dilemma in their effort to manipulate the image of crime in the community. To justify increases in manpower and budget before municipal agencies, they are compelled to emphasize the high volume of crime in the community and the difficulties they face in meeting it with the resources available to them. At the same time, this emphasis can easily be interpreted as failure.

The individual policeman likewise is production oriented; his successes are arrests and acquittals are his failures. The successful policeman quickly learns what the police system defines as successes. These become his arrests. When he is not supported by the judicial system for what he regards as right action, he tends to take the law into his own hands, often by making a decision not to arrest or by making an arrest where there is no intention to prosecute.[14] In this way the police officer sanctions the judicial system for what he defines as its failure to make him a success.

Separation of enforcement from outcome also has an effect on police attitudes. The refusal of the courts to convict or of prosecutors to prosecute may rest on what seem to the police the most artificial of formalities. Police are aware as well that this lack of support attributes failure to them. Their sense of justice may be outraged. Collective subcultural modes of adjustment are a common protective response to such dilemmas and contradictions. For the police this adjustment consists in part in the development of a collective identity wherein the police are viewed as the true custodians of morality and justice. In the words of one police administrator:

> Police get conditioned to the idea that we are the only people with our finger in the criminal dike in this country. They feel that everyone else "lets him go." Police differ from the D.A. The D.A. is satisfied with the conviction, finding him guilty. But police want him punished. They become outraged when the result of their work is ignored. "What if they let him off, I get him tomorrow: those bastards kiss him on the cheek and let 'em go," is their attitude of how the D.A. and the judge handle *their* cases.

Thus the police want an outcome that signifies for them that their effort has been appreciated and that morality has been upheld. This for them is what is meant by justice being done.

Many police see two broad classes of violators—those who deserve

[14] See the sources cited in footnote 8, *supra*.

to be punished and those who do not. For the police, justice is done by *them* when they let a man go; he does not deserve to be punished. But justice must be done by *some other means* when they arrest. This they regard as the moral obligation of the prosecutor and the courts.

Mention has been made that the separation of enforcement from outcome forces the police into a bargaining situation that includes violators, prosecutors, defense attorneys, and courts. The public prosecutor is usually the central figure in this process. Bargaining relationships of the police are undoubtedly more complexly patterned and determined than current information allows us to assess. Three important points can be made here, however. The first is that the police are hedged in by officials whose formal discretion is greater than their own. The second is that although the prosecutor and the judge are the traditional figures, the system of justice has come to include others, such as probation officers and juvenile court officials, with whom the police must also enter into a bargaining relationship. Finally, all of these bargining relationships are ones in which the role incumbents are potentially hostile to the police. As Stinchcombe has recently noted, adjunctive officials of the courts, particularly rehabilitation or welfare officials, are hired wholly or in part as a set of official opponents of the police.[15]

The formal linkage of the police to the prosecutor's office and the court has other implications for their adaptation. Interpersonal contact between police and court personnel involve both an inequality relationship and a reversal of roles. Normally, police are in a position of authority vis-à-vis the citizen; in a substantial number of situations, they are in a superior status position as well. When they are not, police use tactics to assert authority in the situation. Furthermore, police work generally places an officer in the role of interrogator, a role requiring that little information be given to suspects. Now in contacts with the courts, role situations are reversed. Police are generally below the status of officials they deal with in the courts, particularly with men of the bar and bench, and they are interrogated. Under certain circumstances, they are subject to cross-examination. This kind of contact brings with it all the suspicion and hostility generated between status unequals where roles are reversed and authority is displaced. The ambivalence of the police toward both the administration of justice and its role incumbents is further exacerbated

[15] Arthur L. Stinchcombe, "The Control of Citizen Resentment in Police Work." Unpublished paper, no date.

under these conditions. This status reversal plus the generalized lower prestige of police when taken together with the institutionalized distrust of police built into the trial process creates a situation where the police not only feel themselves balked by the courts but perhaps, even more fundamentally, feel themselves dishonored.

The involvement of police in the legal order may also be looked at from the point of view of the legal remedies available in the event of illicit police conduct. For the citizen they are largely civil remedies as against the individual policeman. Usually, the citizen does not sue the police department for false arrest or battery; he sues the policeman. The officer's conduct, however, may have been well within the reasonable limits of departmental policy or regulation. The relatively unpredictable and *ex post facto* nature of judicial decision may exacerbate the problem for the policeman, even though the usually broad wording of applicable provisions of the law of arrest afford the officer much protection. This anamalous disjuncture between authority and liability is presumably one source of the oft-noticed solidarity of police systems. If effecting the department's mission lays the officer open to suit, clearly a norm of secrecy and mutual support is a highly likely result. The blue curtain descends between staff and line and the department and the outer world.

The balancing and correlative fact that police chiefs may be liable to sanctions by political and governmental officials even though immune from suit acts in much the same way. "Formal" informal mechanisms such as secret department trials, requests for resignation, and liability defense funds develop as ways of containing this dilemma.

Although the civil suit is in principle available to citizens, it is rarely used. There seem to be several reasons for this in addition to the fact that policemen are usually not able to pay large judgments. The segments of the population most likely to sue are (or were) least likely to be involved with the police. Those most involved with the police, the "depressed populations," are simultaneously unlikely to use the courts in general, because they are fearful of police reprisal and too impoverished to afford counsel.

The very structure of judicial control of the police means—as in recent U.S. Supreme Court decisions—that rulings about the illegality of police practices toward offenders must come in the form of upsetting the convictions of criminals.[16] Judicial rulings that announce new procedural limitations on the police are of necessity *ex post*

[16] Mapp v. Ohio, 367 U.S. 643 (1961); Ker v. California, 374 U.S. (1963); Escobedo v. Illinois, 84 U.S. 1785 (1964).

facto, and therefore difficult to predict. Given this situation, it is no wonder that in the system for maintaining law and order other people have the law and the police get stuck with the order.

Recent decisions of the Court also highlight basic differences between the police and the courts regarding their organizational requirements for the legality and legal content components and set the stage for organizational conflict. The police organization generally requires high specificity of the legal content component in the decision to arrest but relative ambiguity of the legality component in enforcement and processing situations. The courts, in contrast, insist upon high specificity of the legality component in their position of judicial control of the police (or the protection of citizen rights) while tolerating relative ambiguity in the statement of legal content in the interest of case law.

VIOLATIVE ACTIVITY AND ORGANIZATIONAL STRATEGY AND TACTICS

Police departments are organized primarily to carry out a reactive rather than a proactive strategy. This is in sharp contrast with some intelligence systems geared to a proactive strategy. A majority of the line in any major metropolitan police system is allocated to units that react to communications that the police are wanted at some time and place. The communications center is the heart of the modern operating system. Patrol is the single largest division. Geared essentially to react, patrol belies its name. To be sure, some units, such as tactical patrol, conduct both proactive and reactive operations, and others, such as vice control, are principally proactive, but on-balance patrol is organized to respond to commands that are reactions to requests originating outside the department. To understand how it happens that police departments operate primarily with a reactive strategy, we must turn to the organization of the environing system and the development of police transactions with individuals and organizations beyond its boundaries.

Before the evolution of modern police systems the citizen was paid for giving information on crimes and the whereabouts of criminals to proper authorities. But in Western societies there has been a gradual evolution from the citizen as paid informant and prosecutor to the citizen as a responsible complainant accompanied by a delegation of responsibility to the police for the enforcement of the law and to the prosecutor for pursuing formal charges. As a consequence of these changes the social sources of information on violations have changed. Police strategy and tactics become proactive, and special units—for example, vice and traffic control divisions—are developed to deal with violations where the individual citizen is not directly threatened and hence does not mobilize the police.[17] Information on crimes of this nature must generally originate, therefore, with police work, including the use of the undercover agent and the otherwise abandoned practice of paid informants. Correlatively, where police rely almost exclusively on the citizen complainant for origination of information on crimes against a person or his property, their strategy and tactics are generally reactive. Patrol is the initial unit assigned to respond, and the detective bureau follows.

Only in a superficial sense may police be said to solve crimes or to enforce the law. The organization of the society, the nature of violative activity, and the organization of a police department make it impossible to locate a population of subjects who have violated the law or to solve most crimes.

The social organization of behavior that violates the law and of how it is communicated to the police, when coupled with organizational problems in the allocation of limited resources to the solution of crimes, makes it impossible for the police to generate most of the inputs they process. These conditions also largely determine the internal differentiation of the police department and the strategy and tactics each unit adopts to process violations of the law. We shall turn first to examine ways in which communications about violations of the law create problems for the police in solving crimes and how the police organization adapts to these problems.

In a democratic society, the major volume of police work derives from an external source, the citizen complaint, rather than from an internal organizational source, police detection of crimes committed. The major element occasioning a complaint by an American citizen is that he sees himself as a "victim" experiencing a personal loss. Citizens are unlikely to mobilize the police or to report violations in which they are not actually a victim. In all other cases, the citizen tends to define enforcement of the law as a police responsibility. This means that many violations are known to citizens but not re-

[17] As Skolnick notes, there are those violative acts where the individual citizen is directly offended: there is a crime against him as a private individual or against his property; and there are those violative acts where the citizen is involved only in the collective sense; there is some threat to the social order as defined by the legal norms. See Jerome H. Skolnick and J. Richard Woodworth, "Police, Suspects and Prosecutors." Paper read at the annual meetings of the American Sociological Association, Los Angeles, California, September 2, 1963.

ported to the police because they lack direct personal involvement in the violative activity. Even when the person is a victim, he may not necessarily make his complaint known, since citizen complaint is responsive to public and police norms and expectations about communicating violations of the law.

Police definitions of the status of "victim" constitute one such set of expectations. Certain deviants—for example, homosexuals and prostitutes—do not usually report crimes against themselves, since they cannot afford to take the risk. In other cases, the citizen responds to collectively defined expectations of treatment by the police, as, for example, the Negro's response to expectations of "white man's" justice or police brutality. Indeed, much of the post Second World War reported increase in crime in American cities may be due to the changing relationship between the Negro public and the police rather than to an actual increase in violative behavior. Negroes now seem more willing to report crimes against themselves.

There are a number of norms that govern the role of citizen as complainant. Beyond the fact that enforcement of the law is defined primarily as a police and not a citizen responsibility, there are powerful norms governing the role of informants in our society. Norms about "squealing" and "minding one's own business" control the reporting of citizen information about violations. There are also norms about "not getting involved with the law" and general citizen distrust of involvement with interrogation by lawyers or policemen.

Indeed, the integrity of private systems and relations among them may require that citizens withhold complaint. Such matters as the protection of individual integrity, family honor, or the opportunity to continue in business have priority in the American normative system over obligation to report violations or violators to the police. Finally, though we rely in our society on self-enforcement of conduct, the normative system works against reporting one's own violations. Though the police are charged with the detection of deviation, they are least likely to be sought out for confession of deviation. Deviation from the law may be acknowledged to the self, to the cleric, lawyer, friend, or therapist, but not to the police.

The nature of violative activity markedly affects the way police organization can cope with it. The popular image of how one effectively deals with crimes is through detective work. Yet, in a very important sense, police work does not rest on solving crimes through an inductive process of investigation beginning with evidence that leads ultimately to a violator. Rather, crimes are most often solved through a process of attaching persons known as violators to known violations.

Police work in response to citizen complaint usually begins and concludes solely as an intelligence operation; no arrest is made. The intelligence fed into the police system is on a crime that has been committed with, in many cases, little or no information on who may have committed it. The problem seemingly is one then, as the public says, of solving the crime. Though a majority of crimes must remain unsolved, for reasons under discussion here, even among those solved, only a minority can be said to be cleared through the inductive work of the detective division.

A majority of the cases that are cleared by arrest may be said to solve themselves in the sense that the violator is "known" to the complainant or to the police at the time the crime initially comes to the attention of the police. Whether the prosecutor and the courts will concur is another matter, but there is little doubt that the policeman operates in such situations by having a citizen sign a complaint or by making an arrest. Evidence technicians and detectives may work on such cases, but their task is one of linking the enforcement to the prosecution and adjudication systems by providing evidence, not one of solving crimes.

Though good data are lacking on the matter, there is good reason to claim that the second largest proportion of all crimes cleared by arrest is "solved" by arresting otherwise known violators. The arrest of a person for a crime often results in solving other crimes known to the police, since a major element of police practice is to utilize the arrested person and knowledge of his current offense as a means of clearing other crimes. Such well known police practices as interrogating the suspect to obtain confession to other crimes and presenting him for identification in a show-up are standard practices for clearing unsolved crimes as are less well known ones such as charging the violator with unsolved crimes or simply assigning them to him in the department's records on the basis of a *modus operandi.* It is not uncommon to find that an arrest carries with it the solution to a half dozen other crimes, particularly for crimes of robbery and larceny.

One of the major problems for the modern metropolitan police force, as it centralizes command and control and draws its personnel away from operations that are based in local areas, is to maintain adequate intelligence on potential or known violators. There is good reason to conclude that the pattern of crimes solved by arrest changes with centralization of command and control, since it compels the department to place greater reliance on formal intelligence systems and means of crime solution.

The enforcement of the law is not simply a matter of maintaining an intelligence system on crimes and criminals and allocating organizational resources to deal with them in response to either citizen mobilization or police work. The organization of the larger society affects the organization of operating police units and their strategy and tactics in yet other ways.

Society is organized to make the detection of some violative behavior and the location of some violators more difficult than others. Consider just the matter of how a residential organization can affect the policing of the public. A public housing project with buildings twenty stories high, each containing several hundred families, poses somewhat different problems of crime detection and arrest than policing of the same area when it consisted of tenement houses.

Apart from considerations of the territorial and corporate organization of a population, the legal norms and order exercise an enormous impact on the exercise of coercive authority. A distinctive feature of modern liberal states is their use of the monopoly of violence to guarantee the boundaries of small, autonomous social systems like the private place and the citizen's right to privacy in public places. Police access to private places is guaranteed by the right of surveillance when there is reason to believe that a crime has been committed; and entry, search of the person and of places, and seizure of evidence are warranted under legally specified conditions. The right of the citizen to privacy and the right of state access to private matters forms one of the principle dialectical concerns in the organization of modern states and their police systems.

The laws defining police access to private places have consequences for the organization of staff and line units in police departments and in the strategy and tactics they adopt. Stinchcombe emphasizes that the differential distribution of crimes in public and private places when coupled with the greater legal accessibility police have to public as over and against private places, affects both the volume of police work and structural differentiation within the department.[18] He argues that police are organized through patrol to operate in public places and therefore act much more on their own initiative in them; entry into private places is generally only on complaint or warrant.[19] It is true, of course, that police are in a better position to make an "on-view" arrest in a public rather than in a private place because

[18] Arthur L. Stinchcombe, "Institutions of Privacy in the Determination of Police Administrative Practice," *American Journal of Sociology*, Vol. LXIX (September 1963), p. 158.

[19] *Ibid.*, p. 152.

of norms governing their access to private places. But it is also true that police are more likely to respond to complaints in both public and private places than they are to make an on-view arrest. This fact stems primarily from two conditions: the nature of occurrence of crime, and the allocation of limited organizational resources.

Whenever the nature of the crimes is such that the police cannot readily forecast a high probability of occurrence in a particular public or private location at a particular time, they must be organized primarily as a reactive organization. Many crimes in public as well as private places are of this form. These crimes are most likely to involve coercion in private life and disorders and nuisances in public places. Whether they are homicides, assaults, robberies, burglary, larceny, drunkenness, disorderly conduct, collective disturbances, or traffic accidents, police must in the nature of the case be organized to react to the occurrence of the crime when they are *not* present, for there is usually low predictability of occurrence of these types of crime, given the resources in manpower available.

A major problem police face in norms governing access to private places is the limitation it places on proactive strategies and tactics. Vice provides an excellent example. It operates "in the open" if a police department does not adopt a proactive strategy, since citizens who participate in such activities are unlikely to sign complaints that constitute a legal case. When a department "puts the heat on," however, vice can retreat into private places. This then necessitates an alteration in police tactics for dealing with vice. Progressively, as the legally acceptable means for access to these places become operationally difficult, the police resort to undercover roles or to use tactics designed to control public aspects of vice, for example, harassment.

Police organization and work, moreover, is substantially affected by the ways in which the violation is socially organized. To oversimplify, we might say that the more organized the violative activity, the less effective police are in dealing with the violation. Modern metropolitan police departments are perhaps least effective in dealing with organized crime. The literature on police work and the public press emphasizes that this is largely a consequence of the territorial limitations on operations of a metropolitan police force. By simple deduction, it is assumed that a police force coextensive with the organized activity would "solve" the problem of organized crime. Stinchcombe argues that it is difficult to deal with illegitimate businesses and dangerous organizations because of the barriers of privacy.[20]

[20] *Ibid.*, p. 155.

Though there is merit in both arguments, they oversimplify the problem. While a national police force may well be more effective in coping with organized crime, the fact of the matter is that organized crime is more difficult to deal with precisely because it is highly organized. Similarly, while access to private places limits police effectiveness in dealing with organized crime even when access is gained through warrant or other means, it generally fails because of the difficulty in attacking the higher echelon organization. Operations in private places may be closed only to reopen elsewhere or to take to operating in public places, since the criminal organization adapts its strategy and tactics to those of the police. For the intelligence and operating units of the police, one has the counterintelligence units of organized crime.

We have noted that the more formally organized the criminal activity, the less effective police are in dealing with it. To this we should add that at the opposite extreme, the absence of informal organization of criminal activity, in at least its social patterning, also contributes to the problem of policing. The police are organized principally to respond to stimuli generated by citizen complaint and for surveillance in public places. Furthermore, many of their standard investigative techniques—for example, informants and modus operandi files—presuppose an "underworld," a loosely organized community of persons more or less habitually involved in committing crimes.

Police administrators face a major policy question of how available resources are to be allocated to inputs into the department and their processing within the department. Mention has been made of the fact these problems place limits on the allocation of manpower to situations where crimes may occur and dictate a primarily reactive strategy even for occurrences in public places. The technology of policing now makes possible the mobilization of men to react quickly over relatively long distances so that where possible even foot patrol gives way to mobile patrol. Some police departments organize tactical units to deal with large public assemblies as they occur at various places and times, but on the whole most public as private places do not have police on duty. Most places of business, for example, are left without police on duty as are most public streets; rather, mobile units are assigned to territories to respond to situations requiring police as they arise in public or private places.

Similarly, in the organization's processing of information on crimes, the department faces an enormous problem of allocating scarce resources. A police department must on any day turn out a volume equivalent on the average to its intake. This means that on the average it cannot afford to allocate resources to very many cases on other than a routine basis. Every department will alter assignments within a detective bureau for a particularly "big case" that public pressure presses for solution. But it cannot afford to so assign men for a long time or for many cases without leaving much other work undone.

Although this is not the place to go into the matter, quite clearly both the volume of crime known to the police and the proportion cleared by arrest is some function of how much resources it takes to gain knowledge of a particular crime and clear it by arrest. No department can exceed its resource capacity. Since beyond a certain point the amount of resources necessary to clear a crime exceeds the willingness of the society to allocate additional resources, it perhaps is not surprising that three out of all four crimes known to the police will remain unsolved. One caveat, of course, must be entered to any such statement. There undoubtedly are, in the nature of the case, a large number of crimes that will remain unsolved regardless of the resources allocated to their solution, since the information required to solve them never can become available in the police system. No police department can know more crime than its resources make possible for it to know in that given period of time nor solve more than its resources make possible. From a social organization point of view, the crime in any social system is a function of organizational capabilities to know it.

The heavily reactive nature of police operations means not only that the client-complainant system defines the conditions under which police are called at all but also that the private system that includes the complainant, and in many cases also the offender, dominates the social stage upon which police intervention takes place. The police must react to calls for service by going out into every conceivable kind of social situation. Unlike many modern bureaucratic professions, the police must develop techniques for structuring these social situations, situations over which they ordinarily have little control. The basic tactic for doing so is to "take charge," if only to freeze the situation before any escalation of the offense can occur or evidence of it can be altered. The basic instrument in this strategy is authority. Failing its effectiveness, the basic backstop is force.

Uncoerced responsiveness to police authority in the immediate situation, that is, respect—uncoerced in the immediate situation at least—is the most valuable resource available to the police. Much excessive police coercion can be attributed either to the perception that respect must be reestablished in a situation where it has broken down or to building up future respect credits in populations where police expect disrespect as a routine matter.[21]

Citizen respect for police authority in this context corresponds to the patient's respect for medical competence in the doctor-patient relationship. Unlike medical practice in modern clinics and hospitals, however, many clients of the police on call are not preprocessed by the routines of admission or readmission, nor are the clients always ill in the sense that they are aware of need and dependent upon the physician. Perhaps the proclivity of the police to prefer to deal with persons who have a prior arrest record arises from the fact that they are preprocessed. The use of force by the policeman in a sense is an attempt to create in his clients, usually in offenders but sometimes also in complainants, the same capacity for subservience that the physician can count on because of illness on the one hand and office or hospital routines on the other.

We can discern here one of the fundamental sources of misunderstanding between police and rehabilitation personnel in the system for administering criminal justice. The police are the preprocessing agency that not only enforces the basic transition from independence to subservience but also delivers the newly processed clients to a social setting already dominated by rehabilitation.

CIVIL ACCOUNTABILITY, COMMAND, AND CONTROL

To our knowledge there is no detailed description of the nature of command processes in a police department. It is necessary therefore to rely largely on published discourses that give information on the rhetoric of command and control and that are of variable and unknown validity as descriptions of behavior.[22]

Police literature emphasizes the quasimilitary nature of police command relations, and casual observation in metropolitan police departments indicates that police officials are highly sensitive to "orders from above" and to probabilities of official disapproval of behavior. In principle and in rhetoric, a police organization is one characterized by strict subordination, by a rigid chain of command, and more doubtfully, by a lack of formal provision for consultation between ranks.

[21] William A. Westley, "Violence and the Police," *American Journal of Sociology*, Vol. 49 (August 1953), pp. 34–41.

[22] See for example, Bruce Smith, *Police Systems in the United States*, 2d rev. ed. (New York, Harper and Brothers, 1960), esp. Chaps. 7–9.

Before accepting this description of its structure uncritically, it is necessary to say that such statements are meaningful only by comparison. We have relatively little data comparing the operating as opposed to the rhetorical nature of command in different types of organizations. In many ways policing is a highly decentralized operation involving the deployment of large numbers of men alone or in small units where control by actual command—that is, by issuing orders—is difficult. Furthermore, evidence from the police literature itself suggests that the description is overdrawn, that both internal and external transactions structure the effective range of command and control. Moreover, as J. Q. Wilson points out, it seems quite clear that the variations between "system oriented" as opposed to "professionalized" departments includes fundamental differences in styles of control.[23]

In large police departments, the chief's power to command and control is limited by a complex system of due process that protects subordinates. This, of course, is true of all civil service organizations. The strong interest in keeping the police out of politics coupled with the interest of the rank and file in job security, however, creates a situation where formally at least the department head must contend with legally empowered authorities in the selection, promotion, and discharge of personnel. Even in matters of internal assignment and definition of task decisions may impinge on the civil service classification system. Police employee organizations likewise are quite effective in seeing to it that the system of due process continues to protect them. Lastly, the individual officer when accused of wrong doing or a crime demands all the safeguards of due process, the very safeguards he may deny to those whom he accuses of committing a crime.

The police literature stresses command as the basis of control. Historical changes in the nature of police work and organization have increased the importance of more subtle and perhaps more important developments in methods of control, however. In the dialectic of dispersion versus centralization of command, every development in the technology for police control of the population is accompanied by changes in the capacity of the organization to control its members.

Originally the bell or rattle watches were limited in summoning help to the effective range of their "noise;" the addition of calling the hours served to monitor the behavior of the patrol (quite generally open to question). Here we see evidence of a classic and continuing dilemma in organizations—that to control subordinates they must be

[23] James Q. Wilson, "The Police and Their Problems: A Theory," *Public Policy*, Vol. XII (1963), pp. 189–216.

required to make themselves visible. For the police this means that when they become visible, they likewise become more calculable to potential violators. Control of the dispersed police was really difficult before the call box that simultaneously enabled patrolmen to summon help and enabled commanders to issue calls and require periodic reporting. The cruising car with two-way (now often three-way) radios enabled still greater dispersion and flexibility in the allocation of patrols while at the same time bringing the patrolman or team more nearly within the range of constant control. It is now a fundamental duty of the radio patrol officer to remain in contact, that is, controllable.

More important, perhaps, is the fact that radio communication coupled with the central complaint board makes it possible for top management to have *independent* knowledge of complaints and who is assigned to them *before* the patrolman or patrol team does. At least a minimum of centralized control then is available not by the direct issuance of commands from superior to subordinate but by means of a paper-matching process whereby the complaint board's written record can be matched with the written record the patrolman is required to generate. This pattern of control by centralized communication and internal organizational audit is highly dependent upon the distribution of telephones in the population. The citizen's telephone enables the police commander to enlist the complainant on a *routine* basis as part of the apparatus for control of the policeman. A citizen's opportunity to mobilize the police is intricately balanced with that of the commander.

Not all police operations are constituted in the fashion of this highly oversimplified picture of so-called routine patrol. Detectives, for example, are less subject to such control. But these considerations of due-process bars to centralized command and historical changes in control procedures that rely less on command as a form of control are intended to raise questions about the sociological meaning of the stress on command and to lay the ground for a somewhat more systematic analysis of it.

Thus far, "command" has been used in two senses. In one sense, command refers to a technique of control in organizations that consists of giving commands. The directive communication between superior and subordinate may be called a command, or, if more impersonally clothed, an order. In another sense, however, command means neither a specific technique of control nor an instance of its use but something more general—a principle that legitimates orders, instructions, or rules, Orders then are obeyed *because* they are commanded.

Sociologists are familiar, of course, with discussions of this type ever since Weber.[24] In Weberian terms the police department "as an order" is legitimated by the principle of command. Each form of legitimation, however, as Weber so clearly saw, has a correlative requirement of attitude on the part of those subject to its sway. In the case of an order legitimated by a rhetoric of command, the correlative expectation is obedience—again, not as a situational expectation in the case of a given specific command but as a principle relating member to organization. To be obedient in this sense carries the same general sense of principle as in the poverty, chastity, and obedience of the monk's vow. In a system so legitimated we can expect that commitment to obedience will be displayed as a sign of membership.

It is not surprising, then, that social scientists who are based in organizations where independence is legitimated, rehabilitation workers based in those where professional discretion is legitimated, and police who are based in organizations where obedience is legitimated so often fail to communicate with one another when they are engaged in exchanges of ideologies. It is also no wonder that social scientists and rehabilitation workers therefore find the police hierarchically oriented.

We may point out as well that in orders legitimated by command and exacting obedience, the classic status reward is honor. The morale and public relations problems of the American police can be more clearly understood as an attempt to substitute public prestige sought in an occupational performance market for the Weberian status regard sought and validated in the "honor market." The American police are denied both, for the public seems unwilling to accord the police status either in the European sense of status honor as representatives of the State or in the more typically American sense of prestige based on a claim to occupational competence.

Command as a basis for legitimacy can be located under any of the three basic types of legitimation discussed by Weber—the rational-legal, the traditional, and the charismatic. Inherently, however, command as a principle focuses on the commander, and the exact nature of the concrete order legitimated by the principle of command will depend on the role of the specific commander. Because of this commander focus, the command principle is likely to lead to a mystique of the personal commander and an organizational stress

[24] *Max Weber: The Theory of Social and Economic Organization* Talcott Parsons, ed., (New York, Oxford University Press, 1947), pp. 324ff.

on legitimating specific orders or even general rules as emanating from him.

If the principle of command can vary as a function of the situation of the commander, then it is to the role of the commander that we must attend. In the case of the American municipality, police chiefs, at least traditionally both at law and in practice, are politically accountable officials who ordinarily stand or fall with the fortunes of their civilian superiors (who are lodged in external systems). Given the often controversial nature of police work and the often irrational and unpredictable nature of political fortunes in municipal government, the American police chief who is responsible to a politically elected official comes close to the position of a "patrimonial bureaucrat" in Weber's terms. His tenure as chief, though not necessarily his tenure in the department, depends on continuing acceptability to the elected official(s).

The relations of police commanders to civil superiors are actually more varied and complex than that depicted above. We shall discuss briefly only the two most important dimensions of variation, the security of tenure of the chief commander and the degree to which he is held strictly accountable by a mayor. Given strict accountability plus insecurity of tenure, we can expect a kind of obsession with command and a seemingly irrational emphasis on the twinned symbols of the visibility of the commander and the obedience of the force. Some of the rhetoric of command in the police literature likely arises from an attempt to protect the chief by the compulsive effort to overcontrol subordinates, almost any of whom can get him fired. This amounts to saying that as civil superiors increase the formal accountability of the police chief *without changing* the tenure features of the role, the increasing bureaucratization of the police stressed by J. Q. Wilson leads to the development of an organization animated by a principle of the commanding person.[25] This "personalized subordination" to the hero chief can become an operating, if not a formal, principle of organization.

Increased professionalization can be another accommodative strategy in such a situation, but this time aimed not at control of the force but at control of the mayor by changing the grounds of accountability. One of the first jobs of the professionalizing police chief often is to convince his civil superior that "you can't win 'em all" and that it is irrational and unprofessional to dismiss a police chief or commissioner because of failure to solve some particular crime. Per-

[25] James Q. Wilson, *loc. cit.*

haps in the long run it is hard to have a professionalized police without a professionalized mayor. Perhaps also this would lead us to expect different kinds of command styles where a professional city manager intervenes between the chief and the mayor.

If the civil superior, for whatever reason, does not demand accountability from the chief, the quasiformalized obsession with command as a principle of control may be replaced by a complex system of feudal loyalties. In this situation ties of personal political fealty between chief and mayor—or between chief and the local powers—may become prominent and "keep your nose clean" the principle of subordination. When this trend goes beyond a certain point, the department is commonly described as politically corrupt. Finally, to the degree that the chief is secure in his tenure, we would expect the obsession with command and the emphasis on personalized subordination to decrease.

On the basis of this analysis of command and the role of the chief we may distinguish the following four types of departments:

Relation to mayor	Tenure of Chief	
	Secure	Insecure
Strictly accountable	Command bureaucracy	Personalized command bureaucracy
Feudal allegiance	Command feudality	Personalized "political" feudality

We have chosen all-encompassing words such as "feudality" because the concern here is to direct attention to features of police organization that receive relatively little attention and to questions of fundamental differences in the consequences of organizational membership between police and other organizations.[26] Command, obedience, and honor ring strangely in analyzing organizational life in America, except, perhaps, for the military. Yet it seems to us that meaningful analysis of the police must touch upon them as well as upon duty and courage. The self-image of the police is different because of them. Finally, it is our judgment that some such analysis

[26] This discussion of command and control owes much to the analysis of labor unions in Harold L. Wilensky, *Intellectuals in Labor Unions* (Glencoe, Illinois, The Free Press, 1956).

as this will permit sociologists to analyze implications of variations in the formal control of the police by civil authorities in different cities.

A word about two of these types seems in order. The command feudality type seems a contradiction in terms (and indeed derives from the cross-classification itself). Some small municipal and sheriff's departments, where the tenure of the chief in the local "feudal" political structure is secure, may fall here. Because everyone is secure in a relatively nonbureaucratic system, the operating principle of subordination can be command. Such an arrangement possibly characterizes the exceptionally long-tenure chiefs discovered in Lunden's study in Iowa.[27]

The personalized command bureaucracy seems likely to occur where an insecure reform head is in office. To reform successfully he must bureaucratize and rationalize administrative operations. To do this against the inevitable internal resistance he must emphasize the principle of command. To make clear that status quo oriented commanders have been superseded he must emphasize *his* command and his *capacity* to command. In short, he must exercise what Selznick defines as one of the crucial functions of *leadership* in administration. He must define the emerging character of the institution.[28] Perhaps to cynical persons both in and out of the police department this sounds odd. It would certainly be embarrassing to the men concerned. Yet, it is hard to avoid the conclusion that the fortunes of the American municipal police depend not only on the use of computer technology but on the personal charisma of police chiefs.

CONCLUSION

We have attempted to present a perspective on the metropolitan police that emphasizes the consequences of the external environment on police organization and operations. Such sociological study of the police may be of strategic value both for the sociology of law and of formal organizations. The police provide an unusual opportunity to develop and apply a transaction view of organizations, since, on the one hand, police departments have clearly defined boundaries, and yet, on the other, they must continually engage in the management of highly contingent relationships that arise outside them. At

[27] Walter A. Lunden, "The Mobility of Chiefs of Police," *Journal of Criminal Law, Criminology and Police Science,* Vol. 49 (1958), pp. 178–183.

[28] Philip Selznick, *Leadership in Administration* (New York, Row, Peterson and Company, 1957).

the same time, an organizational perspective that views the legal system in terms of transactions among organized subsystems that include the police rather than in terms of more formal imposition may make for a more viable sociology of law.

Our presentation concentrates on a few broad environmental features and traces their significance for police operations. Inevitably important areas have been scanted. Among those on which we would hope to concentrate more fully are those environmental features that affect the social sources and orientations of police personnel, the changing technologies of communication and intelligence, the increasing development and application of rational planning, and, indeed, the potential impact of sociology itself on police organization and behavior. The rationalization of police systems together with an increased emphasis on professional competence provides many opportunities for research on social organization and social order.

Gang Members and the Police*

Carl Werthman and Irving Piliavin

From the front seat of a moving patrol car, street life in a typical Negro ghetto is perceived as an uninterrupted sequence of suspicious scenes. Every well dressed man or woman standing aimlessly on the street during hours when most people are at work is carefully scrutinized for signs of an illegal source of income; every boy wearing boots, black pants, long hair, and a club jacket is viewed as potentially responsible for some item on the list of muggings, broken windows, and petty thefts that still remain to be cleared; and every hostile glance directed at the passing patrolman is read as a sign of possible guilt.

The residents of these neighborhoods regard this kind of surveillance as the deepest of insults. As soon as a patrolman begins to interrogate, the suspect can easily see that his moral identity is being challenged because of his dress, his hair style, his skin color, and his presence in the ghetto itself.

Negro gang members are constantly singled out for interrogation by the police, and the boys develop their own techniques of retaliation. They taunt the police with jibes and threaten their authority with gestures of insolence, as if daring the police to become bigots and bullies in order to defend their honor. Moreover, these techniques of retaliation often do succeed in provoking this response. When

* This paper is based on data gathered during two separate research projects. The study of the police was supported by Grant MH-06328 from the National Institute of Mental Health at the United States Public Health Service and administered by the Survey Research Center at the University of California in Berkeley. The study of delinquent street gangs was initiated by the Survey Research Center on a grant from the Ford Foundation and was later moved to the Center for the Study of Law and Society on the Berkeley campus where funds were made available under a generous grant from the Office of Juvenile Delinquency and Youth Development, Welfare Administration, U.S. Department of Health, Education, and Welfare in cooperation with the President's Committee on Juvenile Delinquency and Youth Crime.

suspect after suspect becomes hostile and surly, the police begin to see themselves as representing the law among a people that lack proper respect for it. They too begin to feel maligned, and they soon become defensively cynical and aggressively moralistic. From the point of view of a patrolman, night sticks are only used upon sufficient provocation, and arrests are only made with just cause.

After studying the interaction between policemen and gang members for over a year, it became clear, at least to these observers, that behind the antagonism between these two groups lies a number of problems in the sociology of law. First, although the law and local custom overlap considerably in Negro ghettos, the disjuncture that remains brings the boys into conflict with the police, a conflict that has ecological as well as legal dimensions. Second, for a set of structural reasons to be discussed, the methods used by the police to locate suspects tend to undermine their legitimacy in the eyes of many ghetto residents. These cultural and structural conditions affect the nature of expectations in face-to-face encounters as well as the way both parties perceive and evaluate each other's behavior. This chapter is therefore an attempt to analyze the way patrolmen and gang boys first perceive or construct their respective worlds and then respond to the situation created for them by the actions and expectations of the other.[1]

THE PERSPECTIVE OF THE GANG MEMBER

The Meaning and Uses of Streets

It is generally agreed that the transformation of city blocks and street corners into "hangouts," "territories," or "turfs" invests the

[1] The data on policemen were collected by Irving Piliavin, Scott Briar, and Roy Turner, who spent eighteen months observing and interviewing patrolmen and juvenile officers on daily patrols in Oakland and San Francisco. We are deeply indebted to Briar and Turner for the long hours they spent in the field on this project and for the many contributions they made to the analysis. The data on gang members were collected by Carl Werthman in a series of taped interviews with fifty-six "core" members of eleven "delinquent gangs" or "jacket clubs," plus observations and more informal conversations involving over one hundred members of these eleven gangs. The boys were drawn from the clientele of a delinquency-prevention program in San Francisco called Youth For Service, and we owe particular thanks to Orville Luster, Percy Pinkney, and the rest of the staff at this agency for helping us conduct this research out of their offices for a two-year period. Of the fifty-six boys interviewed on tape, thirty-seven were Negro, eleven were Mexican, and eight were Caucasian. This chapter is thus based primarily on a sample of Negro gang boys.

streets with a special meaning to the members of a lower-class juvenile gang. Although much has been made of the unusual patriotism associated with these places and the quasi-military fashion in which they are occasionally defended, there has been little systematic study of the way gang members actually put the streets to use.

Sherri Cavan has suggested that a house is a place where "activities which would be unlawful in public places such as poker games and nudity, and activities which would be a source of embarrassment in public places such as family arguments and love making can be freely engaged in."[2] On the basis of this criterion, the plots of public land used as "hangouts" by gang members must also be considered a sort of "home" or "private place." Activities such as poker games, arguments, lovemaking, drinking wine, and serious reading of comic books and newspapers are considered uniquely appropriate in this setting. As a rule, gang members use street corners for behavior that most ordinary adolescents would confine to a house or a car.

There are even occasions in the "home life" of gang members when the streets become functionally independent of all other settings. One function of expropriating hangout space in front of a doughnut shop or candy store is the ready access to a kitchen and to food. During the periods when entire days are spent in or around private space, gang members typically purchase a doughnut and coffee every few hours. This is often supplemented at regular intervals by food and liquor obtained through extralegal channels. The boys typically know the precise time when all deliveries to grocery stories, bakeries, homes, and liquor stores are made. The unguarded truck appears to be the major source of an unconventional food supply. Goods obtained from shoplifting (a more dangerous enterprise) are also used to stave off hunger, but shoplifting seems more often reserved for luxuries such as clothes, party supplies, and an occasional sporting good. A diet provided from these sources can sustain a boy for days, with the addition of a little cheap wine and a daily ration of about ten cigarettes.

Since all routine life functions are at one time or another performed on the streets, the conventional standards of public decorum are considerably relaxed. Entrance into the private space or hangout is occasioned by a noticeable relaxation of physical posture. Shoulders slump, shirttails appear, and greetings are exchanged with an abandon that is only achieved by people who usually receive houseguests in the

[2] Sherri Cavan, "Interaction in Home Territories," *Berkeley Journal of Sociology*, Vol. VIII, p. 18.

kitchen. A good deal of time is also spent combing hair in front of store windows and dancing to rock and roll (often without a partner and without music) as if completely absorbed in the privacy of a bedroom.

Yet as soon as the boys leave the street corner, they become self-consciously absorbed in the demands of a public role. They pay careful attention to uniform—either casually immaculate ("looking sharp") or meticulously disheveled ("looking bad")—and cover the territory in the characteristic hiking style ("walking pimp"). Most of the boys would no sooner start a poker game two blocks away from the privacy of the hangout than more respectable citizens would think of making love in their front yards. Of course there are many notable exceptions to this rule, and on an irregular basis most boys do both.

The fact that gang members make relatively relaxed and private use of public streets does pose some problems for them, particularly when it comes to controlling the entrance of outsiders. People can take liberties in houses because a house is "an area of restricted entrance,"[3] and those who enter other people's houses either by accident or against the implicit consent of their occupants are potentially subject to physical assault, legal action, or, at the very least, embarrassment.

With the exception of legal action, gang members also have these sanctions at their command. They use every means at their disposal to make outsiders accept the transparent walls they construct around the hangout. In practice, however, there are limits to the defensive measures that can be taken if one's private space is defined by most people, however innocently, as a public street corner.

Since practically every category of person who uses the public pathways is very nearly forced to violate whatever "rules of trespass" the gang members might like to make, it is easily understandable why the situation itself engenders some amount of bitterness among the boys. Over and above the negative feelings associated with this situational shortcoming, however, the gang members do recognize differences among those who actually or might potentially violate the boundaries of the hangout. Moreover, the feelings of hostility directed toward the various categories of outsiders can be ranked hierarchically.

The least disliked category of persons and those most accommodating to the claims made by a gang are the "familiars," mostly residents

[3] *Ibid.*, p. 18.

of the local neighborhood. They walk through even the most boisterous gatherings on private space as though they were not aware of its special character. This response to a potentially difficult situation is correctly interpreted by the boys as a sign that their claims to privacy are being politely accepted. The potential conflict between those who use this physical space as a living room and those who use it as a public thoroughfare is neatly resolved by having both parties studiously pretend to ignore the presence of the other. Occasionally a "familiar" will nod or smile at members of the club. At this time both parties seem to accept a definition of the situation as neighbors whose back doors are always open to one another's unannounced appearance.

More disliked and less accommodating are the "unfamiliars." These persons are not known to gang members, and thus there is no prior mutual understanding as to how the situation of potential conflict is to be resolved. Gang members communicate their claims on the hangout by calling an abrupt halt to verbal interchange in such a way as to suggest that a legitimate setting for private conversation has been rudely intruded upon. The members then begin to stare, and out of the hostile silence may come a wisecrack or a taunt. The boys are usually willing to accept a noticeable increase in walking pace and lowered eyes as sufficient implicit apology. An "unfamiliar" who continues to behave impolitely, either by refusing to hurry out of the space or by challenging the reality offered to him by the boys, becomes eligible for sanctions otherwise appropriate to a common housebreaker.

Usually, however, these illegal sanctions are not invoked. Gang boys have other less legally problematic ways of terrorizing casual observers, and one distinct class of favorites involves riding roughshod over the numerous rules of etiquette that organize routine behavior in public places. The boys may come within short range of a stranger, for example, and ask to "borrow" whatever the person happens to possess, be it tires from a used car salesman, a bicycle from a young boy, or money from practically anyone. This tactic constitutes a dramatic demonstration to most people of how much they are dependent on mundane conventions to maintain the assumption that one is usually safe around strangers. Similarly, the simple act of refusing to move when standing directly in the path of a passerby can destroy the faith of any witness in the orderly character of their immediate social world.

Although intentional violations of etiquette are obviously not crimes, they often succeed in doing considerable psychic damage to their targets. The stranger may give a gang boy money, walk around him if he is blocking the way, or pretend to ignore his antics altogether, but he will be apprehensive because he does not know what lies immediately ahead. With the threat of violence in the air, these situations become "disorganized."[4]

Yet as far as gang members are concerned, both "familiars" and "unfamiliars" share a single redeeming trait; neither can usually avoid trespassing on the street corner. They therefore cannot really be blamed for their presence since they are also the victims of an uncontrollable geographical factor—the awkward arrangement of streets. But there are other categories of persons who, like gang members, make something special out of public space. They are not forced for material reasons to violate the boundaries of the hang-out. They make their own sets of social claims on access to the street corner.

The first of these special people are the members of rival gangs. Like the "familiars," they are willing to support the reality of claims to a private use of the street corner. Given the prestige system that exists among gangs, however, they have a vested interest (although rarely consummated) in obtaining unconditional rights of access both to the hang-out and to the larger "territory" of which it is a part. Next to the rumble, the "surprise attack" on a hangout is considered the ultimate declaration of all-out war. Admittedly these events are quite rare, but should a gang ever win a total victory in one of these wars, the symbol of their success would be unconditional access to the hangout.[5]

The police are the most despised and least accommodating threat to a gang's conception of a hangout. Like gang members, the police have a vested interest in imposing a set of normative claims on the people who use the streets. The very places that are defended like homes by gang members also constitute places of work or "beats" to the police, and the home-like uses to which gang members put

[4] For a systematic discussion of this approach to the problem of "social disorganization" see Albert K. Cohen, "The Study of Social Disorganization and Deviant Behavior," in Robert S. Merton, Leonard Broom, and Leonard S. Cottrell, Jr., eds., *Sociology Today* (New York, Basic Books, 1959), pp. 474–83.

[5] No conflict of this magnitude took place while this study was being done. However, some of the boys studied tell stories about an immediately preceding period in San Francisco gang history when these raids were not uncommon. In fact, a number of boys in the same neighborhood remember seeing a machine gun hidden in a park near the hangout that was used on at least two frequently mentioned occasions to defend the private space. These boys also claim that the machine gun was not used any place else.

the streets are often perceived as threats to the patrolman's task of maintaining the conventional rules that ordinarily govern behavior on them. Although the boys attempt either subtly or violently to convince outsiders that their behavior at the hangout is a strictly private affair, the police tend to insist with equal conviction that all behavior on public property is their legitimate concern. The relationship between gang members and policemen thus has its roots in an ecological conflict over claims to final authority in the same setting. The Chicago police apparently have a phrase that expresses this relationship. When they are annoyed at a gang for their behavior at a hangout, they will say "Gi'me that corner!"

In practice, the police usually do make some concessions to the boys and allow them a privileged use of the streets. Patrolmen often tolerate drinking and gambling at the hangout, activities that become suitable grounds for arrest in other parts of the neighborhood. Under no conditions, however, is the hangout ever considered a completely invulnerable shield against the authority of the police. It is typically under constant surveillance, and the police even stage periodic "shakedowns" as a reminder to the boys that final authority for their behavior on the streets rests with the public's official landlords. For example:

> One time me and a couple of friends, we came down to the corner on Monday night because we was supposed to have our meeting. And we was standing there on the corner bullshitting like we always do, and there was only four of us. Then this cop on a motorcycle pulled over and walked over to us. I seen him before. He rides around the neighborhood a lot. He didn't say nothing. He just zipped down his jacket and there was his big old billy club. And then he started asking questions, identification, what were we doing, and all like that. And he searched us and got our names down on the book and everything. We wasn't doing anything except what we usually do on that corner. (What's that?) Stand there bullshitting. They do anything to get our names on that book. You know. They want us to know they in charge.

Gang Boys and the Law

This ecological conflict thus has a legal dimension. The view of fighting held by gang boys, for example, is clearly a case in which the law and the mores conflict. The police are often called upon to break through layers of screaming girls in order to separate a pair of street-style gladiators, and one patrolman even suggested that the worst injuries he had sustained as an officer had been leg bites received from females on these occasions. Yet to gang boys, most of these fights are both honorable and necessary. They were either challenged, insulted, or hit first, and thus they are always bitter when penalized by the police.

> Like that time that me and this kid from the Sabines was having this big fight up at school. He hit me during gym class. It was sort of accidental, but, see, I said something to him, and then he said something back and so we had this fight. The girls was going crazy. Jumping up and down and screaming and everything like they do. I guess this cop thought there was a riot going on or something cause he really came busting in there. Well, he grabbed us and threw us into the car and all that old shit. We tried to tell him what we was fighting about, but he wouldn't listen. Them cops is something else, man. What he expect us to do? Have one of them duals with guns or something?

There are other situations, however, in which the formal legal status of a disorder is more ambiguous, and these situations can cause trouble when both the police and the gang boys lay claims to the benefit of the doubt. For example, when strangers or "unfamiliars" are being treated to gross violations of etiquette or to other such attacks on their faith in social order, the police quite naturally feel constrained to take action. Yet from a gang member's point of view, the legal issues involved in disorganizing a social situation are not always clear-cut. For example:

> Last Sunday we went to see about buying a car. So we went down to a shop. We were out there parked, and this friend of mine was trying to con the guy into giving him some tires. He was standing there next to this Merc saying, "Why don't you give us the tires?" So the guy says, "No, I'm gonna sell it, and who'd want to buy a car with the tires gone?" So we were trying to open the door, but the guy wouldn't give us the keys to open the door. So there were about ten of us there, and it was in the daytime, and we was just messing around. You know, laughing and everything.
>
> So finally this cop comes by. This fat slob. He was drunk when he got out of the car cause his shirt was out, man. So the dude gets out, and he comes up to me and he say, "What's wrong?" And I go, "What do you mean, what's wrong?" I wasn't

trying to get smart with him. I was just saying it. And he goes, "Don't get smart! I was just asking you what's wrong?" I say, "I'm not trying to get smart!" So then he goes, "Now you are!" I didn't say nothing. I just shut up.

So he walks over to this other friend of mine and he goes, "What seems to be the trouble?" But my friend didn't say nothing. So he pulled out this club, and he came over to me and pushed me against the car and he goes, "So you're a smart guy huh?" So I say, "No." And then I smelled him. He must have been drinking wine cause I smelled it all over his breath so I knew he was drunk. So I moved away from him. But he goes, "Come over here!" I didn't want to get next to him 'cause I knew he was going to try something.

So after that, the jerk, he stands out in the middle of the street and he says, "Well, if there's any trouble and you want it settled, "I'll settle it!" And he starts slapping the club on his hands and walking around to see who he can hit. So we start telling him there ain't no trouble or nothing. And the guy's older brother, he was twenty-one, he came out and said, "What's wrong?" And the cop goes, "Who's asking you? I'm asking the questions, not you!" Smart dude you know. We didn't want to offend him 'cause we knew he was drunk. So he walked up to me again. I don't know what was wrong with the dude! He trying to do something! He says, "I'm gonna give you three minutes to get off the street!" He can't give you three minutes to get off the street when you're not doing nothing, right? So we were laughing.

After a few minutes we got in the car and started driving around. And the first thing you know he started following us. We went around the corner and stopped. And he throw me in the car and goes, "Now I'm taking you down to the station!" I say, "For what?" And he goes, "Because I told you to get out of here and you didn't do it!" So I tried to stick up for my rights, and I asked what he was taking me in for. I say, "Just 'cause I was on the street?" And he goes, "Yeah."

Finally, there is the issue of the role played by the police in protracted conflicts between gang boys and other segments of the community, particularly local store owners, school personnel, and Recreation Department officials. Much of the vandalism in low-income neighborhoods is directed at these targets, and the reasons for attack are often not hard to find. The following quote, for example, was taken from a Negro gang boy whose colleagues had just ransacked a local grocery store and been sent to jail.

> I know why them cats did it, and I bet they ain't sorry. Even now. We used to go to this place all the time to buy cokes and stuff, and this Chinaman who run the place, he didn't like us. He'd sometime call us "boy" and "nigger" and be hollering that we stealing stuff, and when we start talking back to him, he'd quick turn around and start calling the cops. Then the cops would come. You know, like they always do. About fifteen minutes or an hour late. And by that time we just be standing around in front of this place waiting on them. Well, one day we walked in and this Chinaman, he tell us he don't have no cokes. But we can see them. They just sitting there behind this glass. So then he says, "Okay." He gonna sell us the cokes. But he gonna charge us eighteen cents. So Leroy got mad and just grabbed one, and then the cops picked him up. They didn't do nothing to him. Just rode him around or something. But that made Leroy even madder so he went and wrecked the place. Man, you shoulda seen it. Glass all smashed. Cans all over the floor. They got Leroy and them. It was in the papers. But if they get out, I bet they gonna do it again.

The Situation of the Patrolman

As William Whyte observed some twenty-five years ago, the police and the gang boys do not always agree about *what* rules the police should enforce or about *how* they should enforce them. Whyte said:

> The policeman is subject to sharply conflicting social pressures. On one side are the "good people" of Eastern City, who have written their moral judgements into the law and demand through their newspapers that the law be enforced. On the other side are the people of Cornerville, who have different standards and have built up an organization whose perpetuation depends upon freedom to violate the law.[6]

This conflict forces patrolmen to make a decision about which set of standards to enforce, and Whyte's advice to them about this choice was unambiguous. "Under these circumstances," he said, "the smoothest course for the officer is to conform to the social organization

[6] William Foote Whyte, *Street Corner Society* (Chicago, The University of Chicago Press, 1943), p. 138.

with which he is in direct contact and at the same time to try and give the impression to the outside world that he is enforcing the law."[7]

From the point of view of a patrolman, however, this advice is not quite as helpful as it might sound since it still leaves unanswered the question of precisely what "conforming" to local standards involves. It is clear, for example, that the residents of most low-income communities, gang members included, expect the police to stand for *something*. The boys, in fact, are exceedingly contemptuous of patrolmen who know that legal standards are being broken but who are either too frightened or too cynical to act. If a patrolman tolerates all behavior, legal and illegal alike, he is likely to be defined by gang boys either as "chicken" or as "corrupt."

> Man, you should have seen them cops out at the Point on Saturday night. Zeke, and Orville, and Percy (gang workers) and them were there. They can tell you. Five carloads of cops was there, lights flashing and everything. And everybody is just standing around after this party. Fights going on, girls screaming, everything. And then this cat pulls out a gun and starts firing. Man, he was five feet away from them cops and they stood there! Just stood there looking! Somebody coulda got killed or something. Or maybe they just didn't care. Maybe they was saying, "Why not let them niggers go kill each other anyway. They ain't got no sense."

A patrolman can therefore compromise his legitimacy while maintaining order in one of two ways; either by visibly betraying his obligation to enforce *some* rules of law or by fullfilling these obligations in ways that conflict with the moral standards of the local population. If he is too legalistic, he runs the risk of being perceived as arrogant and unjust; but if he tailors his standards to the *practices* of the neighborhood rather than to its *ideals*, he is looked down upon for abdicating his responsibilities altogether. The gang boys are not without their own standards of fairness, and it is these standards that the patrolman must attempt to enforce.

A "good cop" is thus a man who can successfully handle a subtle and narrowly defined moral challenge. He must try to order the life of an ethnic lower-class community from within by holding people such as gang boys to their own ideals, however little these ideals may be reflected in behavior. As Whyte suggested,

[7] *Ibid.*, p. 138.

> Cornerville people and many of the officers themselves believe that the policeman should have the confidence of the people in his area so that he can settle many difficulties in a personal manner without making arrests. . . . The policeman who takes a strictly legalistic view of his duties cuts himself off from the personal relations necessary to enable him to serve as a mediator of disputes in his area.[8]

Whyte's emphasis on mediation certainly applies to the way gang boys expect patrolmen to handle fights. In situations involving violence, it seems that the "good cop" functions as an arbitrator. He does not turn the boys over to a local school principal for "fighting after school," nor does he cart them away to the station. He isolates them in a squad car, talks the situation over with them, and then does what he can to achieve at least a semipermanent peace.

> (Have you guys ever met any good cops?) Yeah, there was two studs out in Lakeview once, not the regular cops, who was pretty straight. Remember when he had that big fight at the playground and those guys from Hunters Point got hurt? Mr. J. (the playground director) sent for the cops only they didn't take us in. They talked to us for about an hour. They asked us what we fighting about and why did we fight and could we use boxing gloves and did we know that fighting was against the law and all that. But they finally let us go, and they got Willie to take the Hunters Point boys home. They was *real* straight, those two. I think they must have lived out there or something, or maybe they was in a club once themselves.

Yet the task of being defined as a "good cop" in the process of handling routine "disorders" involves something more than arbitration. As we have seen, the act of badgering a used car salesman for free tires may be sufficiently annoying to prompt a patrolman to intervene; but if a patrolman makes categorical claims to final authority in these situations, his authority is likely to be challenged.

When gang boys are apprehended for disorganizing a social situation or for behaving badly at a hangout, a "good cop" will therefore remind them of their values while also suggesting that he could claim the right to use force. He responds to formally ambiguous legal situations with an artful ambiguity of his own, and his reward for this delicate maneuver is legitimacy.

[8] *Ibid.*, p. 136.

> Those two studs out in Lakeview wouldn't always be on our back for playing neither. We'd be standing on the corner pulling some kinda phoney shit, and they'd pull up to find out if we was up to something. But they talked to us nice. They wouldn't let us get away with nothing, and, I mean, them cats would bust you if they had to. But they talked to us nice.

Even with the best of intentions, then, it is not easy to be considered a "good cop." Not only must the gang boys be persuaded that a policeman understands and likes them, they must also be convinced that he shares their conception of justice and is fully prepared to enforce it. In practice, most confrontations between patrolmen and gang members thus contain the possibilities of conflict—a conflict over whose conception of proper behavior *will* prevail, a conflict over whose conception *ought* to prevail, and therefore a conflict over whose moral identity is to remain publicly in tact. Furthermore, the fact that most policemen are not defined as "good cops" cannot be accounted for simply by the wide variety of social and personal defects commonly attributed to them. For example, it may be true that the behavior of policemen is affected by a class and ethnic predisposition to prejudice towards Negroes and a psychological predisposition to danger, violence, and authoritarianism, not to mention inadequate education, training, and pay. Yet there are also structural and situational contingencies associated directly with the process of law enforcement itself that make it difficult for even the most enlightened and saintly of policemen to avoid being seen as pariahs by a large segment of the ethnic poor, contingencies that are part and parcel of the methods used by the police.

THE PERSPECTIVE OF THE POLICE

Stated formally, the fundamental problem of police work is the location of a set of criminals that corresponds to a set of reported crimes. The primary resource needed to accomplish this objective is knowledge, and for obvious reasons this resource is limited. With the exception of those who the police can manage to witness in the act of breaking the law, little is generally known about the specific identities of people who have committed crimes in the past. Thus, the police are structurally predisposed to adopt research procedures that will produce this knowledge most efficiently.

In the classic detective story, the police begin the detection process with a crime. The crime itself defines a population of "suspects," and this population is then broken down into smaller and smaller subgroups as "evidence" accumulates, "evidence" being defined as information about the categories of people to eliminate as suspects. At the end of the story, the culprit is finally located by a process of deduction.

In the world of modern police work, however, this procedure is considered hopelessly inefficient. The police attempt to solve particular crimes either by going directly to a population of previously located suspects, or they first locate "suspicious" individuals and then attempt to link them with some item in the set of previously committed crimes. The first of these methods is often adopted by juvenile officers, and the second is standard practice among patrolmen. Moreover, each of these methods creates a unique situation for the various suspect populations involved.

The Situation of Detection

Most juvenile officers actually do begin their investigations by adopting the methods of their fictional colleagues in detective stories. All complaints from schools, parents, citizens, and other policemen about specific infractions believed to involve young people are referred to the juvenile detail, and work proceeds from the crime to a search for the offender.

The first step in this process is usually to exhaust the knowledge of a complainant. A woman whose car has been damaged by thrown rocks, for example, may say that the damage was done by "those boys next door," thereby eliminating in one step everyone but the guilty parties. But she might also report that the car was damaged by "a bunch of Negro boys between the ages of fourteen and sixteen", or worse, if she has no idea who threw the rocks, she may only be able to produce the name of a school or the name of a place where the adolescent troublemakers in the neighborhood are known to congregate. This kind of information, although eliminating a great many boys, still leaves the police with a sizable number of suspects.

In practice, therefore, the juvenile officer often proceeds directly to boys who have proven themselves capable of committing the crime, and then he relies on his skills at interrogation. Although the officer may consult his files on the population of suspects and offenders located during previous investigations, these files are used largely as memory aides.[9] Most of this information is in his head.

[9] These files are often cross-indexed by name, nickname, race, and previous offense. Many juvenile bureaus also keep membership lists of gangs (if available) and a picture or sample of the club jackets currently in use.

The success of this method is suggested by the fact that over 90% of convicted juveniles confess, a rate that testifies both to the competence of juvenile officers at interrogation and the incompetence of gang boys at concealing information. Those boys who have unusual control over words, voice tones, facial expressions, and body muscles can sometimes manage to avoid conviction indefinitely unless they are apprehended at the scene of a crime. Yet these talents are rare. Some gangs contain no such talented members; others contain two or three. It is therefore rarely necessary for a juvenile officer to expend much time and energy collecting evidence in order to build his case against a boy.

Although the procedures used by juvenile officers are unquestionably efficient, the boys on permanent suspect lists do not appreciate the elegance of these techniques. As David Matza has pointed out, efficient enforcement systems contain agents who suspect, apprehend, and interrogate only a few possible candidates. Most of us—the happy few—are rarely if ever contacted or questioned. . . . Thus, even in those cases in which guilt is confessed, the subcultural delinquent may sense injustice because of selective procedures inherent in any efficient system of enforcement. He feels that cognizance is unevenly exercised.[10] This sentiment is often expressed as follows:

> Every time something happens in this neighborhood, them mother fuckin' cops come looking for me! I may not be doing nothing, but if somebody gets beat or something gets stole they always be coming right to my place to find out what's going on!

Encounters

The techniques of interrogation used by juvenile officers can best be viewed as self-conscious variations in the posture adopted towards suspects. If an officer has not been able to compile a good list of suspects after interviewing a complainant, he may simply cruise the local neighborhood asking familiar boys for information. This style of interrogation is usually conducted in a casual, informal, and conspiratorial tone of voice. It is designed to suggest that nothing serious has happened, that the officer is merely curious about a particular incident, or that a "favor" from the boy being interrogated will someday be returned. As far as the boys are concerned, however, this posture is simply "sneaky."

[10] David Matza, *Delinquency and Drift* (New York, John Wiley and Sons, 1964), p. 108.

> Some cops may be nice when you meet them, but as soon as you turn your back they be keeping full tab on you. Like this juvenile officer, Sergeant K. and his buddy. Every time I see him in school the sucker come up to me real nice and start running down his shit. "How's it going? What you been doing?" He gets to interrogating my ass, man, like I done something wrong! And all the time he be coming on nice! You know, like, "It's just between you and me." All that old shit. He sometimes say, "No, we don't expect you to squeal on your friends or nothing. We just want a little help. You do us a favor, we do you a favor. You go on and tell me what boys was involved and I guarantee you I let you go home. Nothing gonna happen anyway. You know. It ain't really serious." All that old shit! And then they turn around and try to book you every damn chance they get! Some of them nice cops you got to watch real careful.

When a juvenile officer has compiled a more promising list of suspects, however, his approach to interrogation is likely to be decidedly less flattering. After confronting a boy with a list of acquaintances, the officer may wait for a suspicious silence to follow a particular name; or he might accuse a suspect directly in the hope that, even if innocent, the boy might get rattled enough to produce the actual offender.

Yet a juvenile officer is likely to give his most deferential and endearing performance when he thinks he has finally located the culprit. By suggesting that the suspect is regarded as a "good boy" and will not be done any harm, the officer attempts to ease him into a confession.

Although a great many gang boys are tricked into confessions, the authority of a juvenile officer is rarely rejected because of the hypocrisy involved in his techniques of interrogation. Since it strikes the boys as reasonable that a juvenile officer would attempt to catch them for the crimes they actually do commit, these defeats are often taken philosophically. As one boy put it:

> If you done something and you be lying and yelling when the boys from juvy come around and they catch you lying, well, what you gonna do? You gonna complain 'cause you was caught? Hell man, you can't do that. You did something, and you was caught, and that's the way it goes.

Yet the sense of injustice created by the actions of a juvenile officer does not necessarily disappear after a confession. In many cases, the equity of a disposition also becomes an issue.

Outcomes

The juvenile officer exercises a good deal of discretion in deciding how to process offenders, a discretion that far transcends the measure of ambiguity ordinarily involved in legal assessments of motivation and intent. Although a truant may not be responsible for his behavior, he may be a touch rebellious, or he may be acting in complete and willful disregard for law, the nature and intent of this crime is not as important to a juvenile officer as what he learns about the attitude of the offender towards the idea of the law itself. For example, if an officer decides he is dealing with a boy who is "guilty but essentially good" or "guilty but sometimes weak," the probability is high that he will decide to let the boy go with a warning about the consequences of committing this crime again. He might feel that contact with the unsavory clientele of a juvenile hall would damage an otherwise positive attitude towards the law or that moral contamination in the eyes of parents and teachers as a result of being sent to jail might weaken an otherwise firm commitment to conventional behavior. On the other hand, if the officer decides that the offender is a "punk," a "persistent troublemaker," or some other version of a thoroughly bad boy, he may well decide to make an arrest.[11]

A "delinquent" is therefore not a juvenile who happens to have committed an illegal act. He is a young person whose moral character has been negatively assessed. And this fact has led some observers to conclude that the transformation of young people into official "delinquents" is best looked at as an organizational rather than a legal process since policemen, probation officers, and juvenile court judges often base their dispositions on a host of criteria that are virtually unrelated to the nature of the specific offense.[12]

The *magnitude of an offense,* of course, can become a factor in dispositions. One responsibly planned and willfully executed robbery, rape, or assault can ruin the moral status of a juvenile indefinitely. Since 90% of the crimes committed by juveniles are minor offenses, however, this criterion is only rarely used.

The number of *previous contacts with police* has a more important effect on dispositions. These contacts are typically recorded on easily

[11] For a more complete discussion of police discretion in dealing with juveniles, see Irving Piliavin and Scott Briar, "Police Encounters with Juveniles," *The American Journal of Sociology,* Vol. LXX, No. 2 (Sept. 1964), pp. 209–211.

[12] The problem of discretion has been formulated and studied by Aaron Cicourel in these terms. See Aaron V. Circourel, *The Social Organization of Juvenile Justice* (forthcoming).

accessible files, and these files contain everything from arrests and convictions to contacts made on the flimsiest of contingent grounds. If a boy confesses to a crime and is not known to the police, he is often released. If he is caught for a third or fourth time, however, the sum total of previous contacts may be enough to affect a judgment about his moral character adversely, regardless of the nature or magnitude of the present offense and regardless of the reasons he was previously contacted. For example:

> Like last night, man, me and Willy got busted for curfew. I mean I got busted for curfew. We was walkin' up the hill towards home, and these cops pull up. It was a Friday night, man, so we didn't want no trouble. When the cops ask us what we was doing and what about our names we was all nice. So then the cop gets on that radio and checks us out. There was a whole bunch of noise comin' over that box. I couldn't hear what they was sayin'. But then the cop comes out and says to Willy, "O.K., you can go." And I say, "What about me?" And the cop says, "You been in trouble before. We don't want you walkin' the streets at night. We going to take you down to the station for curfew." Then I got real mad. I almost ran. Lucky thing I didn't though. I woulda been in real trouble then.

There is even some evidence to suggest that assessments about the type and quality of *parental control* are even more important factors in dispositions than *any* of the offense-related criteria. One of the main concerns of a juvenile officer is the likelihood of future offense, and this determination is often made largely on the basis of "the kinds of parents" a boy happens to possess. Thus, the moral character of parents also passes under review; and if a house appears messy, a parent is missing, or a mother is on welfare, the probability of arrest increases. Similarly, a boy with a father and two older brothers in jail is considered a different sort of person from a boy whose immediate family is not known to the police. As Cicourel points out, these judgments about family life are particularly subject to bias by attitudes related to class.[13]

> See, like if you or maybe one of your brothers, say both of you, been to Y.A.,* or your sister, every time they see you they

[13] Aaron Cicourel, "Social Class, Family Structure and the Administration of Juvenile Justice," Center for the Study of Law and Society, University of California at Berkeley, Working Paper, MS.

* The detention facilities administered by the California Youth Authority.

> get on your back. They know all your family. If they ever pick you up and look at your records, they automatically take you in. They see where your sister been to jail, your brother, or if you ever went to jail. And they start saying, "Your whole family is rotten. Your whole family is jailbirds." Shit like that. And this is what really make you mad, when they tell you your mother don't know how to read!

Although the family situation of a boy and his record of prior police contacts both enter into dispositions, the most important factor affecting the decision of juvenile officers is the *attitude* displayed by the offender, both during and after the confession itself. Cicourel, for example, found that juvenile officers were strongly influenced by the style and speed with which the offender confessed.[14] If a boy blurts out his misdeeds immediately, this behavior is taken as a sign that the boy "trusts" authority and is therefore "under control." If the boy proves to be a "tough nut to crack," however, he is viewed with suspicion. As soon as a juvenile is defined as "hardened," he is considered no less dangerous to society than the adult criminal.

Similarly, the boys who appear frightened, humble, penitent, and ashamed are also more likely to go free. They are often defined as "weak, troubled, and the victim of circumstances" but basically "good boys," an assessment of moral character that may win them a release.

On the other hand, if a boy shows no signs of being spiritually moved by his offense, the police deal harshly with him. Not only has he sinned against a legal rule, but he has also symbolically rejected the normative basis for conforming to it in the first place; and it is this double deviation that has fateful consequences for the way he is treated by the police. Once he gets himself defined as "the kind of person who doesn't respect the law," he becomes a perfect candidate for arrest, detention, and eventual incarceration. Most of the juvenile officers we interviewed felt that the attitude of the offender was the major determinant of dispositions in 50% of their cases, and Nathan Goldman reports that "defiance on the part of a boy will lead to juvenile court quicker than anything else."[15]

It is hardly necessary to describe the way most gang boys feel about the equity of these dispositions. One only needs to imagine the look on a boy's face when he is told that he is about to spend

[14] Cicourel, *The Social Organization of Juvenile Justice, Loc. cit.*

[15] Nathan Goldman, *The Differential Selection of Juvenile Offenders for Court Appearances,* National Council on Crime and Delinquency (1963), p. 106.

a year in jail for an offense committed with a friend who was sent home when he promptly confessed.

The Situation of Suspicion

The methods used by patrolmen are quite a bit different from those adopted by juvenile officers, essentially because a patrol officer or "beat man" is assigned to an area rather than an age group or a special type of crime. Unlike a juvenile officer, the patrolman usually does not launch an investigation on the basis of a specific infraction. His job is to prevent crime, to maintain order, and to locate "suspicious people" who might later be linked to a crime. The last of these functions, however, must be performed from the front seat of a patrol car, and this fact led Harvey Sacks to conclude that patrolmen are engaged in the occupational specialty of "inferring the probability of criminality from the appearances persons present in public places."[16] Their task is to locate suspicious people on sight, and this must be done by inferring moral character from appearances.

David Matza has pointed out that the policeman's methodological problem here "is similar in almost every respect to that faced by sociologists." Both must classify individuals by searching for the particular actors that best fit a set of social or legal categories, and both are typically forced to use indicators of the categories of persons they are looking for since true referents rarely exist.[17] In brief, then, patrolmen are forced to operate like social scientists. In order to locate "suspicious persons" they must use indicators, each with a specific but by no means perfect probability of leading them either to the discovery or prevention of a crime.

Policemen develop indicators of suspicion by a method of pragmatic induction. Past experience leads them to conclude that more crimes are committed in the poorer sections of town than in the wealthier areas, that Negroes are more likely to cause public disturbances than whites, and that adolescents in certain areas are a greater source of trouble than other categories of the citizenry. On the basis of these conclusions, the police divide the population and physical territory under surveillance into a variety of categories, make some initial assumptions about the moral character of the people and places in these categories, and then focus attention on those categories of persons and places felt to have the shadiest moral characteristics. As one patrolman states:

[16] Harvey Sacks, *Methods in Use for the Production of a Social Order: A Method for Warrantably Inferring Moral Character*, MS, p. 4.

[17] See David Matza, "The Selection of Deviants," MS, p. 32.

> If you know that the bulk of your delinquency problem comes from kids who, say, are from 12 to 14 years of age, when you're out on patrol you are much more likely to be sensitive to the activities of juveniles in this age bracket than older or younger youtn. This would be good law enforcement practice. The logic in our case is the same except that our delinquency problem is largely found in the Negro community and it is these youth toward whom we are sensitized.[18]

According to both gang members and patrolmen, residence in a *neighborhood* is the most general indicator used by the police to select a sample of potential law violators. Many local patrolmen tend to consider *all residents* of "bad" neighborhoods rather weakly committed to whatever moral order they make it their business to enforce, and this transforms most of the people who use the streets in these neighborhoods into good candidates for suspicion.

> (Tell me something. Do you guys know anyone up on the hill who doesn't get rousted by the police?) Up on the hill? Everybody gets picked on cause of the reputation of Hunters Point.
>
> (Everybody does?) They sure do. Everybody gets picked on. Even parents. All the time they holler, "You oughta know how to raise your kids! Don't you know how to raise your kids right?"
>
> That's right, man. That's what's happening.

Although many patrolmen believe that some entire neighborhoods are morally inferior to others, they do not enforce their standards with the same severity in all parts of "poor" neighborhoods. According to gang members, the "territory" contains both *safe spots* and *danger spots.* The danger spots tend to be public places of business, such as outdoor drive-in hamburger stands or pool halls, where a great many young people in the neighborhood often congregate and where fights and arguments frequently break out. The probability of being defined as suspicious by the police in these places is quite high, and thus physical presence is more of a risk than in other spots.

> Just like over at the Tick Tock and over in Fillmore where they used to have snacks—and anywhere you go like a public place and a lot of guys be around. I mean everybody would be buying something and most of them do be buying something

[18] Irving Piliavin and Scott Briar, *op. cit.*, p. 212.

and they be eating it, but the police are still sitting on you as long as you're there watching every move you make.

The one condition under which a hangout does become a relatively free place is during the brief periods when patrolmen regularize their appearances at the street corner. Gang members very quickly chart these regularities, and during the periods when they have "the cops figured out" they feel comparatively safe; however, these periods of relative freedom rarely last longer than a few weeks.

(When you guys were on the streets every night, do you think the police came around every night?) We seen the police every night. Not, you know, that they stop us every night, but I seen one every night. Sometimes it was O.K. like when we knew the main streets they'd be on and when they show up. . . . For a while they always be coming around 10:30 so we be waiting for them. So about that time somebody'd start looking out the door and say, "the heat coming!" So, you know, either everybody leave or the ones over eighteen stay. And then after they gone, then everybody just slide on back there and resume where they left off at.

Although the police seem to create a few "safe spots" within "bad neighborhoods," gang members report that the *boundaries of neighborhoods* are patrolled with great seriousness and severity. The police are seen as very hard on "suspicious looking" adolescents who have strayed from home territory.

(Do you guys stay mostly at Hunters Point or do you travel into other districts?) If we go someplace, they tell us to go on home. Because every time we go somewhere we mostly go in big groups and they don't want us. One time we was walking on Steiner Street. So a cop drove up and he say, "Hey! Hanky and Panky! Come here!" And he say, "You all out of bounds, get back on the other side of Steiner Street." Steiner Street is supposed to be out of bounds. (What's on the other side of Steiner?) Nothin' but houses.

Gang members interpret the policy of trying to stop them from traveling into other lower-class neighborhoods as a tactic to stop gang wars, and our research on the police suggests that the boys are right. The police do tend to see all sojourns into neighboring territories as potential attacks on rival gangs.

They don't want us to come out of Hunters Point to tell the truth. Because every time we come out, man, they think we going to fight. But that ain't always true, and it ain't us that always starts the stuff. We on our way home. And they gonna pick us up for fighting back.

In addition to preventing gang members from traveling into neighborhoods of the same class and ethnic status as their own, the police are equally as stringent about preventing the boys from crossing boundaries into neighborhoods of a higher status or a different color. Although the policy of the police is the same in both cases, they attribute different motives to the boys for wanting to enter higher-status areas. When gang members visit other lower-class neighborhoods, the police suspect them of instigating war; when they are found in middle- or upper-class neighborhoods, the police suspect them of intentions to commit robbery or rape.

Me and a friend of mine, we went to a girl's house name of, ah, no, I ain't gonna say her name. You might know her. She was stayin' in a white district. So when we was up there, I guess they saw we was colored. You know, not mostly colored people stay up there. It was about ten o'clock 'cause we was leaving the girl's flat. Just walked out the door. Comin' out the door, and here's the curb. We right there by the curb. Gonna go down the block. Cops come around the corner with an orange light. I believe they just sitting there waiting to nab us. They probably seen us go in there. They come and pull us out. Shake us down. *All* the way down, too, man. They shake us all the way down. And ask us what we doing over here. We tell them we came out to this girl's house. He say, "Where'd you stay?" I say, "Well, you just saw us come out the house 'cause I saw you right around the corner." He say, "Well, she's colored." So they say, "Some girl got raped up here." Or something like that. Some old lie. Then he say, "Where you live?" I say, "Hunters Point." He say, "I'm gonna give you about ten or fifteen minutes to catch the bus, and if you're not off this corner, if I see you over here, I'll bust you." Just like that. If the police catch you walkin' with a white girl, boy, you in big trouble.

Race thus becomes a particularly salient indicator of "suspiciousness" when Negroes or Mexicans are found in white neighborhoods. Being a Negro per se (or being a Negro in a Negro neighborhood) is apparently not as important a criterion of suspiciousness as being a Negro who is "out of place."

> If boys from Hunters Point or Fillmore (Negro neighborhoods in San Francisco) go in all white districts, the police will stop you and ask you where you from. If you say Fillmore or Hunters Point, they'll take you down to the station and run checks on you. Any burglaries, any purse snatchings, anything.

In addition to places associated with the neighborhood, there is another more temporary type of place where physical presence can make a gang member an unwitting candidate for the sample of "suspicious persons." These are *scenes of crimes* or *scenes of potential crimes*—places that only exist for a few hours. It is probably true, for example, that any adolescent standing on the corner near the laundromat described below would have been a target for the same patrolman.

> Me and two partners were standing on the corner near this laundromat and it seems that a few hours before that some teenagers were in this laundromat and broke one of the windows off the washer. So this cop pulled over. He said we were to just shut up and come with him. So he took us to the laundromat and lined us up against the wall. And he called the man that owned the laundromat and asked him which one of us was the one that done it. And it wasn't none of us so the guy said that. So the cops said we could go. But they just picked us up because we happened to be standing on that corner at that time.

It is also possible to become a "suspicious person" by *ecological contamination.* A boy who is standing near a friend who has landed in the situation of suspicion has a good chance of being drawn into the sample himself.

> Remember that day on 44th Street? Remember what them cops did? They caught Arthur and the guys with a false I.D. They was buying beer and they got caught. So I walked into the store just to see what was happening. So they started talking to Arthur and them and they told them to get in the car. So then he points to me and say, "You! Get in the car!" And I said, "Damn! I didn't do nothing!" But he said, "Get in the car!"

In addition to the variety of *places* used to draw samples, however, the police also seem to rely on a number of physical or material *individual attributes*. Certain kinds of clothing, hair, and walking styles seem intrinsically to trigger suspicion. The general description of these styles had best be left to the boys themselves.

> (Why do you think the cops pick you up all the time?) Why do they pick us up? They don't pick everybody up. They just pick up on the ones with the hats on and trench coats and conks.* If you got long hair and hats on, something like this one, you gonna get picked up. Especially a conk. And the way you dress. Sometimes, like if you've got on black pants, better not have on no black pants or bends† or Levi's.
>
> They think you going to rob somebody. And don't have a head scarf on your head. They'll bust you for having a head scarf.‡
>
> (All right, so they bust you for clothes. That's one thing. Is there anything else?) The way you walk sometimes. If you walk pimp. Don't try to walk pimp. Don't try to be cool. You know. They'll bust you for that. (Could you tell me how you walk pimp?) You know. You just walk cool like. Like you got a boss high.§ Like you got a fix or something. Last night a cop picked me up for that. He told me I had a bad walk. He say, "You think you're bad." You know.

Finally, the police also use *themselves* as an instrument for locating suspicious people. Every time an officer makes visible contact with a citizen, the citizen is forced to confront his status in the eyes of the law, and the police soon learn to rely on hostile *looks* and furtive *glances* as signs of possible guilt. A policeman's uniform is a potent symbolic device. It sometimes has the power to turn a patrolman into a walking test of moral identity.

It should not be construed from the above discussion that the process of locating a population of potential offenders always proceeds

* A "conk" is a hair straightening process used by Negroes that is similar in concept to the permanent wave.

† "Bends" are a form of the bell-bottom trouser which, when worn effectively, all but obscure the shoe from vision, thus creating the impression that the wearer is moving down the street with an alarmingly irresponsible shuffle.

‡ Head scarves (sometimes called "mammy rags") are worn by Negroes around the forehead to keep "conk jobs" in place.

§ "Boss" is a synonym for "good."

on such slim grounds. There are a variety of "scenes" that constitute much more obvious bases for investigation. However, since policemen rarely stumble on armed men standing over dead bodies, much of their activity involves a subtle and exceedingly tenuous reading of both appearances and events. For example, when dealing with people who possess the ecological and personal indicators of suspiciousness outlined above, patrolmen may turn a screwdriver into a "deadly weapon" and a scratch on the neck into evidence of rape.

> Like you be walking. Just come from working on the car or something. And if you've got a screwdriver or something in your back pocket, hell, they may beat the shit outa you. They talk about you got a burglary tool or you got a deadly weapon on you.
>
> Remember the time when we was getting ready to go up to the gym? We came home from school one day. He had some scratches on his neck, and the cop pull over and say, "Turn around!" The cop grabbed him. I didn't say nothing. I was walking. I got to the top of the stairs, and the cop holler "Turn around" at me too. So I turn around. And the cop look at my neck and he say, "Yeah. You too. You got scratches on your neck too." So he took us down to the police station. It seem like some girl way over in another district got raped. And the girl say, "I think they live over at Hunters Point and I scratched one of them on the neck." Some stuff like that.

Gang members are very much aware of their moral status in the eyes of the police. On most occasions, they are likely to know that the police have singled them out for interrogation because of the neighborhood they live in, because of their hair styles, or perhaps because they are temporarily "out of place." They know how the police operate, and they are particularly aware of the role played by judgments about moral character in this methodology.

As one might imagine, gang boys thus tend to regard their more or less permanent place in the situation of suspicion with considerable resentment, a resentment that quite often spills over into outrage. Although the boys do not pretend to be moral pillars of the community, they feel, and with considerable statistical justification, that they are much better people than the operation of the crime detection process would otherwise suggest. Not all trips to neighboring territories are undertaken for the purposes of attacking rival gangs or pillaging the houses of the white rich, and most of the time, as the boys put it, "we was just mindin' our own business when the cops came along." Similarly, their resentment at being picked up for the clothes they wear and the hair styles they sport has the same basis in logic. As one boy succinctly put the argument, "Hell man, them cops is supposed to be out catching criminals! They ain't paid to be lookin' after my *hair!*"

The problem, of course, is that patrolmen do have some grounds for questioning the motives of gang boys found in foreign neighborhoods and for viewing clothing, hair, and walking styles as indicators of "suspicion." There are enough gang wars, robberies, and rapes to support an argument that when gang boys are found away from home territory suspiciousness may be warranted, even if the policy of involuntary confinement is not. Similarly, it is commonly understood that personal accouterments such as clothing and hair styles constitute significant elements of communication about how people expect to be treated by those in their visible presence; and, just as parents more or less correctly interpret the heavily made-up faces of their daughters as pleas to be treated as "sophisticates," the police more or less correctly assess the long-hair, black-leather-jacket, blue-jeans complex as fair warning that its owners are making claims to being "tough."

But the problems faced by the police in constructing efficient indicators of suspicion are every bit as tricky as those faced by the social scientist in the privacy of a laboratory. Not only is "suspiciousness" a rather vague and poorly defined category, we can also expect conclusions to be biased by the amount of illegal activity that is visible to the police. We still do not know, for example, how much of the petty crime committed by lower-class juveniles in public is also committed by middle-class youths behind such private barriers to official vision as homes and cars.[19]

In addition, the nature of the data that the police are exposed to is partly a function of the way patrols are organized. The police can only see what the structure of their beats makes it possible for them to see, and lower-class neighborhoods are patrolled with greater frequency and vigilance than neighborhoods in the suburbs. In short, the methodology used by the police to construct indicators of "suspicion" leaves as much room for experimental error and personal prejudice as can be found in the enterprises of social science.

There is one important difference, however, between the social

[19] For a thorough discussion of the emphasis placed on public places by patrol officers, see Arthur L. Stinchcombe, "Institutions of Privacy in the Determination of Police Administrative Practice," *The American Journal of Sociology*, Vol. LXIX, No. 2 (Sept. 1963), pp. 150–61.

scientist and the policeman. The mistakes made by social scientists affect the state of knowledge whereas the mistakes made by policemen affect people. Since patrolmen are in the business of judging moral character from appearances, people who consistently become the targets of this process are pleased in an extremely problematic situation. More often than most of us, they find themselves facing the assumption that they are morally unsound people, and they confront all the inevitable embarrassments that arise whenever routine behavior is scrutinized for criminal motives. If one lives in certain lower-class neighborhoods, frequents certain places in these neighborhoods, dresses a certain way, and belongs to a gang, the probability of becoming the target of interrogation by patrolmen and juvenile officers is high enough to transform this event into an important life contingency.

As one might expect, gang members make various kinds of attempts to avoid the situation of suspicion, and appearances are sometimes altered in order to minimize the prospects of becoming a target for interrogation.

When a large group of boys are congregating on the same street corner and a squad car appears on the horizon, the group often expands the physical space it was occupying and breaks up into subunits of two and three. Gang members seem to feel the police consider a large number of small conversations less suspicious than a single conversation in which many boys are involved.

> (What do you usually do when you see a squad car coming down the street?) If there's just a few of us, we just sit it out. But if there be a lot of guys standin' around, we usually break up into small groups and start walkin' in opposite directions. (Do the police ever see you do this?) Oh yeah, but if they get out of the car they only gonna get one or two boys. Besides, it looks better if you be walkin' down the street with just one or two guys instead of a big group.

When a police car appears, gang boys often attempt to position themselves near females if there are any close by. Gang members argue that the police regard mixed couples with less suspicion than they do small groups of boys.

> Sometimes we jump next to the little ladies. Like one time when we was waiting for a bus and it was after curfew, we saw the heat come cruisin' down the street. And there was this ugly old lady walkin' by the bus stop. Well I just step right

up beside her and start tippin' down the street. She got scared but she didn't do nothin' but keep walkin'. You better off walkin' with a woman. They figure you're not gonna be gettin' into nothing if you with a girl.

Similarly, unmarried older boys will occasionally wear wedding rings in order to bolster their moral status in the eyes of the police. Next to walking beside a girl, gang members feel they can best improve their public image by having it assumed that they are married.

Man, I even took to wearing a finger chain so them cops would think I got an old lady. I figure they less likely to bust you for humbug if they know you got a wife.

Most gang members are also equipped with a battery of socially acceptable reasons for being on the streets. As Paul Goodman has noted, the police in America take a rather dim view of people who are on the streets "doing nothing."[20] Gang members must therefore be prepared to tell policemen during interrogations that they are either going to or coming from some legitimate place. These places, of course, vary with the time of day. At night the boys will usually say they are coming back from the movies or going to see a girl friend. During the day, they almost always have to say they are "looking for a job."

If a cop sees you on the street, he'll say, "What are you doing out of school?" And you just say, "I'm looking for a job." And he'll say, "All right, but if I catch you around here again and you ain't got a job I'll throw you in jail."

As adolescence wears on, the consequences of being picked up by the police become more and more serious; and as months replace days as the unit of sentence, the boys begin to alter their appearances in ways that imply ever increasing compromises with their preferred public identities. The first, and in some ways the most precious, article of clothing to disappear is the club jacket. Most gang members, however, do not decide to stop wearing their jackets all at once. They first decide to wear their jackets "inside out" so that club names on the back or nicknames on the front cannot be seen. Finally, the jackets are abandoned altogether.

[20] Paul Goodman, *Growing Up Absurd* (New York, Vintage Books, 1960), p. 130.

> When we was in high school, we had a club meeting and decided not to wear our jackets any more. It was just gettin' too hot. Everytime something happen, somebody say I saw a boy in a blue jacket and first thing you know, the cops be knockin' on your door. First we wore them inside out. You know, so no names or nothin' would show. But finally we just stopped wearing them at all.

For most boys, the last article of distinctive social identity to disappear is long hair.

> Our whole club is getting this kind of haircut so we can see what they gonna say next. See practically all of us got these short ones. We all had our hair cut. I guess they gonna find something else to pick on now. Most times if you ain't got a hat on, they say, "Conk job! Get in the wagon! You a hood!"

At some point during adolescence, however, a gang boy becomes recognizable to patrolmen by *name*. And when this happens, there is no longer any real escape from constant surveillance by the police. Most of the techniques employed to dodge the situation of suspicion are rendered useless. Even if precautions are taken, the boys usually find they are still trapped. Their place in the situation of suspicion becomes permanent.

> (Let me ask you a question. Let's say you wanted to stay out of trouble. What would you have to do?) You can't stay clear of the cops. You can't get away from them.
>
> Stay in the house.
>
> In the Mission District you gotta get a haircut, and you gotta wear peg pants and tennis shoes. That will do it because the White Shoes (white boys) dress like that.
>
> (Now what if the Negro kids at Hunters Point were to dress like that? Would the police still pick you up?) They'd pick us up and call us "punks." They'd start callin' us "sweetheart" because most colored kids don't dress like that. They wear bends and slacks and black shoes.
>
> (In other words there is no way to make it except to stay in the house?) That's it. Stay home.

Encounters

As soon as a patrolman leaves his squad car to begin an interrogation, his relationship with a gang boy enters a new but related phase. The gang member desires to be treated with civility and politeness.

If he has not committed a crime (of if the interrogating officer is not expected to know about it), he expects the officer to treat him with the respect due any respectable member of the community.

On the other hand, the patrolman has considerable leeway in deciding what view of the suspect to communicate. He can decide to treat the boy with a bureaucratic impassivity and respect, sometimes even with relaxed friendliness; or he can decide to issue commands, back the boy against a wall, and frisk him.

When a patrolman is polite, he can sometimes mitigate the resentment and the sense of injustice provoked by the situation of suspicion. It is almost as though a new reality had temporarily erased the insult to moral character that was implicit when the patrolman decided to interrogate in the first place. To a large extent, therefore, the issue of whether the authority of the patrolman will be challenged hangs on whether this initial insult is compounded or dissipated during the course of interrogation.

Curiously enough, gang boys are often treated deferentially when they are actually caught in the act of violating a law. Patrolmen who are made suspicious by gang boys driving new cars, for example, usually begin their interrogations in a menacing tone of voice. Yet as soon as it becomes clear that the car is stolen, the ensuing interaction is often conducted in a calm and businesslike way. Some patrolmen offer the boys cigarettes as tranquilizers against uneasiness, and many of the boys obey the officer's commands without flinching. In short, when gang members are arrested for clear violations of law and are not insulted in the process, the legitimacy of the arresting officer is often granted without challenge.

This observation is not surprising once it is realized that the essence of suspicion is a frustrated desire for properly validated information.[21] Communicating negative judgments about the moral character of others is one of the job contingencies faced by patrolmen. But as soon as suspicion is either confirmed or disproved, the necessity to make assessments disappears. The professional policeman does not necessarily have contempt for people who commit crimes. On the contrary, he is better positioned than most of us to appreciate the ingenuity, skill, and courage often displayed by people who sometimes break the law.

Both for instrumental and symbolic reasons, however, most patrolmen do not feel they can risk an initial approach that is friendly

[21] For an analysis of suspicion as an "awareness context" see Barney G. Glazer and Anselm L. Strauss, *Awareness of Dying* (Chicago, Aldine Publishing Company, 1965), pp. 47–64.

or polite. A posture of bureaucratic authoritarianism is one of their best techniques of interrogation. By appearing to study a driver's license or an identification card for what feels like an interminable period of time and then occasionally glancing up from these documents to stare the suspect skeptically in the eye, a patrolman has a chance to further assess the suspiciousness of his target.

The police expect law-abiding citizens to express their respect for the law by addressing its representatives with various gestures of deference.[22] It is desired that the suspect's physical presence communicate civility, politeness, penitence, and perhaps fear. In addition, the use of such terms as "Sir" and "Officer" are expected as indications that the humble status of the juvenile in the eyes of adult and legal authority is properly understood. If these deference gestures are forthcoming, the officer has no choice but to assume the suspect is innocent, in which case he usually lets him go. Gang members understand the logic of this gestural vocabulary very well.

> (What responses seem to work for you when the cops pick you up?) If you kiss their ass and say, "Yes Sir, No Sir," and all that jazz, then they'll let you go. If you don't say that, then they gonna take you in. And if you say it funny they gonna take you in. Like, "Yes *Sir!* No *Sir!*" But if you stand up and say it straight, like "Yes Sir" and "No Sir" and all that, you cool.

On the other hand, if a suspect appears nervous and wary or if he looks like he is breaking out in a cold sweat, the patrolman may decide to take him to the station for further interrogation. An experienced patrolman can practically smell concealed guilt. On the basis of evidence that is often completely invisible to the observer, he becomes convinced that a man is hiding something. More often than not he is correct.

In addition, most patrolmen have learned from past experience how gang boys feel about them and how these feelings are socially expressed. If an officer is polite, he becomes vulnerable to a response suggesting that his authority is being rebuffed; and for this reason, most officers decide not to risk a challenge to their honor. They communicate to the gang member that *authority* is *not* the basis on which

[22] For a systematic discussion of the role played by deference in maintaining the ceremonial integrity of routine social life, see Erving Goffman, "The Nature of Deference and Demeanor," *American Anthropologist*, Vol. 58 (June 1957), pp. 473–502.

the encounter is socially grounded but rather that the *power to investigate* is being invoked instead. In effect, this move denies the gang member the option of accepting authority as a basis for participating in the exchange, and the denial of this option is itself a sign of disrespect. Implicit in the "command" to produce identification, for example, is the notion that the suspect is the kind of person who might not surrender his identification voluntarily and is therefore the kind of person who does not believe in the importance of laws or the duty of the police to enforce them.

> Man, they always shouting, "Do this! Do that! Gimme your identification!" All that old bull-shit. They talk to you like you already in prison and that gets me mad!

Yet officers sometimes make their contempt for gang members even more explicit. Instances were observed, for example, of officers commenting on the "nice tan" of a Negro suspect or inquiring after the birth place of a Negro by asking, "Where were you born? Mississippi?" Not all officers utilize these tactics, but most Negro gang members believe that the great majority of police officers are prejudiced, and most can cite personal experiences to document this position.[23]

> Remember that time we was coming from the show? This cop car pulls up and these two cops jump out quick. The first stud says, "All right, God Damn you! All you black Africans up against the mother-fucking wall!" All that shit. So we got up against the wall over there on Market Street. This long house. You know. So then they started. "Where all you ignorant sons of bitches coming from?" We say we coming from the show. "What show?" We say we coming from the Amazon. They say, "Yeah, we got a call there's a whole bunch of shit going on over there! I think I'll call all you mother fuckers in!" So nobody say nothing. So then he starts again. "What's your name? Let me see your I.D.!" Finally, this cop's buddy say, "You want to run them in Joe? They ain't really done nothing." So then Joe stops. He say, "Now all you black Africans pick up your

[23] In defense of patrolmen, eighteen out of the twenty-seven interviewed admitted to being prejudiced but argued that they had become so in the course of their work as policemen. As one officer put it, "They have no regard for the law or for the police. They just don't seem to give a damn. Few of them are interested in school or getting ahead. . . . Furthermore, many of these kids try to run you down. They say the damndest things to you and they seem to have absolutely no respect for you as an adult. I think I am prejudiced now, but frankly I don't think I was when I began police work."

spears and go home! I don't want you guys walking up the street!" Shit like that, man. You know. We wasn't doing nothing. We just coming up the street like we always do coming from the show. That shit happens all the time. There ain't a day that we don't get rousted like that.

When a gang boy finds himself placed in the situation of suspicion unjustly and then insulted in the following encounter as well, he must decide whether to swallow the insult by deferring to the patrolman or whether to defend his honor by challenging the authority of the interrogating officer. To display the ritual signs of deference means suffering the private torments associated with cowardice as well as the public humiliation involved in losing face, and thus most gang members, when faced with this situation, prefer to challenge the authority of the police.

This gestural rebellion takes a variety of forms. The most passive is a posture of sullenness: body muscles tense, shoulders slightly bowed, eyes averted and cast down or directed blankly at the interrogating officer. The voice tones used to answer questions range from silence to a barely audible "I don't know."

If a gang boy manages to hold his body sufficiently still and his face sufficiently sullen, the interrogating officer has great difficulty reading demeanor for signs of possible guilt. The posture itself is not completely inscrutable because it does communicate hostility. But the interrogating officer has no way of knowing whether this hostility has been injected into the encounter as a result of previous experiences or whether it betrays knowledge of a specific infraction.

Rather than adopt a posture of sullenness, however, a gang boy may choose to be insolent, acquitting himself with a straight-forward nonchalance or indifference. This stance requires that bodies be relaxed and the interrogating officer addressed directly, usually with flat statements such as, "Leave me alone. I don't know nothing."

There is also a third stance, more active than both sullenness and insolence, that involves being positively defiant or in some other way aggressively disrespectful. The boy may glare at the officer, move his arms and legs freely in abandoned gestures of anger, and say things like, "What the hell's wrong now? I ain't done nothing! Why do you guys always pick on me?"

The second and third approaches are no less ambiguous than the passive approach, but they are strategically somewhat weaker. By offering to engage in talk, the boys expose themselves to the possibility of being broken down by interrogation.

Outcomes

If a juvenile being interrogated in the situation of suspicion refuses to proffer the expected politeness or to use the words that typically denote respect and if no offense has been discovered, a patrolman finds himself in a very awkward position. He cannot arrest the boy for insolence or defiance, since for obvious reasons no charges of this nature exist. The patrolman is thus faced with the choice of three rather unpleasant alternatives.

First, he can back down, thereby allowing his authority to evaporate. If a patrolman allows his authority to escape, however, there is no guarantee that it can be recaptured the next day or any day thereafter. Since patrolmen are structurally locked into the authority role over long periods of uninterrupted time, any fleeting defeat at the hands of a gang member has the prospect of becoming permanent. In a certain sense, then, gang members have a great deal of power. With the mere hint of impiety they can sometimes manage to strip a patrolman symbolically of his authority.

For these reasons, if a patrolman does decide to back down, he must be careful to retreat strategically by withdrawing from the encounter without a public loss of face. This is usually done by communicating to the juvenile that his innocence is fortuitous, that he is the kind of person who *could* have committed an offense, and that he owes his release to the grouchy good graces of the interrogating officer. If executed artfully, comments such as "keep your nose clean or we'll run you in next time" can pave the way out of a potentially damaging encounter. From the point of view of the boys, of course, this technique simply constitutes an additional insult to moral character.

If a patrolman chooses to press his claims to authority, however, he has only two sanctions available with which to make these claims good. On the one hand, he can attempt an arrest.

> One day we were standing on the corner about three blocks from school and this juvenile officer comes up. He say, "Hey, you boys! Come here!" So everybody else walked over there. But this one stud made like he didn't hear him. So the cop say, "Hey punk! Come here!" So the stud sorta look up like he hear him and start walking over. But he walking over real slow. So the cop walk over there and grab him by the collar and throw him down and put the handcuffs on him, saying, "When I call you next time, come see what I want!" So every-

body was standing by the car, and he say, "All right you black mother fuckers! Get your ass home!" Just like that. And he handcuffed the stud and took him to juvenile hall for nothing. Just for standing there looking at him.

On the other hand, there are a variety of curfew, vagrancy, and loitering laws that can also be used to formally or officially prosecute the informal violation of norms governing deportment in the situation of suspicion.

I got arrested once when we were just riding around in a car. There was a bunch of us in the car. A police car stopped us, and it was about ten after ten when they stopped us. They started asking us our names and wanted to see our identification. Then they called in on us. So they got through calling in on us, and they just sit in the car and wait 'til the call came through. Then they'd bring back your I.D. and take another one. One at a time. They held me and another boy till last. And when they got to us it was five minutes to eleven. They told everybody they could go home, but they told us it didn't make no sense for us to go home because we was just riding around and we'd never make it home in five minutes. So they busted us both for curfew.

In addition to these laws, a boy can also be charged with "suspicion" of practically anything. When the police use suspicion as a charge, however, they usually try to make the specific offense as serious as possible. This is why the criminal records of many gang boys are often heavily laced with such charges as "suspicion of robbery" and "suspicion of rape."

(Could you tell me some of the things you have been busted for?) Man, I been charged with everything from suspicion of murder to having suspicious friends. I think they call it "associates!" (laughter) They got me on all kinda trash, man, and they only make but one thing stick. (What's that?) A couple of years ago they caught me stone cold sittin' behind the wheel of a '60 Pontiac. I said it belong to my uncle, but it turn out that the name of the registration was O'Shaunessee or O'Something, some old fat name like that. The cop knew there wasn't no bloods [Negroes] named things like that.

Gang boys are aware that the police have a very difficult time making these illusory charges stick. They can always succeed in sending a boy to jail for a few hours or a few days, but most of these charges are dismissed at a preliminary hearing on recommendations from probation officers. Moreover, gang members also understand the power of probation officers, and by behaving better in front of these officials they can often embarrass the local authority of patrolmen by having decisions to arrest reversed over their heads. As far as the patrolmen are concerned, then, the boys can make a mockery of false charges as a sanction against impertinence in the situation of suspicion.

Perhaps more important, however, a patrolman's sergeant also knows that most trivial or trumped up charges are likely to be dropped, and thus the police department itself puts a premium on ability to command authority without invoking the sanction of arrest. Unlike the juvenile officer who is judged by his skills at interrogation, a patrolman's capacity to gain respect is his greatest source of pride as well as his area of greatest vulnerability. If he is forced to make too many "weak" arrests, he stands to lose prestige among his peers and superiors on the police force and to suffer humiliation at the hands of his permanent audience of tormentors on the beat.

It is largely for these reasons that many patrolmen prefer to settle a challenge to authority on the spot, an alternative that necessarily poses the prospect of violence. As William Westley has pointed out, in the last analysis the police can always try to "coerce respect."[24]

> They don't never beat you in the car. They wait until they get you to the station. And then they beat you when the first shift comes on and they beat you when the second shift comes on. I've seen it happen. I was right there in the next cell. They had a boy. His name was Stan, and they had beat him already as soon as they brought him in. And then when they was chang-

[24] The above analysis of why policemen retaliate when the legitimacy of their authority is challenged differs somewhat from Westley's analysis of why a large percentage of the policemen he studied "believed that it was legitimate to use violence to coerce respect." Westley argues that disrespectful behavior constitutes a threat to the already low "occupational status" of policemen and therefore comes as a blow to their self-esteem. Westley's hypothesis would suggest, however, that those policemen who *accepted* their low occupational status would therefore allow their authority to be challenged. Although Westley's variables no doubt affect the behavior of patrolmen, there also seems to be more at stake than status as a workman when claims to authority are ignored. In a sense the patrolman whose authority has been successfully called into question has already abdicated a sizable chunk of his honor as well as his job. See William A. Westley, "Violence and the Police," *American Journal of Sociology,* Vol. LIX (July 1953).

> ing shifts, you know, the detective came and looked on the paper that say what he was booked for, I think it was robbery or something like that, and they started beating on him again. See, the police are smart. They don't leave no bruises. They'll beat you somewhere where it don't show. That's the main places where they look to hit you at. And if it did show, your word wouldn't be as good as theirs. They can lie too, you know. All they have to say is that you was resisting and that's the only reason they need for doing what they do.

Resisting arrest is the one charge involving violence that seems uniquely designed to deal with improper deportment in the situation of suspicion. A policeman interviewed by Westley suggests that when the challenge to authority is not sufficiently serious to warrant this charge, the police may continue to provoke the suspect until the level of belligerence reaches proportions that legitimate invoking this category of offense.

> For example, when you stop a fellow for a routine questioning, say a wise guy, and he starts talking back to you and telling you that you are no good and that sort of thing. You know you can take a man in on a disorderly conduct charge, but you can practically never make it stick. So what you do in a case like this is to egg the guy on until he makes a remark where you can justifiably slap him, and then if he fights back, you can call it resisting arrest.[25]

And from a gang member's point of view:

> Another reason why they beat up on you is because they always have the advantage over you. The cop might say, "You done this." And you might say, "I didn't!" And he'll say, "Don't talk back to me or I'll go upside your head!" You know, and then they say they had a right to hit you or arrest you because you were talking back to an officer or resisting arrest, and you were merely trying to explain or tell him that you hadn't done what he said you'd done. One of those kinds of things. Well, that means you in the wrong when you get downtown anyway. You're always in the wrong.

Unlike encounters between gang members and patrolmen, the confrontations between gang members and juvenile officers rarely end in violence. This is because the ability to command respect is not

[25] *Ibid.*, p. 30.

as crucial to a juvenile officer as it is to a patrolman. A juvenile officer is not judged by his capacity to command authority on a beat, and he can therefore leave a situation in which his authority has been challenged without having to face the challenger again the next day. Since he is evaluated largely by his skill at interrogation, he rarely finds himself structurally predisposed to "coerce respect."

On the street, of course, the issues involved in these encounters are by no means as clear-cut as the above analysis might suggest. Much of the interaction between gang members and policeman takes place in scenes that are almost totally chaotic and confused. The following rather lengthy quote from a seventeen-year-old Negro gang leader provides a good illustration of the complex context in which the issues involved in the challenge and defense of police authority typically arise.

> Like the time we went to that dance at the Y.M.C.A. Me and Roger and some more people. First they wouldn't let us in. It was about seven o'clock and everybody that went in, you know, we was about three minutes late and they shut the door.[26]
>
> Richard was at the door. He worked at the Y. He was one of the man's helpers. He say, "Come on in." Then the dude who run the Y he say, "You know that boy?" Richard say, "Yeah. He live . . . ." Then the dude scream, "You live at Hunters Point, don't you!" Richard say, "Yeah." Then the dude say, "No! Shut the door! Shut the door!" Like that. And I say, "Oh man ain't this something." But I didn't say it like that.
>
> We had something to drink that night anyway. So we went and snuck around the back. And we was trying to get into the Y. And the door was locked back there, you know. So I said, "Man, I'm getting into this Y if I have to tear the thing down." So there was a window up there, you know. I was half gone anyway. So I kicked the window in, and then ran around the front. And the dude say, "We saw you when you kicked that window in!" He was the man who owned the Y. He say, "We saw you kick the window in, but we ain't gonna do nothing. You gonna pay for this." So he let me in the Y. I knew he wasn't gonna make me pay for the window. He just let me in 'cause he afraid I gonna break another one.

[26] Agencies that give dances for "troublesome" teenagers often make a policy of refusing admission to boys and girls who come late. This policy rewards promptness, a quality that most gang members severely lack. On the other hand, by making this rule, the agencies also make it possible to break it, thus creating a good issue for "undesirable elements" to exploit at the front door.

And when I come out after the dance the police is there. One cop say, "Is this the one?" And the dude say, "No. That's not the one." He stuck up for me. He said, "It was a much bigger boy." I think the dude afraid of me. He know what I do to him if he tell the cops. So the cops said, you know, "O.K." Then the cops get in the car. They drove around the block. We was going up there to the bus stop, and then the cops told me, "Go on home. It's past the curfew anyway, and we can pick you up." First I didn't say anything. Then I say, "All right. I want to make a phone call." The cop say, "Go on home." I say, "I gotta call my mother, man." I got in a telephone booth, and they drove around the corner. Then I was going up to the bus stop, and I was standing at the bus stop by the pole. There were some more people over there talking. Then the cops come back. One dude done snatch me first, and the other cop come back and said, "Is this the one that's given' us trouble?" He took my hat off and said, "Yep, a conk job. Get in the wagon. You look like a hood." Because I had a white hat on and I had a conk job. You know. And I say, "Hey man! What you busting me on? What's the charge? So the cop say, "Smoking." I say, "Smoking? Look at everybody else with cigarettes!" I said, "Anyway, they even give you cigarettes in jail!" And then the dude looked at me and said, "Shut up!" And I said, "Man, you can't take us to no jail. You gotta tell us what you bustin' us on first." He say, "Congregating." I say, "I can pick up everybody in the party because look at everybody walkin' down the street in big groups talkin' and everything." And then the cop say, "Shut up! We gonna bust you on curfew. I want no more smart talk or I'll hit you in the head with this club!" Then he grabbed me like this. All I say was "Ug." I was getting ready to say something. The dude grabbed me, threw me down, and handcuffed me. Then he say, "Now which one of you smart little punks try to run? I'll shoot the shit out of you! I ain't for no bullshit! We're getting you for curfew." And they snatched us in the wagon. But they couldn't get us for curfew 'cause Roger had a watch on. Roger look at his watch and say, "It's three minutes before eleven, man. Here comes the bus. Let us out." The dude say, "Shut up you little old smart punk!" Like that. He say, "Come on, let's drive them all down to the station."

Then the lieutenant or captain or whatever he was, he was just getting off duty. He say, "Whatcha got these boys for?" The cop say, "Oh, they got kinda smart with us. We're gonna pick them up for curfew." And then the captain or whatever he was say, "Now? At eleven o'clock? Three minutes after? How are you going to . . . ?" Then he say, "I ain't got nothin' to do with it. I'm off duty. I'm going home to my wife." And then he left.

Roger was smokin' a cigarette. So he threw the cigarette on the floor. And the cop say, "Pick it up!" And there was a whole lot of cigarette butts laying on the floor. So Roger say, "Man, look at all them butts on the floor. Why should I pick mine up?" The cop say, "Just pick it up!" So Roger start reaching down there to pick it up and the cop slapped him in the face. I was tryin' to move over so the stud wouldn't hit me, and he said, "What you trying to do?" Then the stud fired on me and went in there and got a rubber hose and beat the shit out of me. Whap! Whap! All on the back of the neck. Then the cop say, "We got business to tend to." And he got in the car. He waited until it was about twelve thirty, and then one of the juvenile officers took us up to the Green House.[27]

And then about one o'clock my mother tell me they called from Juvenile Hall and said, "We just picked up your son for curfew about one o'clock." They do that in a minute, man! They *wait* before they call your house! I told my P.O. He showed me the slip. They had on the slip "starting of a riot." I was trying to start a riot. I said, "Oh man! I was standing at the bus stop and the dude grab me first. I was getting ready to get on the bus and then he smashed me. Took my hat off and said, 'Punk.' Then he began talkin' about my conk job, and then he put us in the wagon. That was all that happened!" My P.O. let me go.

When gang members find themselves *arrested* for insolence rather than for any other specific offense, they are doubly outraged. Not only have they been insulted, but their response to the insult has been the principal reason for their arrest. Under these circumstances, the legitimacy of the interrogating policeman is all but destroyed. The boys have a good word for the factors other than offense that often lead to their arrests. When asked, they will say they got "busted" for "humbug."

Like most people, the boys manage to construct a theory that allows them to "explain" the persistence of police harassment, but this theory is simply a version of their general belief that "everyone is always out for themselves." Most patrolmen are seen as corrupt, prejudiced,

[27] This is the name the boys have given Juvenile Hall in San Francisco.

and sadistic opportunists who exploit their position of power over the boys in order to earn the respect of fellow officers, a theory that is usually formulated as follows:

> Why do they pick us up? Just to be messing with somebody. To get more stripes, that's all, to get more stripes.

Similarly, the fact that patrolmen always seem to demand respect is attributed largely to an idiosyncratic egomania that seems somehow to flourish in the profession of police work:

> You know what cracks me up about them guys, them cops you know, they think you're supposed to do everything they say just 'cause they're cops. They don't even bother about the books. They just think that because they're cops you're supposed to respect them more than anybody else. Does it say that? Does it say in the books that you're supposed to respect them more than anybody else? No it don't! You're supposed to respect everybody, right? And you're supposed to treat everybody equal. They shouldn't be treated as though they were anything special. You should extend courtesy to them the same as you would to your family, the same as you would to your father and mother. I mean you don't have to go out of your way for them. I mean I don't even say "Sir" to my old man. He doesn't expect me to say "Sir!" What a bunch of phony dudes. One time I got arrested for gang activity and they put the cuffs on me, and the officer put them on pretty hard, and they was hurting my wrists. So I told the officer, I told him real nice, I say, "Officer, could you loosen these cuffs a little, they're cutting off my blood circulation." It was really my wine circulation. So he say, "Okay." And he come over there, and when I wasn't looking he squeezed them tighter.

But the above theory of arrogance and opportunism does not provide a basis for the total denial of police authority because it only applies to individuals rather than to the police as an occupational group. The boys continue to believe that patrolmen *should* treat them with respect and that arrests *should* be confined to behavior that is clearly against the law. This is why policemen who treat the boys deferentially and do not arrest them for "humbug" may still on occasion be considered "good cops."

Yet the gang boys continue to have experiences with patrolmen that contradict their conventional expectations about how the police should behave. Moreover, with the exception of the Black Muslims, no one has offered them a comprehensive explanation of their situation. The result is thus a diffuse frustration and fury that occasionally turns into a blind and explosive rage.

On September 28, 1966, for example, a white patrolman in the Hunters Point district of San Francisco spotted three Negro boys in an approaching car and became suspicious when the boys jumped out of the car and began running away. The officer claims he fired three shots in the air before hitting one of the boys in the back with a fourth. The boy was sixteen, and he died on a barren stretch of the rocky Hunters Point Hill just a few feet from his home. The car was reported stolen four hours after the boy was dead.

When the gang boys in the area saw the body, they began breaking windows, burning buildings, and looting stores. The uprising went on for twenty-four hours and only stopped when the National Guard arrived. The citizens of San Francisco responded to the outbreak of violence by attempting to find jobs for the youth at Hunters Point. As far as the general community was concerned, the cause of the riot was unemployment.

Yet it was no accident that the demonstration was triggered by an incident involving the police. Gang boys interpret the way the boundaries of their neighborhoods are patrolled as a conscious policy of confinement, and the police are looked upon as a foreign army of occupation. There are limits to what the natives will take from these troops, however, and there are times when more is needed to express rebellion than artful displays of insolence. These boys have been angry, bewildered, and resentful about the police for as long as they can remember, and they simply decided to strike back the only way they knew how.

> Things don't change. Like day before yesterday. We were sitting down on the steps talking with Joe and them. So here comes the police, coming down there messing with people.
> "Where do you live?" they say.
> "Up on the Hill."
> He say, "Where do you eat at?"
> "Up on the Hill."
> "Where you sleep at?"
> "Up on the Hill."
> He say, "Where you get your mail at?"
> I say, "Up on the Hill."
> He say, "Well don't you think you ought to be getting up the Hill right now!"
> So we went up the Hill.

Bureaucracy, Information, and Social Control: A Study of a Morals Detail*

Jerome H. Skolnick and J. Richard Woodworth

Awareness of infraction is the foundation of any social control system. Whatever the system of normative standards, whether these are folkways or mores, crimes or rules, a transgression must somehow be observed and reported before sanctions can be applied. The potential efficiency of a social control system, therefore, varies directly with its capacity to observe or receive reports of transgressions. For example, socialization at its most primitive level demands the visibility of the asocial act. If the norm requires that shoes or no shoes be worn, depending upon whether one is being presented at court or lying in bed, the socializing agent must be in a position to observe the normative breach. The child who wears shoes to bed must be seen wearing them before he can be told that this act affects civilized sensibilities.

Similarly, when an assault takes place, knowledge of its happening must somehow be communicated to authorities, that is, those who are charged with enforcing the system of rules. If two men fight one another in private and do not report the occurrence of the fight, authorities cannot sanction either, even if the behavior of each violated legal rules. Many violations are, of course, socially managed in this fashion, the disputants preferring to settle matters privately

* Funds for the research were supplied at various stages by the Social Science Research Council, The Russell Sage Foundation, the Walter E. Meyer Research Institute of Law and the Office of Juvenile Delinquency and Youth Development, Department of Health, Education, and Welfare, under Public Law 87-274. Colleagues at the Center for the Study of Law and Society, especially Sheldon Messinger and Philip Selznick, contributed valuable suggestions. The Westville Police Department and Morals Detail, the La Loma County District Attorney and Probation Department, the Mountain City Police Department, and the California Bureau of Criminal Statistics all kindly permitted us to observe their operations and look at their records.

rather than bringing them to the attention of authority. If, however, knowledge of the dispute becomes public—if the fight is noisy, if one of the disputants is injured—authorities must then decide whether or not to invoke the sanctioning process. Nevertheless, before legal controls can be invoked, there must first be official knowledge of the criminal act.

This idea may seem obvious, yet without exploring it, without analyzing the empirical relation between awareness and control, we shall be failing to examine some of the more serious problems and hidden consequences of control systems. Imagine, as an example, a social system where criminality could be accused only if a citizen *complained* that a law was being violated. In such a system we would have a grossly different conception of police than the one commonly held, at least in the United States. In such a system, police would be men who sit in rooms and investigate only when accusing citizens are moved to complain by the occurrence of events regarded as violations of law. Under such circumstances we would not have, for example, surveillance by traffic police. If an automobile were speeding or if its driver made an illegal left turn, it would be up to some other citizen to make a complaint against him, which would be duly investigated and prosecuted by appropriate officials. Awareness of criminal violation would be the responsibility of the citizen, and there would be no concern on the part of police for increasing their capacity to become aware of infractions.

In fact, of course, much energy of police as an organization is devoted to mobilizing resources for awareness of transgression. We are all familiar with signs warning that a section of highway is being patrolled with radar equipment, a warning intended to caution and restrain potential violators by suggesting an extensive ambit of police awareness of violations. Most citizens are less familiar with other technological and structural devices employed by police to learn of transgression. Crimes of vice, for example, typically have no citizen complainants. The man who uses heroin, smokes marijuana, bets on a football game, or patronizes a prostitute does not complain to the police that someone has sold him narcotics, taken his bet, or has offered to go to bed with him for a fee. In order to enforce these laws police must develop an information system.

Those aware of transgressions must be motivated to offer the information to legally constituted authority. There is an exchange, sometimes of money for information, more typically of a reduction or elimination of criminal charges. Policemen learn how to create commodities for such an exchange or the appearance of such commodities. Under these circumstances technological advances become significant. Devices for observing or recording transgression, such as hidden microphones, wiretaps, and high-power binoculars become increasingly important. A body of case law is developed—to the extent that such practices come to the attention to appellate courts—regulating the conditions under which informants, wiretaps, and the like may legitimately be utilized for extending police awareness.

As one observes such a process in action, one becomes increasingly aware of the totalitarian potential inherent in the development of this capacity for awareness. Totalitarianism implies tight socialization. Its conception of man is relatively fixed and inflexible, and its symmetry and conventionalism imply a mandate for developing instrumentalities of conformity. We are not referring here only to such totalitarian social orders as Hitlerism or Stalinism. We are discussing the idea of a totalitarian *potential* inhering in any society, even the most constitutionally protected and democratic, as, bit by bit, legal definitions increasingly standardize the conception of moral man and as the apparatus for social control becomes increasingly refined.

Improvements in discovery apparatus increase the totalitarian potential in proportion to a society's use of law as an instrument for achieving conventional morality. When the discovery apparatus is weak or ineffective or technologically backward, conventional morality enforced through law has a far lesser totalitarian potential. It does not matter very much if criminal law forbids various erotic activities, so long as it is impossible to see through walls. When such vision becomes possible, however, the totalitarian potential is enormous because—constitutional standards of search and seizure notwithstanding—the surveillance potential of those performing police functions will be extraordinary.

Our experiences in observing police in various areas of enforcement have indicated to us that police desire to have as much information as possible, even if much of it cannot be admitted as evidence in court. As an agency charged with enforcing a broad spectrum of rules, they simply cannot know in advance whether stray bits of information will prove useful. Even if enforcement conformed to the citizen complainant model pictured above, the police would feel the need for an intelligence system, although not so strongly as when they are required to enforce crimes lacking in citizen complainants.

Furthermore, our legal ideals demand that all laws shall be equally and fairly enforced regardless of the personal preferences of officials. Of course, in practice there are priorities. These may be more or less articulated, depending on the police force. Nevertheless, their very existence is a source of embarrassment. Only with hesitancy does a police official admit that he is not attending to the enforcement of certain laws. The ideal of law enforcement is universal enforcement, and even if the norm is not always complied with, as it almost never can be, its presence urges the police to enforce all laws. For this reason, therefore, the police are pressed to use their increased capacity to discover crime, even if they should find themselves in personal disagreement with the statute they are legally bound to enforce.

The remainder of this report is concerned with the enforcement apparatus surrounding statutory rape, a violation for which there are few citizen complainants, and which is therefore difficult to discover. We will deal with the procedures used for discovery, the investigation and processing of complaints, and, especially, the relations among various public agencies involved in the discovery and processing of complaints.

CALIFORNIA LAW ON STATUTORY RAPE

Statutory rape occurs when a man has sexual intercourse with a willing girl not his wife, who is under eighteen years of age.[1] The offense can be punished by imprisonment in the state prison for not more than fifty years or in the county jail for not more than one year. The jury, or the court where there is no jury, determines where the defendant shall be confined. If the girl is under fourteen, the male is liable to the charge of child molesting (288 P.C.), for which the penalty is imprisonment for from one year to life. District attorneys, often in exchange for a plea of guilty, will sometimes allow the charge to be reduced to a lesser included offense, most commonly a plea of guilty to statutory rape at the misdemeanor level or to the offense of "contributing to the delinquency of a minor" (272 P.C.). The maximum penalty for 272 P.C. is a year in jail, a one-thousand dollar fine, or both.

METHOD OF STUDY

All statutory rapes reported to the Westville Police Department between January 1962, and October 1963 (235 cases) were studied

[1] During the period of this study no allowances were made if the male honestly and with reason believed the girl to be over the age of consent. Since that time, the California Supreme Court has ruled that the defendant may present evidence showing that he had in good faith a reasonable belief that the girl was 18 years of age or older. People v. Hernandez (1964) 61 A.C. 584.

from the records of the police, district attorney, and probation department.[2] For purposes of comparison, all cases (87) for the year 1961 were examined in the police records of nearby Mountain City. In addition, for a month one author observed the operations of the Westville morals detail (3 detectives) in order to supplement the statistical information.[3] He also observed the activities of the vice control detail for several weeks and spent a month in the office of the deputy district attorney of nearby Cedarville. The other author spent six weeks as participant-observer in the vice control detail, four weeks in the burglary detail, and two weeks with the robbery detail. These participant observations were spaced over a fifteen-month period, including weekly visits to keep up relations.[4] Unless otherwise stated, the observations in this report refer to Westville and not to Mountain City.

[2] Westville is a city of about 400,000 population. When a citizen reports a crime—any crime—it is recorded by either a patrolman called to the scene or by an officer whose job it is to take down the complaints of those who walk into the police building. One copy of this triplicate "crime report" is channeled to the commanding officer of appropriate detail of detectives. He assigns the crime to one of his detectives, taking care to see that work loads are balanced and notes the date of assignment. Approximately two weeks late- the detective is expected to turn in a follow-up report reviewing his activities. Each detective keeps a watch sheet in which he lists all the cases assigned to him during that watch (six weeks) and the date he finishes each. This bookkeeping arrangement prevents any case from simply disappearing under piles of paper. The commanding officer expects regular follow-up reports; when he does not get them and pass them along, *his* superiors complain. From the point of view of the detective, then, his job is to bring the case to a successful conclusion. Ultimately the detective can legitimately dispose of a case only by clearing it in an officially prescribed manner or by reporting that he intends to put the case in the files because all available leads have failed and nothing more can be done until new evidence appears. In practice, the original report is simply forgotten, except, as one detective noted, when a detective recalls a report from oblivion in order to pad his watch report so that he looks busy.

The morals detail which we study is one subdivision of the detective division. Morals, homocide, and robbery details are jointly administered by one lieutenant. Morals investigates most sex-related crimes, particularly child molesting, incest, lewd phone calls, obscenity, homosexuality, school loitering, peeping, and statutory rape. Commercialized sex offenses—prostitution and pornography—are the responsibility of the vice control detail. Their jurisdiction includes transvestites (who frequently pose as prostitutes). Forcible rape is the province of the homocide detail, although rapes of doubtful force involving minors are sent to the morals detail.

[3] See J. Richard Woodworth, *The Administration of Statutory Rape Complaints: A Sociological Study*. Unpublished M. A. Thesis, University of California, 1964.

[4] See Jerome H. Skolnick, *Justice Without Trial: Law Enforcement in Democratic Society*. (New York, John Wiley and Sons, 1966), Chapter 2.

THE LOCATION OF CRIME

Sources of Information

We have argued that sharpening the capacity to discover crime, especially when employed in the enforcement of conventional morality, increases the totalitarian potential of a society, that is, the potential for a standard, rigid form of social control. There are several ways to enlarge official awareness of infraction. The number of people, official or unofficial, set to reporting crimes may be increased, perhaps merely by hiring more policemen. In a more complex form it may involve hiring part-time informants or using the agents, facilities, and records of other public agencies to discover previously unknown crimes. In addition, mechanical devices that extend the senses of existing police personnel may be developed.

Besides utilizing informers and mechanical devices a society may deputize nonpolice to report criminality. Ordinary citizens have both the right and authority to arrest those whom they have probable cause to believe committed a crime. Nevertheless, this citizen honor system has never resulted in a particularly large number of arrests or reports, and police feel that the reports they do get from interested but noninvolved citizens are usually of little value. In Westville, the main sources of statutory rape crime reports are those public agencies whose activities bring them knowledge of infractions that otherwise would be unknown to the police. Since statutory rape generally takes place in secret between willing partners, this increase in the number of unofficial police clearly increases law enforcement's capacity to prosecute the offense. Notable among these agencies are the probation department and the family support division of the district attorney's office. Probation officers are privy to their probationer's not-always-legal activities, as in the following examples.

> CASE 1: Augusta (17) had relations with her boy friend (20). Her probation officer discovered her pregnancy and reported it to the police. The suspect was being held at the California Youth Home on charges of burglary and grand theft, and the district attorney said he saw no reason to prosecute the boy for statutory rape. He suggested that the case be turned over to the family support division for prosecution on nonsupport should the boy refuse to contribute to the support of the child when he is released.

CASE 2. Evelyn (14) told her mother that the mother's husband (40), her stepfather, had been having sexual relations with her. The mother confronted the husband and he admitted the actions; she made him leave the house. He now lives in Juniper and supports his wife and children. Then the mother contacted her doctor and her priest—both advised her to let the matter go since the man had left the home. For some reason she saw a probation officer and was advised to call the police so that there would be a report of the incident on file. The mother reported the incident to the police, but did not want the husband arrested since she would then have to go on welfare. The case was closed as "complainant refuses to prosecute."

The family support division of the district attorney's office and the welfare department are separate agencies. A mother who desires Aid for Dependent Children (this study was made before the advent of Aid to Families with Dependent Children) first applies at the welfare department. It is a policy of the welfare department that when the mother is under 18, she must report to the family support division before aid will be given. Family support division workers ask the applicant for welfare aid about her marital status, age, and the paternity of the child. This information may reveal the violation of one or more laws—nonsupport, adultery, statutory rape.

Usually, the stories told are similar to the point of monotony. Some months earlier the girl began having sexual relations with a boy, generally with just one boy and without contraceptives, and later she discovered she was pregnant. The father either could not or would not support the child, so the girl applied for welfare and ended up in the office of the morals detail. This is the most common story, but there are less frequent variations. Perhaps the girl and boy had intercourse only once or the girl had intercourse with more than one boy. In one case, the father planned to support the child, but the girl's mother's welfare worker threatened to discontinue the mother's aid unless the girl applied for welfare.

Occasionally the police chance across statutory rapes. For example, an officer may investigate a parked car and discover a couple in a compromising position. Generally he will just tell the parties to move along—unless the girl looks underage to him. On one occasion the offense was discovered when an officer stopped a moving car for a traffic violation and happened to see a couple prone in the rear. Other instances of chance include the following cases.

CASE 3. An officer investigating a burglary in an apartment house was told by one tenant that a young girl (13) was pregnant. He located the girl and found that she was, as was her mother. The mother was very uncooperative and annoyed at the policemen's interference. The girl denied that she was pregnant and denied that she had had sexual relations. Detective Frost decided that there was "no information that a crime was committed." (#82)

CASE 4. While on patrol an officer drove up to investigate a parked car and found two males (18, 19) and one girl (15) in the car. One boy had the fly of his pants open; the other's pants were removed. They were arrested for statutory rape. The males at first denied everything but later admitted that they had had sexual relations with the girl. Repeated attempts to contact the girl and her mother failed. The suspects were released and the case closed as "complainant refuses to prosecute."

When a teen-age girl runs away from home, her parents usually file a missing-person report with the police. When she is located, one of the first questions asked of her by the officers, whether police or probation, is, "Which boys were you with?" A signed statement is taken from the girl including the names of the boys she had sexual relations with, if any. These names are then reported to the police department, where a crime report is made.

CASE 5. Diane (13) ran away from home in late January. During the few days before she was found she had sexual relations with four men, two of whose names she was able to give. Since coitus with one of the men (40) took place in a nearby city, he was arrested for child molesting by that city's police. The other man (40) was arrested by the Westville police for statutory rape.

CASE 6. Jean (15) and her boy friend (19) had run away once before. They tried to get to Nevada to be married but did not make it. After that incident the couple was called into the morals office. The boy stated that he had joined the army and was to be sent overseas for two years; he hoped to marry the girl when he returned. No action was taken. About two months later the girl ran off with him again while he was AWOL. They were caught and he was given over to military authorities for trial on desertion charges.

Thirty per cent of the cases are reported to the police by people closely related to the offense and its possible consequences, the girl's parents or relatives. One father called the police after seeing a male jump from his daughter's bedroom window when he investigated suspicious noises in her room. A stepfather called the police after he tried to separate his stepdaughter and her boy friend and was struck by the boy. Several other examples will illustrate this source of complaints.

CASE 7. One father brought his pregnant daughter (15) to the police station after the boy (20) backed out of his promise to marry the girl. The boy was called in and admitted paternity. The father threatened that if the district attorney did not issue a complaint he would "go after" the boy himself. The boy was arrested for statutory rape and the girl charged with being in danger of leading a lewd and immoral life.

CASE 8. Alma (15) was staying with her sister and brother-in-law to get away from difficulties at home. After she left their home, Alma called her sister and told her that the sister's husband had forced sexual relations upon her. The sister called the police and reported the offense. When questioned by the officers, this sister and another sister both stated that they believed that if anything happened, Alma was to blame. The reporting sister is getting a divorce from her husband. Before a complaint could be issued, Alma had been sent to relatives in Louisianna. The case was closed as "complainant refuses to prosecute."

There are also occasional self-reports.

CASE 9. Stella (17) turned herself in to juvenile authorities, saying that she was six-months pregnant and just couldn't stand to live any longer with her mother. Stella named the boy (18) and insisted that she not be sent home; she was transferred to juvenile hall. The boy, called into the police office, admitted the offenses and was also turned over to juvenile authorities.

Of all these sources, only the family support division systematically reports *all* the statutory rapes brought to its attention. The other sources have indeterminate and somewhat arbitrary motives for reporting, resulting in an uneven distribution of the punishment for this offense. Table 1 shows the proportion of cases from each source:

Table 1 *Information Source Reporting Statutory Rape to Westville Police, 1962–1963 (in Per Cent)*

Source	Per Cent Reported
Public agency	
DA family support division	40
Runaway report	11
Probation department	2
Police discovery	8
Total	61
Private person	
Relative reported	30
Self reported	8
	38
Total	99%
	(235)

The sources may be grouped into two large categories. In the first source category, the legally identified victim did not *initiate* the notification of the police. The information was "nonvoluntary," that is, the facts were brought to the Westville police mainly as a result of the operations of *public agencies* not directly concerned with law enforcement.

Factors Influencing the Making of a Complaint

Behind these various sources of reports, one can discern a variety of considerations and motives leading to invocation of police action. Reported crimes are those in which people have a special interest, and these are not necessarily representative of crimes actually committed.[5] Four factors seem to influence the reporting of statutory rapes: pregnancy, poverty, the seriousness of the offense, and righteous indignation. Sixty-six per cent of all the reports are of pregnant girls. It is clearly necessary that the girl be pregnant to apply for ADC; hence, for all of the girls referred by family support, the crime was discovered only because of a certain combination of poverty, illegitimate pregnancy, and the referral policy of the head of the family support division. In over half of the cases reported by relatives

[5] For an illuminating discussion of rules and their enforcement see Howard S. Becker, *Outsiders: Studies in the Sociology of Deviance.* (New York, The Free Press of Glencoe, 1963), pp. 121–46.

Table 2 *Pregnancy and Information Source (in Per Cent)*

Pregnancy	Family Support Division	Police-Probation	Relative or Self
Certain	100	20	58
Not pregnant		10	11
Uncertain		71	30
	100	101	99
	(95)	(51)	(89)

and one-fifth of those reported by public agencies (other than family support), the girl was pregnant (Table 2).

Since, as noted, agencies other than family support do not systematically report offenses to the police and since not all parents of pregnant daughters report that fact to the police, it might be argued that pregnancy alone is not a sufficient explanation of the reports the police receive. Other factors must be invoked to explain the result.

The influence of poverty on the discovery of statutory rapes is obvious: the largest single source of reports is from the family support division (40%). At the time of the study ADC aid could be given to a mother only if her real property was worth less than $5,000 and her personal property less than $600. One social worker reported that most applicants possessed no real property; those who had originally owned such property had exhausted its value prior to applying for aid. Thus, statutory rape is punished mainly among the poor who become visible by applying for maternity aid from welfare authorities.

Another factor taken into consideration when deciding whether to report an offense is the perceived seriousness of the offense. A rough measure of seriousness may be made by calculating the difference between the ages of the girl and the boy. Let us assume that where the difference in ages is large, the relationship is less likely to be an ordinary teen-age sexual relationship and more likely to involve some exploitation of youth by experience. Since the family support division reports *all* cases that come to its attention, its cases might be expected to involve proportionately more equal-aged partners. By contrast, groups that do not report systematically should more often report more serious offenders. Relatives should be able to handle most affairs of equal-aged partners; those where partners are not of equal age are considered more exploitative and are more likely to be referred to the police. Table 3 supports these suppositions.

Table 3 *Age Difference and Information Source (in Per Cent)*

Source of Report	Age Difference (*in Years*)			
	2 or less	3–4	5–6	7 or more
Family support division	56	46	32	18
Nonwelfare agency	7	24	24	38
Relative or self	37	30	44	44
	100	100	100	100
	(71)	(67)	(50)	(45)

Similar reasoning leads to the inference that relations between equal-aged partners will not be reported as *quickly;* the parties will try to devise other solutions, in the meantime waiting to see if the girl is pregnant. Relations between unequal-aged partners, on the other hand, will tend to be reported sooner, and less often will anyone wait to see if the girl is pregnant (Tables 4 and 5).

Finally, there is a small group of parents whose dominant motive is a sense of righteous indignation. These parents are angry at the boy and want to see him punished. In view of the commonly held belief that this group constitutes most statutory rape complainants, its small size is especially notable. The purest form of indignation is found in a small group of 27 cases (11%) in which the parents reported the offense without waiting to see if the girl was pregnant.

Table 4 *Age Difference and Time Elapsed between Offense and Report (in Per Cent)*

Time between Offense and Report	Age Difference (*in Years*)			
	2 or less	3–4	5–6	7 or more
Day	6	7	14	27
Two days to one month	10	21	18	20
More than a month	84	72	68	53
	100	100	100	100
	(71)	(67)	(50)	(45)

Table 5 *Pregnancy and Age Difference (in Per Cent)*

Pregnancy	Age Difference (*in Years*)			
	2 or less	3–4	5–6	7 or more
Certain	84	69	66	38
Not pregnant	4	4	2	18
Uncertain	11	27	32	44
	99	100	100	100
	(71)	(67)	(50)	(45)

Variations in Discovery Procedures

It is instructive to compare discovery procedures for statutory rape with those of another police detail that handles crimes in which the victim does not usually complain—the vice detail. The most enterprising vice unit, the narcotics squad, energetically seeks out informers who will tell them of drug crimes. When "business" is slow they may liven it up by going out into the street and talking with their regular informants attempting to discover who is selling and who is "dirty." Sometimes this is done with such frenzy—stopping addicts, questioning, driving fast—that the addict community refers to this mode of gathering information as "maniacing." Viewed in more neutral terms, however, it is merely an exaggerated example of the initiative character of narcotics enforcement. Likewise, other details charged with enforcing "victimless crimes" typically reorganize so that they can discover offenses for themselves, for example, by systematically traveling from bar to bar, by watching the places prostitutes hang out, by following the men who get picked up, by trying to get picked up themselves, or by introducing agents or willing informers into gambling operations. Unlike these enterprising detectives, morals detectives have typically taken no steps to create special sources of information. They only respond; others supply the stimuli prompting them into action. This is not uncommon within the police department as a whole; most detectives must await the report of a crime before taking action. But it is unusual for those charged with enforcing laws where the victim cannot be expected to report the offense. The morals detail has retained an organization similar to that of theft and robbery in a field where it is less effective.

The relations among the welfare department, the family support division, and the police constitute a significant public policy. Using welfare department records, the family support division maintains the policy of reporting crimes to police over and above those they were specifically created to uncover—fraud and nonsupport. Perhaps it seems completely appropriate that any publicly supported agency or institution report whatever crimes it learns of; yet as a general policy—that public agencies share criminal information regardless of the purpose of the agency—its wisdom is questionable. For example, imagine public schools as being included under such a policy. Many acts routinely dealt with by school officials under the label of school discipline—petty theft, carrying of knives, assaults, sport "pools"—could conceivably be reported to the police for criminal processing. If one maintains the consistent position that a criminal offense, wherever it comes to light, should be brought to the attention of law enforcement agencies, a serious burden may be placed upon the internal capacity of publicly supported institutions to reach their primary goals. In the conclusion we shall deal with the wider public policy implications of the sharing of criminal information.

INVESTIGATION OF COMPLAINTS

Clearing the Report

To satisfy his superiors, the detective aims ultimately for a "clearance." "Clearing a report" has a precise meaning, but the methods by which it is accomplished are not precise. A crime report is cleared (1) when it is fully readied for prosecution and delivered to a higher authority (the district attorney or the probation department), or (2) when a legitimate reason is given why prosecution, by Westville at least, should be carried no further. The first alternative is familiar, involving arrest, trial, and judicial disposition. In the second, the police department itself, following general suggestions by the FBI, decides which reasons are legitimate; whenever a situation fits one of the following classifications, the case can be cleared.

Each of these categories means about what it appears to mean; the officer's task is to find a category covering his case. Most of them apply to clear situations. Within limits of the available outcomes, however, the detective may be called upon to engage in a variety of discretionary assessments. Detectives are usually most interested in clearing cases by arrest and prosecution, and a good portion of their ability is measured in terms of knowing how to manipulate

Table 6 *Police Disposition of Accused Males (in Per Cent)*

Police Disposition	Per Cent
Arrest and prosecution of adult	34
Juvenile dispositions	
Turned over to juvenile authorities	23
Reprimanded and released	0
Complainant refuses to prosecute	25
Complaint refused by district attorney	3
Prosecuted for another offense	2
District attorney citation	0
Prosecuted by outside department	1
Occurred in another jurisdiction	1
Turned over to military authority	0
Death of offender	0
Unfounded (reported crimes believed not to have happened)	5
Not cleared	6
	100
	(250)

resources in order to achieve this goal. Occasionally, however, other commitments prevail. Police are not only workers but authorities as well, and they seem to enjoy making judgments and exercising discretion according to their personal conceptions of what constitutes a reasonable disposition.

Several discretionary forms of clearance are regularly used to ease the administrative burden of prosecution. Police are allowed to drop a suspect against whom another agency has a more serious charge. Sometimes, too, the offender will be in custody for prosecution on another offense; the usual policy, especially if the other offense is more serious, is to forget about prosecution for statutory rape. Statutory rape is considered less serious than homicide, forcible rape, robbery, burglary, auto theft, grant theft, and aggravated assault. The morals detail lost 4% of their statutory rape cases in this way. The formal legal responsibility of the morals detail does not end when this administrative alternative is selected; conceivably the report could be held until the offender is again free, at which time he could be charged with statutory rape. But there is general administrative acceptance of this device as a reasonably just way of treating the multiple offender.

Two other clearance categories can be administratively manipulated: "complainant refuses to prosecute" and "complaint refused by district attorney." Does the complainant have to refuse verbally? Apparently not; in one case the failure of repeated attempts to contact the mother and girl were a basis for clearing the case in just that way. In another case, the detective walked into the office of District Attorney Patten and informed him, "You just refused me a complaint. Goodbye." When Patten called, "Wait a minute. Tell me about it," the detective just continued walking. The district attorney did not question further.

The police are not asked to decide whether sufficient evidence is present to convict the suspect; technically, they decide only whether there is evidence that the crime occurred. Decisions concerning sufficient evidence are in theory left to the district attorney. In large part, however, the police also make the decision with regard to evidence, first by putting cases in their files until they believe the evidence is adequate; and second, by persuading insistent complainants that their cases would not stand a chance in court and that they should therefore drop them. For example, the father of one girl insisted that King prosecute the accused boy, who denied the offense. King told the father that he must think of what would happen in court, pointing out that the girl was incorrigible and that her parents could not handle her. In court it would be her word against the boy's, and no jury would believe her. The father still insisted that the boy be prosecuted. King ended the interview by ushering the father out the door and saying that if the father could not get any more evidence, the district attorney would not issue a complaint. "If you can find me someone who heard him admit it, I'll prosecute."

California law provides an additional structure through which the police may exercise discretion. The detective in such a circumscribed area as morals offenses is typically quite sophisticated regarding the dispositional consequences of his charge. The tactics of charging were explained as follows by Detective King.

> Are you learning much about sex crimes? It's really pretty simple, isn't it? You see, for each code section there is an escape section. We can charge a guy 314 [indecent exposure], and he has to register with the police department in whatever county he goes into. That's rough. So we can charge him with 650½ [injury to public health or decency], and he doesn't have to register. (Do you decide what to charge?) Yes. I think a great deal about it, trying to decide whether to be rough or not.

> Guys I know like Alvin Moone [who had intercourse with a girl under 14], I don't charge hard. He was only after a little piece and is not a sex criminal. That damn guy [pointing to Frost's desk] will charge all of them 288 [child molesting]. I never charge a 288 unless I'm sure that the guy is a sex criminal. It's a tough section. Not that I care if he has to register; but I hate to clutter up our file of pictures with these non-sex-criminal guys.

On another day Frost complained to King that he "fouled up" a possible "288" by only asking the district attorney for a "261.1" (statutory rape). Frost tried to persuade the district attorney to amend the complaint but without success.

The district attorney has final control over the charge to be made against the offender, but the police attempt to sway his judgment in the direction of the charge they prefer. They appear to choose that felony charge which most specifically describes the behavior being considered. Usually they would be unwilling to ask the district attorney for a lesser offense in a clear-cut case of statutory rape because the lesser offenses are less behaviorally specific, for example, "contributing to the delinquency of a minor." On the other hand, when the offense is equally well described by several penal code sections, their choice seems influenced especially by personal attitudes toward sexual conduct. For instance, when the girl is under fourteen, both "child molesting" and "statutory rape" accurately describe the physical behavior; when there appears to have been no exploitation of the girl, King prefers the lesser charge, Frost the harsher. Even among the police themselves, therefore, the norms of the charging process vary with differences in police attitudes toward sexual morality.

Sustaining the Interest of the Complainant

One of the persistent problems of detectives in all details, and not just morals, is making sure that the complainant will continue to support the police action. Police are often cynical regarding family "beefs," for example, because husbands and wives frequently decide that they would rather not go through with prosecuting a charge of assault. Although it is technically possible for the prosecution to continue after the complainant has lost interest, in practice prosecutors do not relish cases in which their chief witness takes the stand reluctantly. For the police who are exercising discretion, this feature of criminal law administration requires that they develop an understanding of the motivation of complainants. This is an especially important feature of statutory rape cases. Motives prompting third parties to report the offense are varied, and certain motives come to seem more reliable to the detectives. Third parties, especially public agencies, bow out of the criminal process after reporting the crime to the police; sometimes even the parents are hesitant about signing a complaint and testifying in court. It is therefore sometimes necessary for police to attempt to create and utilize resources for motivating the interests of the complainant. We discussed in the introduction the resources of the burglary detail. This section will attempt to show how the attributes of the girls and their parents are utilized to maintain and enhance their motivation to serve as prosecutorial witnesses in cases of statutory rape.

Reliable Motivations. One drug seller will sometimes inform on a competitor to put him out of business, and vindictive girls have been known to accuse boys falsely. The police recognize that informers are impelled by motives of varying purity; when the informant gives narcotics officers information in exchange for money to purchase drugs or to avoid a penal sanction, his motives tend to be regarded as reliable. It should also be noted that these motives—the ones the police trust—are the ones they made possible and hence to some extent can manipulate and control

Morals detectives tend to suspect purely righteous motives. In the abstract they agree that indignation is the proper motive for parents who discover that their daughter has been violated. In practice, however, the detectives often treat indignation—especially when asserted by Negroes—as an affectation, and parents who express indignation are at best considered woefully ignorant of their daughter's active role in the crime. Several times detectives were observed to deflate indignation with pointed observations to the parents about the girl's character. Moreover, indignation is less acceptable from those whose daughter is pregnant; in these cases the police feel that indignation was too slow in appearing and too contaminated with other motives to be honest.

Paradoxically, then, although indignation is considered a more *proper* motive than pregnancy or the need for welfare funds, the latter two are in practice received more favorably by detectives. When dealing with a mother who reported the offense only because she believed it necessary to obtain welfare aid, the detective feels no need to deflate a phony motive; such mothers are treated more gently than those who are both welfare applicants *and* indignant. Detectives, therefore, tend to be "hard-nosed" in assessing motives;

they prefer necessity over what they regard as a false sense of propriety.

Induced Motivation. Most statutory rapes are reported by public agencies which then withdraw their interest; they do not want to sign the complaint or to give evidence in court. In this regard they bear a certain similarity to narcotics informers, who do not wish to be exposed ("burned"). Thus, if the police and district attorney decide to prosecute a statutory rape, they are compelled to locate someone else to sign and testify. Generally, the police attempt to make the statutory rape victim and her mother (or, less often, her father) the signatories and witnesses. Although the police themselves *might* sign a complaint against the boy, they do not. In contrast, the narcotics detail often tries to structure the situation of arrest in such a way that a police officer can become the complaining witness; this officer then signs the complaint and sees the case through the court. This gives the officer some control over the degree of enthusiasm with which the case will be prosecuted and also maintains the anonymity of the informer.

Morals detectives, however, require mothers to sign the complaint. Apparently, signing is taken as an indication of willingness to cooperate in court. With such a policy it sometimes becomes necessary for the police to convince mothers to sign; reluctant or unwilling mothers require special persuasion similar to that undertaken by vice officers when dealing with reluctant informers. The vice officer persuades reluctant informers by arrest, followed by a reduced charge or no prosecution at all in exchange for the informer's identification of and help in trapping a drug salesman. In short, by manipulating the situation so that they control important sanctions, they *create* resources for motivating cooperation. Morals detectives similarly create motives in reluctant mothers. It might indeed be suggested that whenever police deal with willing "victims" they will find it necessary to hold threatened punishment in the background for those who will not cooperate. When communication among those so threatened is relatively good, as it is in the addict population, police will occasionally need to carry out the threat to show to all that they mean business. When communication does not exist, as among statutory rape victims reported by the welfare department, it need never be used; since the person is not sure if the police will carry through, threat alone may be sufficient.

The size of the motivational problem facing the morals detail may be seen in the fact that fully 61% of the statutory rape cases were reported on the initiative of someone other than the parents. The parents must now be convinced that it is in their interest to continue the prosecution of the adult male for the offense. (No complaint is needed for a case handled in juvenile court.) The primary indicator of willingness is the parental signature upon the complaint issued by the district attorney. The police are relatively successful persuaders, for, even in those cases in which the girl's family did not become voluntarily involved, as great a percentage (44 per cent) supported prosecution as among those who voluntarily reported the offense (43 per cent).

Police persuasion first takes the form of emphasizing the guilt component of the mixed feelings held by the parents. Parents are sometimes annoyed that they must deal with the police, often against their wills, yet few can entirely escape feeling guilty for their daughter's actions or, at least, escape feeling that they ought to feel guilty for her violation of the law. So the police speak throughout, perhaps unconsciously, as though they assume the parents are interested in righting the violation of the law by punishing the lawbreaker. Guilt is effectively encouraged by hewing to the straight and narrow, the letter of the law. The detectives are masters at feigning indifference to extenuating circumstances, particularly the equal involvement of the girl. They say, "It doesn't matter if she does look older. . . ." "It doesn't matter if she knocked him down and took it away from him. . . ." "It doesn't matter if they do plan to get married . . . the law is the law." They argue that violation is supposed to be followed by punishment, and even if your daughter's complicity does not lead you to desire punishment, the law requires it.

Also increasing the readiness of the parents to sign the complaint is the organization of the initial interview with the girl and her parents. Upon receiving a statutory rape crime report, the detective first calls in the girl and one of her parents, usually the mother. He then routinely attempts to take a signed statement from the girl. The detective begins by asking about the circumstances of the crime, the time and place, the name and address of the boy, whether contraceptives were used, whether there was penetration, how often the offense occurred, whether the boy knew the girl's age, and the names of any witnesses. Then he goes through each question a second time, this time writing down the girl's answers in the form of first-person declarative sentences, for example, "I had sexual intercourse with Jimmy Jones, 272 Place Street, in his apartment." The girl is then asked to read the statement and sign it, after which her parents are asked to witness her signature. After this detailed, intimate questioning, the detective suggests that signing the complaint is merely a formality.

This listing of the steps of the interview, however, does not convey the emotional tone, which combines elements of righteousness, irony, and contempt. Far from being the impersonal bureaucrat, the detective usually emphasizes the guilty and sordid aspects of the crime. At the end, the signing of the statement may seem like the promise of redemption at the end of a confessional. Some feeling for the flavor of the interview can be gotten from these extracts from two interviews, one with a girl, the other with a defendant.

> The girl, who was pregnant, had been reluctant to answer the detective's questions dealing with physical intimacy. "Those who play must pay. Did he use any preventatives?" (No.) "Did you have intercourse with anyone else?" (No.) "Did he discharge in you?" (No answer.) "Well, come on now, a little pelican didn't do it. Or maybe you wash your undies in Duz—Duz does everything."

In another case, a boy came into the office with his mother. He admitted to having four sexual acts with the girl, who is pregnant, and wanted to take responsibility for the child.

> Frost asked the regular question: "Didn't you use contraceptives?" (No.) "Didn't you even think about it?" (Uh, uh.) "At the time you didn't, huh?"

When the detective meets with failure, several further inducements may be employed. One might be called the appeal to future contingency. Paraphrased, it runs, "All right. We'll let you drop the case, but don't bother us with it again. If you later decide you want the boy punished because he doesn't help support the child or because he continues to have intercourse with your daughter, we aren't going to be very interested. We'll be sure that you aren't going to carry that complaint through either." Anything might happen in the future; how can a parent be sure that he or she will not need the morals detail again? This is a potent threat, even though the system of police supervision might not permit detectives to carry it out.

Cases referred by the family support division of the district attorney's office (40% of the cases) are especially troublesome. *Before her welfare check will be released,* the girl must report to the police department and obtain a detective's signature on a duplicate form which reads, "_______ has agreed to sign a complaint charging _______ with _______." That is, the girl must notify police that a crime has been committed and give evidence of the notification. Girls referred by the family support division usually want *only* to have the form signed and to turn it in at the family support division. The detectives, however, are interested in pressing a criminal action. From the detective's point of view, his problem is that even if such girls—94% of whom were Negro in the period studied—promise to sign a complaint, they frequently try to avoid further cooperation with the police department and the actual signing of the complaint. "All they want is for us to sign their slip so that they can get their money," was a plaint common to the morals detectives. Under these circumstances, the complainant's poverty is an important resource for the detective. Express or implied threats to have funds withheld if the complainant does not cooperate may serve to "persuade" a reluctant impoverished family to carry through with the complaint, whereas a wealthier family may escape this particular pressure.

Influences on Processing Decisions

Although police attitudes toward Negroes may vary little from those in the white population as a whole, their official position enables them, if they desire, to give more effect to their attitudes. One must distinguish, then, between bias (attitude) and discrimination (showing favoritism in treatment) and ask whether the police discriminate. The main discrimination takes place before the case reaches the detectives: because of their economic position, more Negroes apply for welfare aid, thereby increasing routine contact with morals police. Although the detectives dislike Negroes, they do not send more of them along for prosecution (66% of arrested white males compared to 55% of arrested Negro males are prosecuted). Why, then, do they express dislike for the Negroes they process? They typically reply that Negroes are on welfare "taking our money," or that they only report the crime because they have to.

Most important perhaps is a persistent theme mixing elements of sexual interest, jealousy, and revulsion. As one morals detective put it, "These black apes fuck too much. They just have no morals. They fuck like animals." The sort of language detectives use, of course, varies with the setting in which it is spoken. In court, or even in the district attorney's office, the police talk in euphemisms, sometimes in a stilted jargon. A fight is an "altercation," a Negro is a "minority-group person." What we are reporting is office language, private language, and should be understood as such. In fairness to the police, it should be pointed out that such language is commonly used in informal male settings, such as barracks and ballfields. It is important to report it verbatim because it expresses the essential feelings of the police on the job and also because it sometimes spills over into interactions with those accused of morals crimes. Thus, it may be that attitudes have less of an effect upon the *outcome* of cases than upon the manner in which such cases are handled *interactionally*. It is worthwhile noting that the chief of the Westville department handed down an order in the summer of 1965 stating that departmental police forbade the use by police of derogatory language 'in the course of their official duties or at any other time. . . ." And he listed the forbidden words: "boy, spade, jig, nigger, blue, smoke, coon, spook, headhunter, jungle bunny, boogie, stud, burrhead, cat, blackboy, black, shine, ape, spick, mau-mau."

A factor which might be expected to account for much of the apparently discretionary behavior of the detective is whether the girl is pregnant. We indicated above that pregnancy is a strong influence on police discovery of the offense. Moreover, a pregnant girl has *legal* significance. She is a walking *corpus delecti;* her age and her condition provide proof for subsequent criminal processing. But we find little difference in the treatment of those who definitely are pregnant and those for whom the condition is still uncertain. "Rapists" of pregnant girls are arrested less often (52%) than "rapists" whose victims did not know if they were pregnant (68%).

The seriousness of the offense, measured roughly by the difference in ages between the male and the female also appears to have an effect contrary to expectations: offenders who are older than the girl (that is, the more serious offenders) are not prosecuted as often as those of the same age. Among those couples separated in age by two years or less, the male is prosecuted 66% of the time, whereas among those differing by seven years or more he is prosecuted only 46% of the time. As the age gap widens the portion falling in the category "complainant refuses to prosecute" grows. One explanation might be that mothers fear the traumatic effects of a trial upon their daughters. If so, one would expect mothers of younger daughters to withdraw more often, but they do not. A more likely explanation is that since the main interest of many of the complainants is to cope with the girls's pregnancy, older defendants may be in a better position to provide financial assistance than juveniles. When the male offers such aid, the mother and daughter may be less inclined to press their complaint.

Arrest

Once it has been decided to clear the case by arrest and prosecution, the detectives begin to make arrangements to take the principals into custody. It is not widely known that in statutory rapes the girl is typically arrested as well as the male, for she is considered to be "in danger of leading an idle, dissolute, lewd, or immoral life . . ." (602 W&I Code). Her arrest is usually technical. Unless she is arrested for running away from home or for an offense observed by the arresting officers she is quickly released to her parent's custody after being given a date to appear in court.

Arrests of male juveniles are similarly handled. Once a statement is taken, the inspector calls the probation department to set a date for the boy's appearance in juvenile court. The boy is technically arrested, then released to his parent's custody until the court date.

The arrest of the adult male is also carried out in a casual, even considerate, manner. Depending on their moods and on how busy they are, the detectives will often first inform the accused that they have a warrant; they will hold it for several days if necessary so that he can arrange to make bail. If the suspect does not voluntarily appear for questioning or arrest, they give the warrant to the police warrant or fugitive details to serve. These arrest practices suggest that detectives do not consider the adult statutory rapist a serious or dangerous criminal, one likely to escape if he can. In child-molesting cases they are more businesslike, considering the molester more dangerous.

SOCIAL CONTROL AND BUREAUCRATIC EFFICIENCY

Social control depends not only upon prevailing policies of pooling or insulating information among agencies but also upon the ability of the agencies to make use of such information when it is available or potentially available. In this respect administrative efficiency is a catalyst for social control through bureaucracy. The rewards and punishments available to the police in the processing of statutory rape cases, for example, are dependent upon unwritten agreements and understandings among the police and district attorney, judges, family support division, probation department, and parole agencies. The narcotics squad keeps these arrangements well oiled and ready to use. One or another of its members can regularly be found in the district attorney's office; their visits there are more frequent than those of any other police detail. The narcotics squad holds weekly meetings with probation officers and assigns one officer to act as permanent liaison.

The relation between the morals detail and the family support division of the district attorney's office provides a contrasting case. The family support division reports nearly half the statutory rape incidents processed by the morals detail and is the only agency systematically reporting all the offenses it discovers. Yet the members of the detail view the family support division with ambivalence. The detectives generally dislike public welfare, and they are pleased that the family support division lets them know about law violations among recipients; it gives them a legal chance to exercise their hostility; perhaps they can even discourage some girls for attempting to receive welfare aid. On the other hand, they are restrained by the fact that the law primarily punishes the male and not the girl, by the conviction that teen-age intercourse is really not terribly evil, and by the feeling that their activities make them no more than an extension of the welfare department, a feeling that saps the enthusiasm of an anti-welfare policeman. When the family support division sends a girl to them, the detectives first record the circumstances of the crime and then takes sworn confessions from the boy and the girl. They know, however, that the family support division has, perhaps moments before, taken exactly the same admissions. Their own efforts to get confessions on paper are regarded as pointless duplication. The situation confirms their dislike of paper work and their belief that it has little to do with "real police work."

Their hostility to the cases reported by the family support division, both covert and overt, is intensified by the inability of family support division to back up the threats of the morals detail. The family support division does insist that the girls make out a police report of the offense and a promise to sign a complaint. But they *do not require* that the girl or her mother actually sign the criminal complaint issued by the district attorney's office. The detectives also report, however, that they are able to create some "static" through the family support division and through the welfare workers themselves. When a welfare recipient refuses to sign a complaint, they sometimes telephone the case worker and report that the attitude of the recipient is uncooperative. The welfare department presumably takes note of these evaluations, but it was impossible to trace out precisely what actions are taken as a result, because access to welfare records was not made available.[6]

[6] Irving F. Reichert, Jr. recorded the law enforcement complaint that social workers do not report crimes they run across in their case work, but he pointed

To persuade the girls and mothers to follow through on criminal charges, the detail often informs welfare recipients that aid will be cut off unless they sign. The family support division cannot back this threat, for it can recommend that aid be withheld only when the recipient will not cooperate with the district attorney in finding the absent, nonsupporting father. Under the circumstances, then, the threat of cutting off funds works so long as the recipient believes it will be carried out. Of the ninety-five welfare cases studied, twenty-eight refused to sign.

The morals detail cannot fully exploit its *other* potential sources of information. Parents, of course, are likely to have only one offense to report and are unlikely to be useful as future sources of information. Probation officers unsystematically report offenses known to them; unlike the family support division officials, probation officers are not housed in any single office building, making it difficult for the morals detail to establish a uniform relationship with them. In addition, probation officials have some discretion about what action to take on the cases reported to them verbally by the morals detail. In their final reports on cases involving four male juveniles, for example, the police indicated that the probation officer had been told each time of the offense, and that he had promised to add statutory rape to the charges on which the boy was being taken before the juvenile court. We were unable to find any indication in the probation records that the charge had been added. Thus, the possibilities of utilizing "negative" information seems to be related to bureaucratic efficiency. In those areas where communication is difficult, haphazard, or inconstant, the possibilities of social control through bureaucracy are reduced.

Finally, the morals detail has contact with the district attorney's office. It might be thought that the district attorney and police are not separate agencies, since both are part of law enforcement. It is important to understand, however, that police and prosecutor are separate agencies, with distinct hierarchies of administration, pay,

---

out as well that both the Federal Social Security Act, Title IV, Sec. 402 (a) (8), and the California Welfare and Institutions Code, Sec. 118, forbid the use of such information for purposes other than the administration of aid. Reichert recommended that workers be required to report crimes to the county welfare director who would then decide whether they should be related to law enforcement officials. In Westville this safeguard is effectively bypassed by the policy of telling the family support division of all welfare applications involving minor girls. "Relationships Between Welfare and Law-Enforcement Agencies in California," *California Welfare Study Commission Report* (Feb. 1963), pp. 302–3.

and responsibility to city government. Each agency could be quite hostile to the other—especially if one agency publicly criticizes the other—and in some communities this has occurred. The relations between the Westville police department and the Westville deputy district attorney's Office—in turn, the major municipal subdivision of the county district attorney's office—were regarded by both police and deputy district attorney as exceptionally smooth and untroubled.

Members of the morals detail regularly talk with one member of the district attorney's staff—Patten—although others are sometimes involved as well. In general, the police know what evidence the prosecutor requires, but technical legal questions frequently arise for which they seek his counsel. When an investigation is completed and the case is ready for prosecution, the district attorney prepares the complaint and obtains an arrest warrant. Between January 1962 and October 1963 the district attorney issued eighty-five complaints and refused to issue eight more. As might be guessed, some of these refusals were a source of friction between the police and the district attorney. Most of the denials were accepted by the police, probably because they realized that the available evidence was insufficient and yet wanted to clear the case from their files.

One denial brought Detective King into conflict with District Attorney Patten. A girl of 12 years had been impregnated, and King had gathered statements from all parties. He asked Patten for a complaint and was refused; the statement from the boy (19 years) had been taken by an officer at the Carson Home for Boys (which was holding the boy on another charge), and Patten wanted to be sure that no promises had been made. King contacted the officer who had taken the statement. At King's behest, the officer obtained a written statement from the suspect that no promises had been made and offered to testify in court himself if necessary. When King reported this to Patten, Patten became angry, accusing the police of not doing their job, of shirking their responsibilities. Apparently Patten expected King to spend a day traveling to see the boy, to get the statement himself. Exasperated, King reported the conversation to his lieutenant and openly wondered how detectives could be expected to go to that effort when the district attorney would "let the guy plead to contributing to the delinquency of a minor anyway." Lieutenant Richards interrupted King's diatribe and remarked, "As far as the detectives are concerned the district attorney is God. I wish we had as much discretion as they do. God, wouldn't it be nice to be able to decide which cases to handle and which not to? Don't let him make you mad at him. Just ignore his digs at the police force."

Table 7 *Action of Municipal Court and Superior Court on Adult Statutory Rape Defendants*

Action	Per Cent
Municipal Court	
Held for superior court	46
Plead guilty to misdemeanor	40
Dismissed	9
No action (warrant out)	5
	100
	(85)
Superior court	
Plead guilty to statutory rape	49
Plead guilty stipulated misdemeanor	44
Acquitted	2
Convicted by court	5
	100
	(39)

Despite such occasional friction, a situation of mutual confidence usually prevails. The district attorney usually takes the detective's word that a case is ready for prosecution and often issues a warrant without reading the report.

Differences seemingly based on personality are perhaps symptoms of a more central conflict, namely, that higher authority resides in the district attorney, which leads to the sort of resentment frequently encountered in relations between a skilled craftsman and a foreman. For example, each detective judges from the crime report how serious the offense is and then expends his effort proportionately. He signifies his estimate of its seriousness by the penal code number he assigns it on his report, and generally these code numbers are accepted by the district attorney. Even when the district attorney accepts the policeman's estimate, however, he may invoke the more severe felony charge of statutory rape only as a level in bargaining; for a plea of guilty he may be willing to reduce the charge to an included misdemeanor. If this happens very often, the police may feel that they have been "sold out," that they were put to needless effort to obtain what has become needless evidence.

Table 7 shows that a large portion of those charged with statutory rape are allowed to plead guilty in municipal court to a misdemeanor (40%); of these 39 cases sent to superior court, 44% were allowed to plead guilty with the stipulation that they were pleading guilty to statutory rape at the misdemeanor level. In short, the district attorney conducted a lot of bargaining for pleas of guilty. When these reductions are not assented to by morals detectives, they constitute a fundamental source of friction between the district attorney and the detectives.

CRIMINAL PROCESSING AND THE NONVOLUNTARY CLIENT

The findings of this study raise questions about the relations between individual goals and organizational ends. Organizations providing services often take client goals for granted. When the client's request sets in motion the activities of the organization, the client is usually assumed to desire an end identical with the declared goal of the organization. But let us suggest the idea of a nonvoluntary or ambivalent client—someone who comes to an organization, who asks for its service, but who lets the organization know (verbally or through demeanor) that he was compelled to come and that he would rather not be served. How will an organization respond? Let us guess that the quality of service (measured by whatever goals the organization espouses) will be lowered whenever the organization's officials believe (1) that the client did not voluntarily ask for the service in the first place or (2) that, despite his original intent, the client does not *now* desire the service.[7]

Statutory rape cases illustrate organization problems associated with hesitant or nonvoluntary clients. As already noted, most statutory rapes are not reported voluntarily to the police by the girl or her parents, that is, by someone personally interested in the act and its consequences. Most (61%) are discovered instead in the course of the operations of other agencies and referred to the morals detail from these agencies. One question raised was: What notice do legal officials take of the fact that the complaining witness did not come to them of her own volition? Our prediction was that the police,

[7] Blau discovered a type of nonvoluntary client among those recipients of unemployment insurance benefits who did not want to find a job and yet were required to accept any suitable job unless they had an acceptable cause for refusal. Blau found that a newly introduced technique of performance evaluation induced employment interviewers to discourage job refusals by the use of threatened sanctions—that is, disqualification for unemployment funds—even though this was forbidden and generally lowered the quality of interviewing for job placement. See Peter M. Blau, *The Dynamics of Bureaucracy* (Chicago, University of Chicago Press, 1955), Chap. 6.

Table 8 *Information Source and Final Disposition (in Per Cent)*

Disposition	Information Source	
	Voluntary	Official
Disposition of Males by Police		
No action; case dropped	24	28
Male sent to DA or probation	76	72
	100	100
	(58)	(97)
Disposition of Males by District Attorney, Probation, or Courts		
Dismissed	21	22
Probation	57	56
Confinement	23	21
No action or no record	—	1
	101	100
	(44)	(70)
Disposition of Females by Police		
No action; case dropped	35	22
Female sent to probation	65	78
	100	100
	(54)	(93)
Disposition of Females by Probation and Juvenile Court		
Dismissed	29	25
Probation	69	62
Confinement	3	8
No action or no record	—	5
	101	100
	(35)	(73)

district attorney, and courts would press voluntarily initiated cases harder than those originating out of other public agencies; consequently, defendants in voluntary cases should *more often* be passed along to the district attorney for prosecution and should more often receive heavier penalties in court.

Table 8 portrays the general outcome of the legal disposition of

[8] It might be objected that some accused males were not guilty of the crime. For this reason the only cases shown in Table 8 are those in which the male signed a confession to the sexual acts; presumably these cases could have been successfully prosecuted.

both parties involved in statutory rape cases. Instead of finding as we predicted, that voluntary cases would be more vigorously prosecuted, we found little difference between these and officially initiated cases. Two after-the-fact explanations can be suggested for the unexpected finding.

First, the voluntary cases are more or less left to take care of themselves in the criminal process; the police and district attorney need only guide them through to the courts. In contrast, officially initiated cases do not propel themselves. Legal officials are therefore faced with the choice of either dropping these cases entirely or getting behind them and pushing. Once committed, they try to exact the full measure of legal punishment, much as they do with the prosecution of other victimless crimes where the state is the real complainant.

Second, the "willingness" of a voluntary complainant is tenuous. The parent's original demand for punishment of the offending male may be undermined upon hearing a detailed account of their daughter's complicity. It begins to seem less fair to press a criminal complaint when one's daughter consented, perhaps even pursued the male. In one case, for example, a sixteen-year-old girl admitted during questioning, with her parents present, what they had not known before pressing charges: that she welcomed her eighteen-year-old lover over a period of months by keeping her bedroom window open.

THE NONVOLUNTARY CLIENT AND POLICE MORALE

When a policeman can engage in real police work—act out the important symoblic rites of search, chase, and capture—his self-image will be affirmed and his morale enhanced. In our survey, detectives, whose jobs generally involve these elements, preferred their present jobs more than other policemen. Detectives have police jobs without equal; for the most part they are active and nonsupervisory. Few of the detectives wanted higher rank and the greater responsibility of supervision (only 12%). In contrast, morals detectives uniformly disliked their work.

Lowered morale, however, is not common to all police details enforcing conventional morality. On the contrary, members of the vice squad expressed the greatest preference of any police unit for their present assignment.[9] In spite of the difficulties inherent in enforcing laws that produce few citizen complaints, the high morale of the vice squad may be attributed to the extent to which the vice squad police are able to identify themselves fully with the policeman's role in carrying out routine functions. This, in turn, is closely connected to the perceived menace of the criminal being pursued.

Certain kinds of offenders more than others possess attributes which the police see as menacing. In crimes against person or property the menace is immediate and clear. There is more variation among crimes with willing "victims." We suggest that at least four factors are selected by the police as evidence of the potential menace of the offender. These factors might be most instructively presented by means of a contrast between the statutory rapist as "victimizer" and the drug seller, the bookmaker, the abortionist. First, each of the last group are involved in criminality entailing organization, there is a degree of regularity in behavior location, source of supply, and lines of information. Such organization is interpreted as a greater menace than the labile situations and patterns of interaction which surround statutory rape. Second, unlike the heroin addict, for example, who engages in theft or pimping to support his habit, the statutory rapist need not engage in instrumental or supportive criminal activities. The wider these criminal ripples spread from the central crime, the more the police regard it as a menace.

Third, in contrast to statutory rapists, these other offenders are distinguished by affiliations with subgroups that share values, beliefs, and symbols which are considered both foreign and dangerous by the police. By contrast, police, like most males, can empathize with the role of statutory rapist. Finally, menace is associated with the potential of the criminal act for altering the identity of the victim. Public morality is seen as menaced by the homosexual; through seduction he may convert a normal male to homosexuality; drug users are converted to addiction; abortionists convert life to death. The seduced or seducing underage girl, however, has not radically altered her identity; she may no longer be "pure," but this is a value of uncertain social importance.

Where the police perceive the menace of the criminal as great, morale among policemen tends to be high. In the absence of menacing attributes on the part of the pursued, the policeman feels cheated. He cannot properly play the police role because the criminal and the victim do not play the proper supporting and complementary roles. There is no suspense, no chase, no investigation, no danger. In most statutory rape cases the detectives feel as if they have been reduced to stenographers, recording trivia rather than apprehending criminals.

When attributes can be viewed as menacing, the police will tend to don moral colors; more than usual they will see themselves as guardians of morality or perhaps even as moral entrepreneurs in Becker's

[9] And this preference does not result, as might occur to the reader, from the possibility of graft. See Skolnick, *op. cit.*, Chap. 2.

sense.[10] They will work hard to make enforcement effective, seeking sources of information. There will be strong self-justifications, and they may become legislative lobbyists for harsher penalties. By contrast, police who deal with nonmenacing deviants tend to lack this interest. Complaints will be heard about the nature of the job and the law. Rationales will be weak. Perhaps they will even engage in some sabotage of the law, if not directly, then by the device of failing to do all they *might* do to prosecute the crime. For example, a morals detective might contact homes for unwed mothers and might sign criminal complaints himself, but he typically does not.

Finally morals detectives express frustration that their activities produce little appreciation from the victim and no beneficial results. Furthermore, even when the offender is successfully prosecuted, the detectives themselves often wonder if they have really done any good. They are skeptical of the benefits of prosecution, for the statutory rapist is difficult to interpret as a danger to the community. His *act* is often understandable, and it suggests neither punishment nor rehabilitation. They therefore tend to dislike their work, expressing themselves through irritation with each other and with those whom they are required to interrogate—*required to* ultimately because they are workers and must do their job.

MORAL RESPONSIBILITY AND STATUTORY RAPE ADMINISTRATION

When conventional morality is written into the law, when the law prohibits certain transactions willingly entered into by all involved, a decision has been made about where the desired but illegal exchange of goods and services will take place in that society. Henceforward they will take place in secret, under continuous moral and legal threat; approval will not be given to these transactions or to those who supply and receive them. This initial decision, even though it is rarely made consciously or at a single point in time, molds both the subsequent criminal processing of offenders and the attitudes of those who carry out that processing.

Generally, these observations apply no less to offenses involving drugs, gambling, prostitution, abortion, and homosexuality than to statutory rape. But statutory rape has one peculiarity that sets it apart from the others. The sexual act is illegal only because of the age of the girl; in some cases a few additional months would be sufficient to remove the penal threat. In none of the other crimes

[10] See Becker, *op. cit.*, pp. 147–63.

mentioned is there so sharp a break between legal and illegal. One can be certain that many girls less than 18 years of age possess sufficient sophistication to know what they are doing and that some over that age may not. This arbitrary dividing line denies the obvious variations in the speed of human development. One can better understand this law, however, if one examines its original intent. The common law sought to protect a minor female child from sexual exploitation, but it defined child as one who was under the age of 10 years. In its laws of 1850 California followed this standard, as did many other states. Subsequently, California, like other states, has continually pushed the age of consent higher, to 14 in 1889, then to 16 in 1897, and finally to 18 in 1919.

By prolonging for eight years the age of innocence the law now does more than protect minor females. It lends legal sanction to the double sexual standard. Under such a standard men and women are held to different moral codes, and women who behave like men are considered loose or fallen. Yet, at least under the double standard of *morality*, women are designated as saints or sluts according to their behavior. The extended age of *legal* consent creates a class of saintly women whose purity is beyond challenge; the male may not produce evidence in court about the girl's moral character. In other words, the law firmly established the girl's right to trouble, her claim to be considered a victim based on her *status* and not on her *acts*. Despite the concern of the juvenile court with the female, the male is presumed to be the offender, and his punishment is potentially the more severe.

As should be clear by now, however, this assessment of relative blame may be defeated by a day-by-day practical acquaintance with factual situations. Police are supposed to ignore the circumstances; they should attend only to whether one specific act was committed and whether the girl was under age. Both police and parents, however, are used to a dispensation of blame founded on acts rather than on status. No matter how hard police try they find it impossible to ignore the circumstances. When they discover the character of the girl's involvement, often even hardened policemen are dismayed. In the end the police mediate between the formal law and the demands of the situations presented to them.

BUREAUCRACY, INFORMATION, AND SOCIAL CONTROL

Our central findings analyze and describe the process whereby the formal rule of state law is modified by the local agencies assigned to administer it. These agencies mediate between actual conditions and attitudes and the formal rigor of the law. As the various agencies of the federal, state, and local governments all extend their activities into spheres formerly occupied by private interest groups and, most importantly, *increase their capacity for awareness,* we expect this mediating function of local administrative units to become increasingly significant.

The importance of sharing becomes manifest when one compares the operation of the Westville morals detail with the operation of the corresponding unit in nearby Mountain City. Despite the fact that Mountain City's population outnumbers Westville's by more than two to one, during 1961 there were forty fewer cases of statutory rape reported to the Mountain City police. The Mountain City family support division does not systematically report violations it discovers while taking welfare applications, and it is largely to this difference in policy that the different outcome is attributable. (Ironically, of the two Mountain City reports that were identifiable as resulting from a welfare application, one was a referral from the Westville family support division.) As a result, many of the features of the Westville cases are lacking in Mountain City: fewer reporting persons wait until they are certain the girl is pregnant before reporting the offense (67% compared to 22%); offenses are reported more quickly (44% within one day of the offense, compared to Westville's 13%); and Negroes are involved in far fewer of the cases (35% compared to 78%).

Since the proportion of Negroes in Westville is more than two times that in Mountain City, this last finding would not seem to be directly attributable to the welfare policy of sharing information with the morals detail. However, as percentages approach 100 per cent they cannot be expected to rise at the same rate. This ceiling effect is expressed in the formula, percentage change = $(P_2 - P_1)/(100 - P_1)$, where P_1 is the initial percentage (proportion in population Negro) and P_2 is the final percentage (Negroes in morals detail caseload).[11] Using this formula the percentage increase in Negroes in the morals detail case load over those in the population is 70 per cent in Westville and 28 per cent in Mountain City.

Westville also receives more reports of offenses from public agencies other than the Family Support Division. Excluding welfare-originated reports, 70 per cent of Westville reports compared with 41 per cent of the Mountain City reports come from these other public agencies.

[11] See Carl I. Hovland, Arthur A. Lumadaine, and Fred Sheffield, "A Baseline for Measurement of Percentage Change," *The Language of Social Research,* Eds., Lazarsfeld and Rosenberg. (Glencoe, The Free Press, 1955), pp. 77–82.

To put the matter another way, if all cases discovered by public agencies (including welfare) were removed from the Westville total, there would be, in the two cities, a similar rate of statutory rape cases per hundred thousand population. It is the addition of cases originating in welfare and in other public agencies which produces the extraordinarily high proportion of Negroes involved in the Westville statutory rape case load.

These differences in the composition of the statutory rape case load are reflected in police investigation procedures. In Westville the encounter between police and suspect appears less adversary, since the case load contained a greater percentage of cases where the participants themselves felt their behavior to be socially acceptable. The Westville police make use of subjective feelings to incriminate. They *invite* the suspect in to talk with them, and he is likely to comply. By contrast, the Mountain City police usually must arrest the male and then interrogate him, thereby arousing his suspicions. Consequently, a lower percentage of the Mountain City males confess to the crime, so greater effort must be extended to discover other factual evidence which will ready the case for prosecution.

Over all, the Westville morals detail is a far more effective agency of legal control with regard to this offense than is the Mountain City detail. Yet it is well to ask about the consequences of this increased competence. The great obstacle to repressive dictatorships has always been the limited competence of the rulers. But, as pointed out by Philip Selznick, this poses a conflict between the value of equal justice and the threat of despotism:

> The idea of equal justice seems to require that all offenders be treated alike. Yet there is evidence that the police routinely attempt to distinguish, especially among juveniles, the apparently casual offender from the committed delinquent. Lawyers and other social scientists may see in this a violation of evenhanded justice. And indeed, this is so, especially where racial and class biases are operative. But confronted with these facts I am moved to ask: . . . Do we need or want agencies of control so efficient and so impartial that every actual offense has an equal chance of being known and processed? In considering this point we should bear in mind that offenses of all kinds are probably very much more numerous in fact than in record.
>
> . . . I am concerned that we do not respond too eagerly and too well to the apparent need or more effective mechanisms of social control. In the administration of justice, if anywhere,

> we need to guard human values and forestall the creation of mindless machines for handling cases according to set routines. Here vigilance consists in careful study of actual operations so that we may know what will be lost or gained when administrative changes are proposed.[12]

Selznick's concern seems especially relevant where increased police efficiency is used to reinforce conventional morality. We would like to examine briefly the possible consequences of the administrative changes whose beginnings have been described.

Eventually most record systems—school, census, income tax, employment, military, criminal, welfare, recreation, etc.—will be computerized and centralized.[13] A strong possibility is that access to records will be granted to those groups that can present socially legitimized needs for access. Justifications are already in existence. The police and the district attorney may say that they are charged with enforcing the law and that certain law violations come to light in the records of such organizations as the welfare department. "Either we are serious about enforcing the law or we are not," they may assert. "If we are serious, then inform us whenever a violation is uncovered." One finding of this paper is that information is already shared between welfare and the police, and the rationale is exactly that stated above.

Consider those public agencies which maintain rehabilitative, therapeutic, and even preventative ideals—welfare, probation, the courts. "We are concerned with the whole individual in his social milieu," they may assert, "and unless we can consider all available information we cannot adequately fulfill our socially approved purpose" Education similarly considers itself the guardian of the whole child. These claims are hard to deny precisely because they make true assessments of need. But approval of these claims means that the selection and shaping of a person's roles is taken from his hands. Among those sectors which have pooled their data, the individual has no secrets.

[12] Philip Selznick, "Foundations of the Theory of Organization," *American Sociological Review*, Vol. 13 (Feb. 1948), p. 84.

[13] Nine nearby counties are now building a computer center which will handle police data retrieval for them. Ultimately the plan will include police, court, probation, and possibly welfare and health records. Sharing the information among *private* secondary groups would probably result in a polarization of memberships; a person would belong to a set of groups where his roles would involve the least conflict. To the extent that certain major roles in a person's life—his job, for example—are dependent upon the government, this polarization becomes fixed on a single pole.

When bureaucratic criteria define them as important, conflicts among roles cannot be concealed.

A cry of alarm is perhaps not yet warranted, for there are opposing tendencies. First, modern governments operate through a multitude of agencies, and these are often openly in conflict about goals and means. Just how far such agencies are controlled by central policies and finances and how far their concerns are directed by their specialized task is not clear. Second, the accepted doctrines of privacy and privileged communication (or the organizational equivalent, confidentiality of records) operate against widespread sharing. Finally, we may put some confidence in the protections afforded by the "natural" inefficiency of bureaucracy. That a system based upon the ideal type of rational administration posited by Weber is not truly efficient is an increasingly general theme of sociologists of organization.[14] Nevertheless, our data have shown that the Westville morals detail is significantly more successful in locating "crime" than its Mountain City counterpart simply because it taps welfare records. Although its efficiency could be further heightened by adopting the techniques of other police units, much more of its success is attributable to the policy of routinely pooling information than to enthusiastic administration. The policy of routinely pooling information is found to more than compensate for the inefficiency of human officials. No matter how much they may personally dislike the laws they enforce, petty officials are also puppets of policy. Ultimately, we are faced with the issue Selznick poses: "Do we need or want agencies of control so efficient and so impartial that every actual offender has an equal chance of being known and processed?[15] The combination of dependence upon criminal sanctions as an instrument of social control, increasing involvement in individual lives by government, and an increasing capacity to discover, record and transfer information, invites us to spell out and examine the fundamental assumptions of our system of social control.

[14] See, for example, Reinhard Bendix, *Work and Authority in Industry* (New York, Harper Torchbooks, 1956) pp. 444ff.; also same author's "Bureaucracy and the Problem of Power," in *Public Administration Review*, Vol. 5 (Summer 1945), pp. 194–209. Also Selznick, *op. cit.*, pp. 25–35.

[15] Selznick, *op. cit.*, p. 84.

Police Morale, Reform, and Citizen Respect: The Chicago Case

James Q. Wilson

During the first two years of this decade the American public was treated to a series of police scandals in Boston, Chicago, Denver, Kansas City, New York, and elsewhere involving police officers charged with theft and corruption.[1] In 1965 and 1966 the police are in the newspapers again but now more commonly because of the role they play in the current civil rights struggle. In many cities the police are accused of brutality as a result of the actions they take toward civil rights demonstrators (many but not all of whom have in fact broken the law) or in the course of subduing riots in Negro sections of Los Angeles, Rochester, and New York or while apprehending or searching suspects who are members of minority groups. A few years ago Boston police packed a large hall to hear a cardinal defend them against charges that they had been corrupted by bookies. In 1965 a large number of New York City police picketed city hall to protest plans for creating a civilian review board to hear charges against police officers of misconduct, especially mistreatment of Negroes.

There is as yet no evidence that both phenomena—dishonesty and

[1] Support for this research was received from the Center for Programs in Government Administration (formerly at the University of Chicago) and the Joint Center for Urban Studies of M.I.T. and Harvard. Statistical analysis was aided by National Science Foundation grant GP-2723 to the Harvard Computing Center. Valuable comments on earlier drafts were received from Edward C. Banfield, Martha Derthick, Herman Goldstein, Seymour Martin Lipset, and Jerome Skolnick. I wish especially to thank Superintendent Orlando W. Wilson and his associates in the Chicago Police Department for giving me the opportunity to conduct this study. I, of course, take sole responsibility for the data and their interpretation.

harrassment—are but two expressions of the same underlying problem, yet a plausible theory to this effect can be devised, and until more is known about the "police problem" in America, it is worth considering. In an earlier article, I set forth such a theory to account for various aspects (particularly corruption and criminality) of the police problem in large American cities:

> To the individual officer, the police problem is largely a morale problem. Stated more exactly, the problem for him is to find some consistent and satisfactory basis for his self-conception. . . . The problem of morale, or self-respect, is created by at least two aspects of the policeman's role. First, the policeman is frequently in an adversary relation with his public. . . . The policeman in the *routine* case is often (though not always) dealing with his clientele as an antagonist: he issues summonses, makes arrests, conducts inquiries, searches homes, stops cars, testifies in court, and keeps a jail.
>
> Second, powerful demands are made on the policeman to serve incompatible ends. This happens both because his public cannot make up its mind what it wants and because it wants certain ends to be only symbolically served (e.g., "the community shall not tolerate gambling") while other, contradictory ends are actually served ("citizens should be allowed to place bets with honest bookies").[2]

In some ways, of course, certain causes of the police problem are being mitigated by fundamental social changes. The entry of the lower classes, particularly the immigrant lower classes, into the large "respectable" American middle class has lessened the demand for—or the tolerance of—the exchange of petty favors and the provision of commercialized vice in municipal politics. This may reduce to some degree the incompatibility of ends which the policemen is expected to serve. But in other respects the policeman's morale problem may be getting worse. The recent acceleration in the tempo and scale of the civil rights movement is one reason; the announcement by higher courts of their intention to enforce certain restrictions on police investigation and the uses of police evidence is another.

The policeman's sense of alienation from society results in the development of a distinctive "subculture" or "code" among police officers by which they can live, thus providing a basis for self-respect independent to some degree of civilian attitudes. Whether that subculture

[2] James Q. Wilson, "The Police and Their Problems: A Theory," *Public Policy*, Vol. XII (1963), pp. 189–216.

or code is based on a commitment to highly professional, austere, and impersonal standards of police conduct or is based on a celebration of the highly personal and particularistic fraternity of police life (with a tolerant attitude toward misconduct by officers provided that policemen "stand together" against outsiders) depends on many factors. One is the quality of police leadership; equally important is the extent to which one police code or another is supported by the political and civic ethos of the community. Maintaining a highly professional police force is probably impossible in a city that does not have a political and civic leadership that attaches a high value to honesty, efficiency, impartiality, and the impesonal application of general rules. By the same token, communities which prefer a politics of personal friendship, of favor-giving and favor-receiving, are likely to have police departments which reflect this ethos.

In our large cities where the population is economically and racially heterogeneous and where different political styles contend, the morale problem is likely to be especially critical; here also the political arrangements are likely to make a commitment to either thorough-going professionalism or police fraternalism both more difficult (competing pressures on the force will make either choice hard) and more necessary (the morale problem will be severe enough to make the development of *some* code important).

Obviously, there will be many cities (particularly smaller ones) and many occasions within all cities in which the police officer senses little or no hostility and detects few important inconsistencies in goals. Furthermore, in many routine matters the policeman is likely to be a peace officer rather than a law officer; that is, he is likely to provide assistance rather than to make arrests or enforce laws.[3] And finally, many police administrators argue that a professionalized force will be a respected force, even in the most conflict-laden large city.

Thus, there are at least three aspects of the theory I have presented on which evidence is particularly desirable. First, to what extent do police officers perceive citizens as hostile? Second, to what extent does this perception affect their morale and their attitude toward various aspects of police work? Third, to what extent can highly professional police administration and wholesale reform within a department affect perceptions of citizen hostility and thus affect the morale problem?

A unique opportunity to gather facts on all three questions arose several years ago. When the Chicago police department was under-

[3] Michael Banton, *The Policeman and the Community* (London, Tavistock Institute, 1964), p. 7.

going intense public criticism and beginning on a course of root-and-branch reorganization and upgrading under new leadership, I was able to distribute a self-administered questionnaire to all the sergeants (over 800) then serving in the department.[4] Four years later, after the reorganization was virtually complete and the force was judged by various professional associations as highly competent, I was able to readminister essentially the same questionnaire to the sergeants then serving.[5] In addition, I was given an opportunity to observe the workings of the force and to interview informally many key members. The focus of the questionnaire was on police-citizen relations and on police evaluations of their own department.

In 1960, as the new superintendent, O. W. Wilson, assumed his duties, it required no survey to know that police morale was very poor, that many officers of all ranks were dissatisfied with the way the department was run, and that the force sensed, rightly, that many citizens held them in contempt. From my own observations and interviews which preceded the administration of the questionnaire, as well as from newspaper accounts, there is little doubt that the superintendent took charge of a demoralized and suspicious organization. The officers were under almost daily attack by newspapers and civic leaders; the politicians whose meddling in the force had once been taken for granted could not now be counted upon to defend the force from these attacks; and superintendent Wilson was himself an "outsider" in every sense of the word—he had never been on the force; he was from out of state; he had been a "beat" cop for only four years and that was almost forty years ago; he brought with him an eager group of young "experts" who took over the top staff positions; and he was obviously allied with those civic forces most critical of the department. The scandals and mismanagement which had lead to the arrival of the reform superintendent were conceded by many officers to be indicative of a need for change, but the change that they got was more than they had bargained for, and it made them deeply apprehensive.

Given his commitment to change, almost every action Superinten-

[4] The self-administered questionnaire was distributed and collected during 1960 to 1961 at a two-week training school which all sergeants, lieutenants, and captains were obliged to attend. Virtually all the sergeants (a total of 818) completed the questionnaire. The number of lieutenants and captains (121 in all) who also completed it was not a sufficiently large proportion of all officers of those ranks to warrant including their responses in this analysis.

[5] About one-fourth the sergeants in 1964 to 1965 recalled having completed the questionnaire four years earlier; another fourth could not recall; half were sure they had not.

dent Wilson took was bound to increase rather than allay these anxieties. Many of these sergeants (to say nothing of the lieutenants and captains) had been on the force for thirty years or more. During this time they had come to know in detail how it was operated and what a man must do to hold his job, to earn a promotion or better duty assignment, to avoid trouble, and to become eligible for a pension. Some of this knowledge of procedure was incorporated into the formal rules of the organization, but most of it came from the decades-old informal understandings and conventions which governed almost every aspect of life on the force. The new superintendent, being an outsider and committed to reform, was quite obviously not bound by these norms. His power was great—not only did he have, as do all commissioners, great formal authority, but he also had the backing of the powerful Mayor Richard J. Daley. The superintendent used this power vigorously and by so doing created great uncertainty and thus deep anxiety and anger. The rules that the officers knew and understood were all now in jeopardy; no one knew what the new rules would be, what new changes were yet to come, or what effect these rules and changes would have on the career chances and pension rights of the officers.

Since the officers knew the system and the city and the new superintendent did not (at least at the outset), many members of the Chicago force quite understandably assumed that they knew much more about police work as well. Many found it impossible to believe that the new superintendent understood anything about catching criminals and preventing crime; accordingly, their anger at his anxiety-inducing organizational changes was expressed in terms of a disdain for his competence at police work. Superintendent Wilson clearly had to prove himself.

Certain of the superintendent's reform strategies were seen as particularly threatening. The leadership of the Chicago department was by and large in the hands of a small clique of very senior captains, many of whom were well beyond the normal retirement age. The former commissioner had had little effective control over these men. Such control as he did have was further reduced by the political organization of the department. Each rank had its own organization (for example, the Chicago Patrolmen's Association) dedicated to defending the interests of its members. Leaders of these groups were often police politicians who spent more of their time on association matters than on police duties. These groups were often allied with elements of the city's political parties; the department, after all, contained several thousand voters who through their family connections or because of their intimate knowledge of and influence in the affairs of many neighborhoods could wield electoral power all out of proportion to their numbers. The system tended to be static, for promotions and the entry of new faces into critical supervisory and command posts were rare. (For example, no promotion list for sergeant had been established for thirteen years preceding the arrival of the new superintendent.) The new leadership of the department quickly understood the importance of this internal political structure and took steps to destroy it and replace it with a structure loyal to, or at least willing to accommodate, the reform superintendent. Examinations were held for promotion to all posts. Great care was exercised in picking as command personnel (the top seventy officers in the department) men who appeared to be honest and reform-minded. Senior officers were "encouraged" to retire. Within a year 260 men were transferred to new assignments; within four years over 870 new sergeants were appointed from among the patrolmen. Some of the younger and abler of these new sergeants were very shortly appointed lieutenants. By 1964 there were 226 new lieutenants and 94 new captains. After years of stagnation promotions came suddenly for many and with dizzying speed for a select few. Soon a majority of the men in each senior rank owed their promotion to the new superintendent. The effect of this was not only to alter completely the status system within the department but also to change radically the composition of the various protective associations. Thus, in the informal as well as formal aspects of departmental affairs, change and uncertainty were rampant.

All these changes must surely have affected how the sergeants responded to the questions which sought to assess their perception of "citizen hostility." Many of the officers who expressed some pariah-like attitudes may well have been projecting on the citizenry as a whole the hostility they found in the statements and actions of the new superintendent and his allies in the newspapers, the civic associations, and city hall. A plausible hypothesis—indeed, a theory of reform—might take this into account. Uncertainty, anxiety, and hostility—both real and perceived—are the inevitable consequences of rapid and drastic change. Once the changes are completed and those unable or unwilling to accept them weeded out, the theory goes, the benefits of the new order will be such as to strengthen morale and to bring the officer and the citizen into a proper and sympathetic relationship. A thoroughly professional police department—one that is honest, competent, impartial, and ably led—will command the respect and cooperation of citizens and will thus produce in the members of such a department pride and a confidence that they have the support and understanding of the citizens whom they are required to protect.

This theory gains strength from the fact that even as the new superintendent began his work, a majority of the sergeants felt that the department in the preceding five years had been run "poorly" or "not so well." These men did not see themselves as defending a well-run department against an outsider; on the contrary, they were willing to admit its deficiencies. Since they at least agreed with Superintendent Wilson that the department then was not well run, might they not also agree later on—after the reforms had been instituted—that the department had been improved, and might not this sense of improvement affect their perception of what the citizenry thought of them?

There is another hypothesis, however. This asserts that in a large, racially heterogeneous city such as Chicago the police officer senses citizen hostility for reasons having little to do with how well his department is managed. Perceptions of the quality of the department and of citizen hostility are to some significant degree independent of one another; thus, a great change in the former may produce little change in the latter. If this is true—if in certain cities police officers feel themselves alienated from the public and if highly professional police administration cannot eliminate such feelings of alienation—then the problem of public safety in such cities is more complicated and less amenable to solution than we may suspect.

This chapter offers evidence in evaluation of these competing hypotheses. It first shows the changes that occurred over a five-year period in the sergeants' evaluation of the department, in police perception of citizen respect (or hostility), and in police morale. Next we show to what extent morale was linked to both evaluation of departmental quality and perception of citizen respect. The first survey covered all sergeants serving in 1960; the second covered a sample (approximately one-half) of the sergeants serving in 1965.[6] In both

[6] The questionnaire was administered in 1964 and 1965 to 554 of the 1,046 sergeants then serving on the force, or 53 per cent of the total. As before, these men were attending an in-service training program run by instructors from outside the department. The questionnaires were filled out midway through the week-long course. The sergeants who responded were those who attended during the last half of the program. Commanding officers assigned sergeants to the courses on a more or less random basis, approximately 35 attending each week over about a year's time. Several tests of the data—for example, a comparison of the answers of the first 250 against the last 250 sergeants—revealed no error attributable to sampling bias. Somewhat fewer sergeants completed the questionnaire from the traffic division than from the patrol and detective divisions, but tabulating responses against duty assignment revealed no differences arising from this factor.

surveys the same questions were asked in the same setting: midway through a required one-week in-service training course run by instructors from outside the department.

CHANGES IN ATTITUDES, 1960 TO 1965

After four to five years of reform, there was a substantial improvement in how well the sergeants thought the department was run (Table 1) but little or no improvement in their morale (Table 2) or in their perceptions of citizen respect (Table 3).

In 1960 over half the officers felt the department was poorly run; less than a tenth thought it was run very well. By 1965 those believing it was poorly run fell to less than a fifth; those thinking it very well run rose to almost a fourth. There was, in addition, general agreement that discipline had improved. (Most thought it too lax in 1960; by 1965 two-thirds thought it about right.) And the speed with which promotions had been made in the reform period was not lost on the sergeants: over 93% thought they were too slow before, less than a third thought that five years later.

Of interest to the observer—and perhaps of distress to the police administrator—is the fact that after five years of change, the men were persuaded that the department was better run but not persuaded that it was more fairly run. A substantial majority, then and now, refused to believe that duty assignments were passed out fairly. In particular, politicians are still seen as influencing those assignments, though there has been some decline in the percentage of sergeants thinking that politicians had a lot of influence. In this the men may be mistaken; it seems quite clear that the superintendent was reasonably successful in reducing the interference of the party officials in the department. (In this he had the absolutely essential support of Daley, who was both the Democratic party leader as well as the mayor.) Perhaps to the policeman, "politician" means anyone, in or out of uniform, who makes decisions other than as fairness and the needs of the department require. Members of any organization are disposed to find ulterior or self-serving motives behind the decisions of superiors; the policeman, given the very great power of his superior over him, has this disposition perhaps to an exceptional degree.

In 1960 a majority of the sergeants said they liked their work very much (Table 2) and that their department was better than that of most other big cities (Table 1). The overwhelming majority (84%) said they were very interested in their own assignments. Such findings seem at first glance to be inconsistent with the officers' belief in 1960

Table 1 *Sergeants' Evaluation of How Well the Police Department Is Run, 1960 and 1965 (Per Cent)*

	1960 (N = 818)	1965 (N = 554)
1. In general, how well do you think the police department has been run in the past five years?		
Very well	9.3	24.0
Pretty well	31.5	53.0
Not so well or poorly	54.2	19.4
Undecided	4.9	3.5
2. What do you think of the discipline in the police department during the last five years?		
Not strict enough	58.8	14.7
About right	27.9	65.9
Too strict	7.0	18.2
No answer	6.4	1.3
3. Most duty assignments are passed out fairly in the department		
Agree	31.9	38.5
Disagree	66.0	60.3
No answer	2.1	1.3
4. Promotions in the department are too slow		
Agree	93.6	32.9
Disagree	4.9	66.6
No answer	1.5	0.4
5. If a man wanted a better duty assignment in the police department, politicians have		
A lot of influence	53.7	33.9
Some influence	32.9	53.2
Very little influence	10.6	10.5
No answer	2.8	2.4
6. How do you rate this police department as compared with police departments in other big cities?		
This is the best	19.9	[a]
This is better than most	40.0	
This is about the same as most	26.9	
This is worse than most	3.6	
Don't know or no answer	9.4	
7. Police work is pretty much the same no matter who is at the top of the department		
Agree	53.1	59.9
Disagree	45.2	39.4
No answer	1.7	0.7

[a] Not asked in 1965.

Table 2 *Sergeants' Morale in 1960 and 1965 (Per Cent)*

	1960 (N = 818)	1965 (N = 554)
On the whole, do you think the police department is giving you a chance to show what you can do?		
Very good chance	24.6	20.9
Fairly good chance	43.0	54.8
Not much chance	28.7	22.3
Undecided or no answer	3.6	2.0
How well do you like your present job?		
Like it very much	58.2	61.7
Like it fairly well	33.9	32.3
Indifferent or dislike it	7.6	5.8
No answer	0.4	0.2
Being a policeman tends to make you cynical		
Agree	66.5	69.5
Disagree	31.7	29.4
No answer	1.8	1.1
If you were starting all over again, would you still join the police department?		
Yes	50.1	40.5
No	28.4	35.9
Don't know or no answer	21.3	22.0
How good is morale in the police department today?		
Very good	5.4	6.7
Fairly good	45.4	57.4
Low	48.0	35.8
No answer	1.2	0.2
How has the morale of the department changed in the last four or five years?		
Has improved	[a]	38.8
Stayed about the same		30.3
Gotten worse		30.1
No answer		0.7

[a] Not asked in 1960.

that the department was poorly run. In fact, they are probably not inconsistent at all but reflect the difference between judgments about the *police role* and judgments about *police organization*. Interviews and observations, together with these data, suggest that men become police officers in large part because they like the work. (The security of the job is the other major reason.) Cruising in a patrol car, con-

Table 3 *Sergeant's Perception of Citizen Hostility in 1960 and 1965 (Per Cent)*

	1960 (N = 818)	1965 (N = 554)
Do you think the police department has the respect of most citizens of this city?		
Yes, of most	33.7	45.9
Of some but not most	52.2	48.6
Of very few	13.5	5.1
No answer	0.6	0.4
Do any of your civilian friends ever criticize the police department to your face?		
Many do	39.6	24.1
A few do	49.4	62.8
Hardly anyone does	10.6	12.9
No answer	0.4	0.2
Civilians generally cooperate with police officers in their work		
Agree	43.3	37.4
Disagree	55.5	62.3
No answer	1.2	0 2
Most civilians think you are a policeman because you were not good enough to get a better job		
Agree	32.8	28.9
Disagree	64.1	69.3
No answer	3.2	1.6
Most people obey laws simply from fear of being caught		
Agree	38.6	46.1
Disagree	59.4	53.7
No answer	2.0	0.2
It is important that a policeman be liked by the citizens with whom he comes in contact		
Agree	79.0	59.0
Disagree	19.8	39.9
No answer	1.3	1.1

ducting an investigation, running a station house—these activities have some intrinsic satisfactions. They are manly, they often take an unexpected turn, and they can be done with some degree of independence and freedom from close supervision. All officers naturally complain about "dull routine," "paper work," and regulations, but I have met few officers who thought that the routine, paper work, and regulations of a safe, clean desk job in a large office was any more bearable. On the contrary, many have volunteered that unless the pay were a lot better, they could not stand to be tied to a desk shuffling papers all day; they wanted to get outside and be on their own. These day-to-day aspects of police life, and thus the degree of individual job satisfaction, do not change radically with changes in police administration. As Table 1 shows, a majority of the sergeants agreed that "police work is pretty much the same, no matter who is on top," and this view remained unchanged by five years of reform. On the other hand, administration can affect—profoundly—chances for promotion, the level and fairness of discipline, the availability of equipment, and the standards of training.

Since the nature of the job in its day-to-day routine changes relatively little, morale as measured by satisfaction with the job does not change significantly. As Table 2 shows, there was little difference between 1960 and 1965 in reports about how well the men liked their job and whether they felt it gave them a chance to show what they could do; the responses were generally favorable at both times. Morale as expressed in judgments about the tendency of police work to make one cynical, the morale of the force as a whole, and one's willingness to join the force today if one were starting over again also did not change much. It was low in 1960 and it remained low in 1965. Two-thirds agreed both times that police work made them cynical. Barely half were willing to join again in 1960; by 1965, the number had fallen slightly to 40%. Half thought that morale was low in 1960; that proportion had only fallen to a third by 1965, and the proportion believing that morale was very good had scarcely increased at all. Indeed, the force was evenly divided on whether morale had improved or not over the four years: a third felt it had, a third felt it had gotten worse, and a third thought it was still the same.

The meaning which these men attach to the word "morale" may be sufficiently vague, and the subjective scale on which they measure it may have sufficiently changed, so as to call into doubt what such responses, then and now, actually signify. Even if we discount these findings to allow for such factors, it is nonetheless striking that after four to five years of sweeping changes—including substantial pay raises, rapid promotions, and new equipment and buildings—so few men felt that morale was good or even that it had improved very much.

This suggests that morale is to some extent dependent on factors over which the police administrators have relatively little control.

One of these, obviously, is the extent to which the men find the citizenry lacking in respect or feeling hostile to the police. Table 3 indicates that the sergeants acquired during this time slightly more positive feelings about citizens, but only slightly. The greatest change was the decline (fifteen percentage points) in the proportion of men reporting they had friends who criticized the department to their face. This probably reflects the cessation in Chicago of the countless popular jokes and stories about policemen robbing stores and shaking down motorists. The anticop jokes of five years earlier ("the police don't drive squad cars, they drive pick-up trucks"; "the cops patrolling the highways are the last defenders of free enterprise"; "kids don't play cops and robbers, they play cops and cops") had by and large disappeared (to be replaced, needless to say, by jokes about "gung ho" cops). This must have made life a little easier for the average policeman.

There was also some improvement in the proportion of officers who felt that most citizens respected the department, but in 1965 it was still less than half of all the respondents. Moreover, there was a slight but significant increase in the proportion of sergeants who felt that civilians would not cooperate with the police and a sharp increase in the proportion who believed that only a fear of being caught deterred most people from breaking the law.

If, in the eyes of the sergeants, the department had clearly become better run but the citizenry had not responded with greater respect and cooperation, then to the extent that the police value citizen respect, their morale must suffer—either that, or the police must themselves change by attaching less importance to citizen attitudes. In fact, both things happened; morale did not improve commensurate with the magnitude of the departmental improvements, and the sergeants professed themselves less dependent on citizen attitudes. The proportion agreeing that it is important for an officer to be liked by those civilians with whom he comes in contact fell dramatically from 79% in 1960 to 59% in 1965 (Table 3).

SOURCES OF THE MORALE PROBLEM

In 1960 the principal sources of discontent with the way the department was run were the young, recently promoted sergeants. Of the sergeants who had joined the force within the previous ten years, nearly three-fourths (73.0%) felt the department was poorly run; of those who had joined before 1936, only about one-third (35.8%) were as critical. Similarly, 61.9% of the men who had just become sergeants at the time of the first survey thought the department poorly run; only 36.8% of those who had held the rank for ten years or more had similar views.

It is, of course, not surprising that younger men, until recently excluded from power in the department, felt that the men who wielded that power were not doing a good job. And it would not be surprising to learn that after this younger group had been in power for a few years, their opinion of the way things were run—which is to say, their opinion in large part of themselves—would show a marked improvement. This is indeed the case. By 1965 not only had the overall evaluation of departmental management improved substantially, but age, date of entry, and date of rank (all of which tend naturally to be covariant) no longer significantly affected this evaluation.

If discontent about the way things were done in the department was largely confined to the younger sergeants, the various measures of perceived citizen respect and of morale were not. Reports of low morale and of a sense of citizen hostility were equally common among sergeants of every generation. Of course the low morale of different generations may have had different causes. The newly minted younger sergeants may have been dismayed to discover that upon acquiring their new supervisory rank, the affairs they were to supervise were generally a mess as a result of the rapid changes and the conflict then raging between the old guard captains and lieutenants on the one hand and the new superintendent and his aides on the other. The older sergeants may have been depressed because they saw their power in the force slipping away. Whatever the reasons, differences in generation as such made no difference in morale in 1960; this was still true in 1965.

Nor did any of the other obvious personal characteristics—education, religion, or ethnicity—make any difference in 1960 or 1965 in either morale or judgments about how well the department was run.[7] One factor did affect perceptions of citizen hostility in 1960: the more education the sergeant had the less likely he was to agree that most citizens respected the police department. By 1965, however, education had ceased to be a significant influence on his perception.

It is also interesting to note that feelings of citizen hostility were not mitigated by being a member of a " cop family." In 1960 over

[7] Age and ethnicity do affect other aspects of police life, including, apparently, the reasons why one joins. See James Q. Wilson, "Generational and Ethnic Differences Among Career Police Officers," *American Journal of Sociology*, Vol. LXIX (March 1964), pp. 522–8.

half the sergeants had one or more relatives who were or had been policemen also. Over one-fifth had fathers who were officers. In 1965 these proportions were still about the same. But having police relatives made no difference in perceptions of citizen hostility or, for that matter, in any of the other attitudes of which we have been speaking.

In sum, the morale problem was and is a generalized phenomenon to be encountered among sergeants of all ages, duty assignments, levels of education, religious preferences, and ethnic affiliations. It is a problem that exists because of some aspect of the police experience rather than as an expression of some obvious personal attribute.

Morale may be affected by how well the men think the department is run or by the respect which they believe the citizenry has for them or by both. Tables 4 and 5 indicate the extent to which various measures of morale—liking one's job, satisfaction with one's opportunities, a willingness to rejoin the force, and one's estimate of departmental morale—are affected by attitudes toward the department and the citizen.

In 1960 perceptions of citizen respect were far more important than evaluation of departmental management in determining officer morale (Table 4). The differences between sergeants who agreed that the department was either well run or poorly run but who disagreed as to whether citizens respected the department were greater than the differences between those who disagreed as to how well the department was managed. For example, there was no appreciable difference in the willingness to once again join the police department between those who thought the department well run and those who thought it poorly run; in each case, about half the men were still willing to become a police officer. But within these two groups, about two-thirds of those who believed that most citizens respected the department were willing to rejoin; less than half of those who found citizens hostile were willing to do so.

Those aspects of morale most affected by perceptions of citizen hostility in 1960 were the willingness to rejoin the force and estimates of departmental morale—an estimate which presumably, though not certainly, was as much a statement about one's own morale as it was a statement about the morale of one's colleagues. The judgment of experienced police officers about the desirability of a police career was more affected by what people think of policemen than it was about how well the department was run. Those aspects of morale somewhat less affected by citizen hostility were job satisfaction and opportunities directly related to police organization rather than to police status. Since such factors can be altered by departmental

Table 4 *Morale of Police Sergeants as Influenced by Their Perception of Departmental Management and Citizen Respect, 1960 (Per Cent)*

	PD Run Very Well or Pretty Well		PD Run Not So Well or Very Poorly	
	Citizens Respectful	Citizens Hostile	Citizens Respectful	Citizens Hostile
On the whole, do you think the police department is giving you a chance to show what you can do?				
Very good chance	38.1	28.1	31.0	17.1
Fairly good chance	50.4	48.1	39.7	41.5
Not much chance	11.5	23.8	29.3	41.5
N:	(139)	(185)	(116)	(316)
How well do you like your present job?				
Like it very much	73.0	63.0	67.2	46.9
Like it fairly well	23.4	27.0	29.4	44.4
Indifferent, or dislike it	3.5	10.0	3.4	8.7
N:	(141)	(189)	(119)	(322)
If you were starting all over again, would you still join the police department?				
Yes	63.8	46.0	68.1	42.1
No	17.0	33.3	18.5	34.1
Do not know	19.1	20.6	13.4	23.8
N:	(141)	(189)	(119)	(323)
How good is morale in the police department today?				
Very good	10.6	4.3	9.2	2.8
Fairly good	55.3	33.9	63.9	42.4
Low	34.0	61.8	26.9	54.8
N:	(141)	(186)	(119)	(321)

policies, as in fact they were, it is not surprising that management more than citizen attitudes affects, in the eyes of the officers, this component of morale.

After five years of reform, estimates of the Chicago department's management had improved, meaning, in effect, that a large number of sergeants had moved from columns three and four in Table 5 into columns one and two, either because their own attitudes had

Table 5 *Morale of Police Sergeants as Influenced by Their Perception of Departmental Management and Citizen Respect, 1965 (Per Cent)*

	PD Run Very Well or Pretty Well		PD Run Not So Well or Very Poorly	
	Citizens Respectful	Citizens Hostile	Citizens Respectful	Citizens Hostile
On the whole, do you think the police department is giving you a chance to show what you can do?				
Very good chance	31.9	19.0	0	3.6
Fairly good chance	56.2	62.1	61.9	41.7
Not much chance	11.9	19.0	38.1	54.8
N:	(226)	(195)	(21)	(84)
How well do you like your present job?				
Like it very much	72.4	63.8	40.9	37.2
Like it fairly well	24.6	32.1	45.5	50.0
Indifferent, or dislike it	3.1	4.1	13.6	12.8
N:	(228)	(196)	(22)	(86)
If you were starting all over again, would you still join the police department?				
Yes	57.5	34.9	22.7	21.2
No	23.0	40.6	50.0	57.6
Do not know	19.5	24.5	27.3	21.2
N:	(226)	(192)	(23)	(85)
How good is morale in the police department today?				
Very good	11.8	3.6	0	1.2
Fairly good	78.9	58.4	18.2	18.6
Low	9.2	38.1	81.8	80.2
N:	(228)	(197)	(22)	(86)
How has the morale of the police department changed in the last four or five years?				
Has improved	66.5	30.8	4.5	1.2
Stayed about the same	25.1	40.0	21.8	24.4
Gotten worse	8.4	29.2	63.6	74.4
N:	(227)	(195)	(22)	(86)

Table 6 *Attitudes toward Outside Groups as Influenced by Perception of Departmental Management and Citizen Respect, 1965 (Per Cent)*

	PD Run Very Well or Pretty Well		PD Run Not So Well or Very Poorly	
	Citizens Respectful	Citizens Hostile	Citizens Respectful	Citizens Hostile
Civilians generally cooperate with police officers in their work				
Agree	48.9	31.5	36.4	24.4
Disagree	51.1	68.5	63.6	75.6
N:	(227)	(197)	(22)	(86)
Most people obey the law only from fear of being caught				
Agree	36.6	53.8	31.8	57.0
Disagree	63.4	46.2	68.2	43.0
N:	(227)	(197)	(22)	(86)
It is discouraging to be a policeman because the courts let off so many people with little or no punishment				
Agree	57.7	78.8	68.2	73.8
Disagree	42.3	21.2	31.8	26.2
N:	(227)	(193)	(22)	(84)
Newspapers are too critical of the force				
Agree	55.8	76.9	54.5	70.9
Disagree	44.2	23.1	45.5	29.1
N:	(226)	(195)	(22)	(86)
Politicians' influence on assignments within the force				
Much	22.6	37.8	28.6	56.5
Some	59.7	56.0	57.1	40.0
Not at all	17.6	6.2	14.3	3.5
N:	(221)	(193)	(21)	(85)

changed or because new men with a different evaluation of the leadership had been promoted to sergeants. Table 5 shows that about 80% of all the respondents could be categorized as having a favorable opinion of the management in 1965 as opposed to approximately 42% in the earlier period. Morale continues to be profoundly affected by perceived citizen respect—less so with regard to immediate job satisfaction and personal opportunities, more so with regard to a willingness to join the police force and to think departmental morale high, but significantly in all cases. Interestingly, however, citizen respect now affects the morale only of those officers who think *well* of the department; the morale of those who still think it badly run is not affected by their perception of citizen attitudes. This small minority is bitter on all scores.

In short, nearly half the sergeants who think well of the department and over a third of all sergeants on the force experience what is probably a serious perceptual conflict: they think the department is well run but believe that the citizens either are unaware of this, fail to give the department credit for it, or for some other reason hold the force in contempt. To live with such conflict requires either a strong conviction as to the rightness of what one is doing, a willingness to attach a low value to popular opinion, or both. As we have already seen, the importance that the officers attached to citizen attitudes did decline markedly over the five-year period. It should be noted that the value these sergeants attach to being liked does not depend on whether in fact they think they are liked; those who believe the citizens are respectful assign no higher value to this respect than do those who believe them hostile.

The evidence which the officers adduce in explanation of their belief about citizen attitudes is about what one might expect: those who find citizens lacking in respect are significantly more likely to believe that citizens obey the law only out of fear of being caught, that the courts let off too many people with little or no punishment, that politicians have a great deal of influence on assignments in the force, that civilians do not cooperate with the police, and that the newspapers are too critical of the force (Table 6).

For all the items reported in Table 6, there is no significant difference in response that can be attributed to evaluation of departmental management; all the differences which are significant are introduced by distinguishing between officers who feel that civilians respect them and officers who do not.

IMPLICATIONS OF THE MORALE PROBLEM

The impact of judicial opinions or citizens' attitudes on the effectiveness of law enforcement is widely discussed. Since so little is known in a systematic way about the process of law enforcement in our large cities, discussion of the impact of, say, court-imposed exclusionary rules on crime prevention and arrests has been in part a heated but uniformed debate. Because senior police officers believe that court attitudes and public opinion are incompatible with effective law enforcement does not make it so; on the other hand, if they act on this belief, the effect may be much the same. Perhaps too much attention has been focused on the legal consequences of court opinions and of political pressures to respect civil liberties; the more important consequence—one harder both to detect and to remedy—may be the effect of such opinions and pressures on the morale of the police.

There is, of course, no necessary trade-off between morale and civil liberties. There is no reason yet to accept the discouraging inference that a highly motivated police force can only exist at the expense of community control and effective legal guarantees of individual rights. Other ways can surely be found to deal with the morale problem without sacrificing civil liberties or civilian control over police conduct. But this study at the very least should suggest that devising such solutions is likely to be difficult, for police morale is not simply a function of technically competent police management. Other studies have shown that morale and job satisfaction are affected as much by the status of the occupation as by its internal arrangements[8]; this study confirms those findings. It underlines again the importance of Chester Barnard's observaton that one of the essential aspects of executive responsibility is inspiring morale in an organization, but it also calls attention to the difficulties which arise when morale is dependent not only on what the organization does but also on what opinion the clients of the organization have of it.[9] In changing an organization in which morale is externally as well as internally influenced, the executive must find some way either of obtaining control over those external factors (for example, by educating public opinion or mobilizing community support) or of producing some internal substitute for unobtainable respect.

One internal substitute is to create in the force a complete subculture which is independent of the larger community and in which the officer can find ample esteem, self-respect, and a belief in the value of his work. One might therefore expect that a police department with a particularly keen morale problem would encourage the off-hours socializing of its officers, thereby protecting them from civilian hostility and fomenting a sense of solidarity. In fact, there

[8] Cf. Michel Crozier, *The Bureaucratic Phenomenon* (Chicago, University of Chicago Press, 1964), pp. 28–30.

[9] Chester I. Barnard, *The Functions of the Executive* (Cambridge, Mass., Harvard University Press, 1938), p. 279.

was no change between 1960 and 1965 in the extent to which the sergeants interacted with one another rather than with civilians. At both times fewer than 10% reported that they visited the homes of other officers "very often," though over half said they did "occasionally." About one-fourth at both periods indicated that they spend off-duty time with other officers as often as once or twice a week. Over half when asked to list their three closest friends did not include a police officer. Nor was there any relationship between morale or perceptions of citizen attitudes and the degree of interaction with other officers: those who had a high morale or who found citizens respectful spend about as much time with other officers as those who had the opposite attitudes.

Another internal substitute is the deliberate inculcation of morale by various institutional devices, such as vigorous in-service training programs, the dissemination of information, the distribution of newsletters and brochures explaining the improvements in the force and the reasons why such improvements are a legitimate source of pride for all members, and the careful enforcement of internal regulations in a way that demonstrates that the leadership stands behind the men without fear or favoritism. The Chicago department has tried to do all of these things and more, and that the men feel discipline and promotions to be fairer and their job somewhat more satisfying may be due in great part to the success of these measures.

An important constraint on the success of these programs has probably been the increased size, activity, and militancy of the Negro community in Chicago. While the police department was being reorganized and upgraded, various Negro groups—which previously had been comparatively quiescent—began to increase the tempo and vigor of agitation on civil rights issues, particularly the issue of *de facto* school segregation. Many protest marches were held and picketing increased. At the same time, the Negro population of Chicago continued to grow (Negroes now account for more than one-fourth the total population), increasing the incidence of real or potential racial tension in various neighborhoods and the number of Negroes who come into contact with the police as suspects. (In 1963 Negroes accounted in Chicago for about three-fourths of all persons arrested for murder, forcible rape, and robbery; for about two-thirds of all those arrested for aggravated assault; and for well over half of those arrested for manslaughter, burglary, and theft.) It was not possible to devise questions for this survey which would give a valid measure of the relationship between perceived citizen respect (and thus morale) and the race problem in the city; personal interviews leave little doubt, however, that there are strong feelings on this score. Although the police force has received commendations from various groups—including the city's human relations commission—for the way it has handled various racial problems, it is not by any means clear that the officers would vote a similar commendation to the people of the city. White police officers in the North, after all, are drawn from that segment of society (working-class Catholics) least likely to favor rapid social change on behalf of Negroes. This resistance is intensified by the fact that police officers are personally involved in racial conflict in a way few others are. Not only do they arrest Negro suspects but they also must handle civil rights demonstrations, protect Negroes who move into white neighborhoods (in which white police officers or their friends may have homes), deal with charges of "police brutality," confront demands that the police department rapidly integrate, and accept the fact that rapid promotions for all have meant in some cases the rapid promotion of Negroes to supervisory and command positions. In even a professionally led department the fraternal aspects of police life loom very large: assignment to squad rooms and patrol cars is not simply an administrative matter but a decision that profoundly affects the character of those close personal relations on the basis of which police work is conducted.

Police officers do not see the citizenry as a homogeneous group with a single attitude toward the police; on the contrary, they carefully distinguish between law-abiding and criminal groups, between "decent citizens" and "bums." In the past such a distinction may well have been identical to the distinction between citizens who had respect for the police and those who did not. Today it is not so clear that both distinctions are the same to the police. The civil rights movement has brought noncriminal elements into conflict with the police; the courts, by various rulings on criminal evidence and police procedure, seem to be restricting police authority and thereby allying themselves (in the eyes of the police) more with the criminal elements and the "bums" than with the decent citizens; and the decent citizens themselves, because of the widespread use (and misuse) of the automobile, are coming increasingly into conflict with the police. The fact that the police can no longer take for granted that noncriminal citizens are also nonhostile citizens may be the most important problem which even the technically proficient department must face.

This problem may be especially acute in Chicago because although the police department has changed significantly, the other elements of the system of justice—the courts and prosecutors—have not. As Herman Goldstein has pointed out, the police are engaged in a battle between the "good guys" and the "bad guys" in which success is measured by the number of "good pinches" that result in the apprehension, conviction, and sentencing of criminals. Procedural safeguards and judical behavior are often regarded by the police as troublesome "technicalities" which constrain and sometimes frustrate winning victories in this battle. But when, as in Chicago, the courts are still heavily influenced by the political parties, are deeply involved in bargaining over charges and sentences, and are staffed (in some cases) by persons of low professional competence, police irritation at the failure of society to support the police function is magnified. Police morale may therefore suffer not only because citizen attitudes are thought to be hostile but in addition because the other elements in the system by which society deals with crime are defective.

Whether police *morale* affects police *behavior* is, of course, a question on which this study can shed little light. It is quite possible that officers with low *esprit* may nonetheless function reasonably well in the police role. Studies of the American combat soldier during the Second World War indicate that the attitudes of infantrymen about how well the Army was run and whether or not it gave them a chance to show what they could do were not significantly and consistently related to the men's combat performance.[10] Policemen are not, of course, soldiers. They rarely face combat and thus are rarely exposed to an experience so powerful that it might well make general attitudes toward the organization irrelevant, at least as constraints on behavior. Police morale may, one might conjecture, be a greater influence on police behavior in matters of *routine* police contact with citizens; which make up such a large part of police work and which may, precisely because of their routine nature, be governed to a greater extent by the attitudes of the officer.

The way a professional police department copes with the morale problem in a city like Chicago is in part to reduce, intentionally or unintentionally, the extent to which police value public opinion as manifested in face-to-face contacts. This is a result both of what professional doctrine requires (substituting patrol cars for officers walking beats, increasing the size of police districts, rotating men among assignments, and discouraging police involvement in political affairs) and of what the ethos of professionalism assumes (that the impersonal rules of law enforcement are correct and appropriate re-

[10] Samuel A. Stouffer, et al., *The American Soldier* (Princeton, N.J., Princeton University Press, 1949), Vol. II, pp. 37–41.

gardless of what a hostile or indifferent citizenry may think). The substantial decline in the proportion of officers who believe that it is important that they be liked by civilians and the significant increase in the proportion who believe that only fear of being caught keeps people from breaking the law suggest that this process of withdrawal has begun.

The way a member of an old-style or fraternal police force dealt with this problem was to maintain respect for himself through informal means in his day-to-day contacts with civilians, good and bad. The techniques employed ranged from occasional violence to a deep involvement in neighborhood affairs, from having a variety of personal relations with criminal elements to participation in political activities. A professional force, in principle at least, devalues citizen opinion *as manifested in personal relations;* professionalism, in this sense, means *impersonalization.* Relations with the community are no longer handled by the officers' informal contacts—some legitimate, some illegitimate—with neighborhoods and individuals but are given over to a specialized and bureaucratic agency within the police organization. The officers are instructed to do their duty impersonally and with minimum involvement, especially with suspects; community relations are bureaucratized in the form of offices created to handle public affairs and publicity, human relations, and citizen complaints. Such organizations deal primarily with other organized elements of the community: civic and voluntary associations, other government agencies, businessmen's groups, newspapers, and the like. In one sense, as measured by money and effort devoted to community relations and by the awareness among police leaders of the importance of organized community support, a professional force appears to value public opinion very highly. But in another sense, as reflected in the attitudes and behavior of rank-and-file officers, public opinion is valued less than before, and the nature of police-public relations shifts from the informal and the personal to the formal and the impersonal.

Because the nature of the police job on the street does not change radically in a professionalized police department, the officer can only go so far in maintaining an aloof or impersonal attitude toward the public. In the large American city the police officer must feel he has a reasonable chance to either win or compel the respect of the citizens with whom he comes in contact. This is particularly necessary when, as in the United States, assaults on police officers are common, and thus police-civilian contacts always have a potential for vio-

[11] Federal Bureau of Investigation, *Uniform Crime Reports* (1962), p. 111.

lence. (In 1962 there were over 17,000 reported assaults on policemen or one for every ten officers. The rate was, of course, highest in the largest cities. Seventy-eight officers were killed.)[11] Michael Banton has clearly explained why, in America, the normal symbols of authority, the badge and uniform, are insufficient to control the behavior of both police and suspect and why, therefore, an officer's confidence in those symbols is not a sufficient support for his morale. Professional behavior—that is, uniform, rule-defined behavior—toward civilians becomes very difficult in even a highly professional force:

> The establishment of uniform and predictable modes of action is not a matter for the police alone. They cannot respond in a standard fashion unless they know their behaviour will be correctly interpreted by subjects. The officer in the United States is less predictable than his British colleague partly because, in a heterogeneous population, common understandings are less inclusive. The American officer cannot rely upon the authority of his uniform, but in dealing with subjects must establish a personal authority by proving what a good guy he is, or what a dangerous one.[12]

The American police officer finds himself today on the grinding edge between the need to maintain his authority on the street and the increased community pressures against that authority.[13] A police force may improve greatly because of professionalization, but if at the same time the popular image and authority of the police officer have deteriorated, the two changes may cancel each other out, producing no net gain in police morale and creating a continuing police problem. In order to maintain morale the officer may have to rely increasingly on police doctrine, a perhaps exaggerated conception of the rightness of what he is doing, and a contempt for both the criminal and hypocritical noncriminal elements of the population. Under such pressures it is not surprising that many police officers have shown themselves amenable to extremist political positions. (No

[12] Banton, *op. cit.*, p. 168.

[13] J. Edgar Hoover succeeded in turning a badly organized and ineffectual Federal Bureau of Investigation into a highly skilled, elite group with, apparently, very high morale. The rigorous application of professional law enforcement doctrine succeeded in this case in part because the FBI is not generally exposed to the sources of citizen hostility: it does not enforce those laws which bring the police into an adversary relationship with its public. In particular, it has stayed out of such conflict-laden fields as gambling, organized crime, and (until very recently) civil rights.

one knows how many officers are members or sympathizers with the John Birch Society, but few knowledgeable people think the number is negligible.) For all this, the community must bear some responsibility. New ways, and not simply the exchange of publicity releases, must be found to bring police officers and neighborhood groups together for nonbureacratic and meaningful communication. The task of sustaining police morale cannot be left to the police themselves; it requires a community effort. The alternative may be a police force which, however competent, functions as an army of occupation.

Uncertainties in Police Work: The Relevance of Police Recruits' Backgrounds and Training

John H. McNamara

UNCERTAINTIES REGARDING LEGALITY OF POLICE ACTIONS

Along with the heterogeneous normative structures associated with urbanization and industrialization there has been a marked proliferation of substantive laws. These laws have developed, in great part, solely as an attempt to create limits, per se, to action and interaction. It is often assumed that in this manner the ultimate values of a society will be protected since, it is further assumed, a body of substantive laws acts as a deterrent to evil doing or as a crystallization of consensus concerning appropriate forms of conduct. Furthermore, many feel it to be sufficient to rule against a given form of behavior in order to do away with the behavior. The clamor that follows upon a particularly unsavory and socially visible act for new laws or for the broadening of laws and the increase in severity of sanctions associated with the laws frequently abates shortly after the passage of such laws. The feasibility or effectiveness of these laws in reducing the behavior in question often seems to be a secondary or irrelevant issue. Thus this process can be seen as an attempt to induce a sense of certainty regarding what is possible in the way of conduct.

With this proliferation of substantive laws there has also been an accompanying growth in procedural laws aimed at supporting the values potentially threatened by the enforcement of substantive laws. Particularly of interest are those concerning civil liberties and rights of the citizen, such as the "search and seizure" laws. Within the American common law tradition these laws have frequently developed in such a way that many conflicts or tensions can be found both within and between procedural and substantive laws. Different segments of the community and the nation have had their interests codified, and competing legal ideologies have become institutionalized with a marked consequence for police: an uncertainty on their part with respect to the legal basis for their authority and their actions. It is difficult not to find frequent expression of this uncertainty in the mass media. What has been characterized above as uncertainty is more likely to be described by law enforcement officials as incomprehensible, unpredictable, and inconsistent restrictions placed on police by legislatures and courts that are seen at best as lacking in understanding and at worst as financially, politically, or ideologically corrupt.

Coupled with this large source of uncertainty for law enforcement organizations in general is the diverse nature of tasks that have become the responsibility of metropolitan police departments. Although the mass media, for the most part, stress enforcement of the criminal law by police, by far the major part of police work lies elsewhere. Police have assumed large administrative functions of licensing and inspecting and the very large task of traffic control. Moreover, in metropolitan areas police are called upon to fulfill a "service function" for members of the lower socio-economic strata. Police perform the functions of family counselors, obstetricians, agents of socialization for potential delinquents, and myriad roles associated in other socio-economic strata with the family or with more specialized agencies of social control.[1] This mixture of enforcement and service functions creates conflicts and uncertainties that are only partly resolved by attempts to segregate the two functions. This conflict is probably experienced by almost all members of the force at one time or another. It is likely, however, to be most keenly felt by police assigned to lower-income areas where both criminal law enforcement and service functions are maximized.

A further problem for police working in lower income areas, another area of uncertainty, has developed in recent years. As courts have de-emphasized property rights in favor of the rights of persons, the degree to which members of the lower income groups are considered criminally responsible in courts for their actions has become blurred for police. This uncertainty is most marked in the case of present police handling of the Negro segments of the population. Negroes

[1] See E. Cumming *et al.*, "Policeman as Philosopher, Guide and Friend," *Social Problems*, Vol. 12, No. 2 (1965), pp. 276–86 for a description of these functions in one department. See also A. E. Siegel and R. C. Barker, *Police Human Relations Training*, Applied Psychological Services (Wayne, Pa., 1960) for a similar analysis of the Philadelphia police.

have probably always been subject to a "double standard" treatment both by police and courts. In the past they have been quickly apprehended and given severe sentences for crimes against whites, often with little or no concern for the rights of the accused. On the other hand, there was notably less concern when the victim of a crime committed by a Negro was also a Negro. Although this double standard undoubtedly still exists to some extent in northern as well as southern cities, it seems to be less marked than before. For example, police have more frequently found that simply because a Negro walks on the streets of an exclusively white neighborhood it is not legal, "reasonable grounds" for assuming he has committed a crime, much less that a crime has been committed.

Similarly, police have shown more concern in recent years with preventing crimes of Negro against Negro and with apprehending persons suspected of such crimes. This concern has resulted from an increased number of Negroes on police forces, from the realization on the part of white police officers that it is possible for some persons to be both Negro and "respectable," and from the pressures stemming from the courts and civil rights organizations. According to police, however, these latter pressures have not been consistent. For example, police in New York City report that the local N.A.A.C.P. first asked that more Negro police be assigned to the Harlem area and then later asked that more white officers be assigned to the area and that a large number of Negro officers be transferred to other areas.

At present there seems to be little agreement among police about the proper police concern with crimes committed by Negroes. This lack of consensus is further aggravated by the militancy of contemporary Negroes, with the result that the individual police officer is often uncertain about what his course of action against crime should be, and this uncertainty in turn produces a hesitancy or indecisiveness that is highly inappropriate to much of police work. We might also hypothesize that at the other extreme the affective consequences of such uncertainty for the police officer would increase the likelihood of hostile action against Negroes as the perceived source of ambivalence.

In addition to uncertainty regarding lower income groups in general and Negroes in particular, police face a similar problem of assessing the degree of criminal responsibility or accountability of youths suspected of delinquencies or crimes. As criminal law has evolved, a less voluntaristic view of juvenile offenses has emerged, often in an inconsistent or complex manner. Attempts to establish the limits of criminal responsibility of juveniles have produced, for example, a number of varying ages for different offenses at which a juvenile can be legally held to have committed a crime rather than a delinquent act. Consequently, the extent of police authority or discretion has been reduced, particularly in regard to the "lawful use of force." Legislation aimed at clarifying police authority in the handling of juveniles is put forward, but much of this legislation seems to add a further element of uncertainty for police. We could assume this uncertainty underlies the inappropriate reactions of police withdrawal from the situation of juvenile misbehavior or of the use of an unnecessary degree of force in correcting the situation or in taking a juvenile into custody. To complicate matters further, many juveniles are aware of their relatively sensitive position *vis-à-vis* police and by their actions cause individual police officers to feel they are being "abused" by the juveniles. In this respect, Piliavin and Briar have described how "verbal abuse" and other extra-legal characteristics of juveniles become criteria for the determination of guilt by a police officer in handling juveniles.[2]

UNCERTAINTIES REGARDING POLICE PRESTIGE

A further source of uncertainty is that police feel their occupation has suffered a loss in prestige since the Second World War. Police in New York City talk nostalgically about the indefinite past when police were "looked up to and respected." Some older police point to the educational level of entering officers immediately prior to the war as contrasted with the present-day educational level. During the depression the department was able to recruit from a population which included many unemployed or low-paid college graduates as well as graduates with professional or advanced degrees. As general economic conditions have improved, however, the job of police officer has become less attractive to college graduates. In New York City in 1963 a police officer entering the force could expect a salary of $8000 per year automatically after three years, a six-week paid vacation each year, unlimited sick leave, and a retirement at one-half of his salary drawn at the time of retirement. For the incoming recruit with little specialized training or experience and with little more formal academic training than high school the work offered attractive economic benefits. Nevertheless, the department reports a marked difficulty in recruiting a sufficient number of new officers.

[2] I. Piliavin and S. Briar, "Police Encounters with Juveniles," *American Journal of Sociology*, Vol. 70 (1964), pp. 206–14.

At the same time that police inveigh against the loss of respect for their position, the general public on a national scale has favorably changed its view of the "general standing" of the occupation of policeman. Hodge *et al.*[3] in their recent replication of the North-Hatt-NORC study of occupational prestige, report that the rank of policeman changed from that of fifty-fifth in 1947 to forty-seventh in 1963 in the ranking of the ninety listed occupations. This improvement in rank is exceeded only by the improvement in rank of the occupation of nuclear physicist, the latter improvement being largely a function of an increased awareness of the meaning of the occupational title.

Regional variations in the amount of prestige assigned to police work might partly account for the discrepancy between New York police officers' feelings that their occupation has been gradually downgraded and the above findings regarding occupational prestige. It appears, for example, that police work in the western regions of the country is assigned more prestige than in the eastern regions.

This feeling of lowered prestige may further be understood as a product of an increased number of conflicting or uncooperative contacts between police and the increasing proportion of lower income groups that reside in the central districts of metropolitan areas. These contacts are ambiguous for police not only because of the implied loss of police authority but also because the lower income segments of metropolitan areas tend to report a more favorable opinion of the police in their communities than do the middle income segments.[4] This inconsistency between a favorable attitude toward police and the more dramatic (or more dramatized) resistance to police on the part of members of lower income groups, added to the maximized "service function" served by police in these areas, must provide another large source of ambiguity or uncertainty for police in the implementation of their duties. That police are not objective in their estimates of the degree to which lower income groups are criminal or law abiding has been demonstrated by Kephart in a survey of 915 police officers in the Philadelphia Police Department.[5] Seventy-five per cent of his respondents overestimated the percentage of arrests

[3] R. W. Hodge, P. M. Siegel, and P. H. Rossi, "Occupational Prestige in the United States, 1925–63," *American Journal of Sociology*, Vol. 70, No. 3 (1964), p. 291.

[4] See G. D. Gourley, *Public Relations and the Police* (Springfield, Ill., Charles C Thomas, 1953) for a survey of attitudes toward the Los Angeles Police Department and also see A. I. Siegel and R. C. Baker, *op. cit.*, for a similar survey of attitudes toward the Philadelphia police department.

[5] W. M. Kephart, "Negro Visibility," *American Sociological Review*, Vol. 19 (1954), p. 464.

involving Negroes made in the districts to which the officers were assigned. Only 11.2% of the officers correctly estimated or underestimated the percentage of Negro arrests.

UNCERTAINTIES REGARDING EFFECTIVE INTERPERSONAL TACTICS

Another source of uncertainty, and one that seems to be relatively ignored in discussions of police problems, stems from the lack of systematic and reliable knowledge concerning the appropriate interpersonal skills that can be used by police officers in face-to-face encounters with citizens. In the heterogeneous milieu of metropolitan areas, the range and number of values and norms incorporated into vaguely differentiated subcultures present police officers with a variety of offenses against a primarily middle-class legal structure conditioned by the offenders' memberships in these subcultures. Perhaps equally important from the standpoint of police work is that these subcultures also condition the manner in which their members will respond to variations in police handling of citizens. Thus, a police officer whose background is likely to be middle or lower-middle class in nature cannot rely on his common sense or his past experiences within the middle-class segments of the community when he attempts to gain voluntary compliance from those whose common sense is predicated on values and norms at variance with his own.

In a three-year study of the New York City Police Department the author, in reviewing "critical incidents" involving police and citizens, was initially struck by the extent to which the handling of relatively minor incidents such as traffic violations or disorderly disputes between husbands and wives seemed to create a more serious situation than existed prior to the police attempt to control the situation.[6,7] A family dispute might have been merely noisy prior to the entrance of a police officer; after his entrance, personal violence often became more likely to occur in all possible combinations and permutations of assaulter and assaultee. In this type of situation police often found it difficult to be an impartial and disinterested third party.

[6] The study was supported primarily by the Russell Sage Foundation and conducted in cooperation with the American Institute for Research and the New York City police department and personnel department. Some funds were also initially provided by the Rockefeller Brothers' Fund.

[7] For an initial statement concerning other aspects of these critical incidents and a description of the methodology, see L. R. Eilbert, J. H. McNamara, and V. L. Hanson, *Research on Selection and Training for Police Recruits: First Annual Report,* American Institute for Research (Pittsburgh, Pa., 1961).

Patrolmen were often assaulted by a wife armed with a frying pan when they used "necessary force in restraining" a husband who, moments before, had been roundly denouncing his wife and publicly calling into question her species membership. The consequences of inappropriate handling of citizens by police was well documented in the summer of 1964, during which a number of race riots occurred in northern cities. It is interesting to note that the majority of these riots seem to have been triggered by the handling of Negro women or children by white police officers. By their handling of persons in these more dependent roles, the police seem to be "altercasting" Negro males into the role of protector.[8]

Further analysis of additional critical incidents in the New York study led to a number of hypotheses concerning the most frequent difficulties encountered by police in face-to-face interaction with citizens. The major problems for police in gaining voluntary compliance revolved about the following: (1) the gathering of an adequate amount of relevant information about a situation and the citizens in it both prior to and during the interaction between the officer and the citizen(s); (2) the clarification of police expectations for the citizen; (3) the exploitation or utilization of the values of the citizen(s); (4) the officer's presentation of himself as decisive and impersonal.

Information Gathering

The problems concerning the appropriate kinds and amount of information were generally of two sorts. First, officers frequently failed to gather information prior to the beginning of their interaction with citizens. In the ordinary conduct of his police duties an officer is able to gather a good deal of information about a neighborhood, the general values of its inhabitants, the particular manner in which police are viewed, the identity of persons most likely to require his attention, and myriad other relevant facts. His sources are many: other officers, storekeepers, janitors, children, newspaper venders, and persons labeled as "police buffs," who apparently can be found in almost any neighborhood and in exchange for social approval from police officers will barter their store of neighborhood gossip and rumors. Of course, there also exists a large store of knowledge independent of any one officer's experience about how persons of varying statuses or roles are likely to view police requests for cooperation.

[8] See E. A. Weinstein, "Some Dimensions of Altercasting." Paper read at American Sociological Association Meetings, Washington, D.C., 1962.

For example, the knowledge that delinquent gang members are sensitive to any indication they are being treated or are seen as children seemed to be necessary in order for a police officer to act as a buffer between two rival gangs which are threatening warfare.

Another set of problems regarding information gathering prior to interaction with a citizen had to do with the information that was available from witnesses or complainants who had requested police assistance. In part because of time restrictions on the use of police radios, officers in police cars were frequently unable to get needed information at the time they were dispatched by the communications personnel. In addition, officers on foot patrol often felt such urgency to find an immediate solution to such problems as a dispute that they ignored or overlooked such potentially useful sources of information as the person reporting the existence and location of the dispute. This tendency was most marked for younger or less experienced officers and was clearly shown in role-playing exercises involving police recruits designed and conducted by the author after the completion of the recruits' formal recruit training.

The second general set of problems concerning information gathering had to do with the information that could be gathered *during* interaction with citizens. This set of problems, of course, is often identified as a consequence of a lack of empathic or role-taking skills. For the purpose of the research, the skills were conceptualized as those of "interpersonal testing." This conceptualization proved useful in designing and conducting the role-playing exercises aimed at improving police skills in gaining compliance.

It was hypothesized that police officers frequently failed to assess the motives and behavior of citizens with whom they were interacting because of the categories they used in classifying these citizens. Classification based on legal categories particularly reduced the likelihood of accurate interpersonal testing. Concern with establishing the appropriate legal category to which a citizen belonged often detracted from the process of estimating the citizen's response to the police officer's requests or commands simply because of the time taken to do so. Perhaps more important, however, is the putative nature of deviant labels. Lemert has pointed to the tendency to impute additional characteristics to persons identified as deviants other than the characteristics used as the basis for assigning the deviant role.[9] He has further hypothesized that law enforcement agencies relative to

[9] E. M. Lemert, *Social Pathology* (New York, McGraw-Hill Book Co., 1951), pp. 55–6.

other agencies of social control are particularly likely to maintain policies concerning the treatment of deviants ". . . conceived with no allowance whatever for individual variation."[10]

Data concerning the handling of citizens by the police do not justify the assumption that police are completely unable to allow conceptually for individual variation among persons labeled as wrongdoers, but the data do indicate that legal labels, independent of the actions of the citizen, often tend to govern the police officer's decision regarding the proper handling of a situation. One striking instance of the principle operating retroactively involved a patrolman directing traffic in the middle of an intersection who fired his revolver at and hit an automobile whose driver had not heeded the officer's hand signals. The driver immediately pulled over to the side of the street and stopped the car. The officer then realized the inappropriateness of his action and began to wonder what he might offer as an explanation to his supervisors and to the citizen. The patrolman reported that his anxiety was dissipated shortly upon finding that the driver of the car was a person convicted of a number of crimes. The reader should understand that departmental police did not specify that any person convicted of crimes in New York City thereby became a target for police pistol practice.

Perhaps more relevant is the tendency to formulate initially a plan of action based upon whether a citizen is labeled a criminal. In this respect the legal categories often had an effect similar to that of stereotypes. That is, criminals were selectively perceived by officers in terms of (1) the legal prescriptions and proscriptions regarding appropriate police authority and procedures relative to the type and degree of the crime, and (2) the actions past and future that were considered to be associated with the type and degree of crime. This labeling, in turn, provided a base for a "self-fulfilling prophecy" in situations where the labels and their imputed or associated characteristics were communicated to citizens who responded with indignation and often physically assaulted the officers.

The legal categories also interfered with the process of predicting a citizen's response to a police officer simply because of the salience for police officers of the legal categories when applied to citizens. That is, officers acted as though their understanding of the citizens with whom they were interacting were complete once they found the appropriate legal and/or departmental designation for the citizens. Some problems for police officers in such seemingly simple tasks as

[10] *Ibid.*, p. 69.

serving traffic tickets can be seen as the result of an officer's inability to see beyond the label of "speeder." For example, a few incidents were reported in which a Negro woman was able to make life difficult for a white officer by claiming to bystanders that the officer had made remarks of a sexual nature while issuing a traffic ticket to her. Some of these reactions to officers could be traced to the woman's feeling that she had received a ticket primarily because she was a Negro and not because she had violated any traffic laws. If the officer had this information prior to attempting to issue a ticket, he would have been in a much better position to avoid the public claim of interracial lechery. (Of course, this tactic on the part of women attempting to avoid a ticket often worked effectively for women, regardless of their ethnicity.)

Clarification of Expectations

The second general area of problems in face-to-face attempts to gain compliance by officers had to do with the manner in which they succeeded or failed at making clear to citizens what they expected. The problems, for the most part, involved either a misunderstanding on the part of citizens or their view of the officers' expectations as inappropriate or undesirable. The problem of simple misunderstanding is, of course, most obvious in the case of persons who understand little English. In New York the growing Puerto Rican population, which has, for the most part, formed into ghettos, presents the single largest language problem for police. Officers are issued small pamphlets which contain phrases such as "What is your name?" translated into a phonetic version of Spanish, for example, "KAY ESS-TAH FAH-MILL-EEYAH?" Few officers used these aids. Rather, they fared better if they asked another Spanish-speaking person to act as translator. But in order to avail themselves of another Puerto Rican in this manner, the officers had to assume at least that not all Puerto Ricans are engaged in a concerted effort to undermine law and order and that some could speak English. In some officers' view the first assumption was not justified.

One role-playing exercise required police recruits to handle two Puerto Ricans played by other recruits. One role, that of an alleged thief, contained the instructions to speak no English, only what Spanish phrases or words that could be mustered. The other role was that of a friend of the thief for which the instructions read that he could speak English but he was not to do so unless asked if he could or would by the recruit playing the role of the police officer. The majority of recruits playing the part of the police officer failed to ask for the assistance of the friend and instead increased the volume of their voices as they repeated the same phrases in English. The chagrin, upon finding that the suspect's friend could speak English, was almost expressed audibly. The extent to which this handling of the problem is customary for experienced police officers was not clear from the critical incident data.

Another difficulty concerning the misunderstanding of the officer's expectations is that the officer frequently does not have a clear notion of what his specific expectations should be in a given situation. Thus, officers were unable to communicate simple directions that moved the situation toward a solution. For police this is particularly problematic, since the persons with whom they are dealing are likely to be under some psychological stress. In this respect, the mere presence of a patrolman creates stress for many people. Hence, expectations that were vague or general were not likely to be met by a citizen who is in a relatively poor condition to do any original problem solving because of the "narrowing of perception" that characterizes excessive stress. Officers frequently encountered difficulty in gaining compliance, therefore, because their requests or directives were vague or too general to be comprehended by citizens with whom they were interacting.

The other general problem in clarifying expectations concerns the undesirability of the officer's expectations as they are presented to the citizen. The specific nature of the desirability or undesirability of the officer's expectations will be discussed in the next section, but there was one interpersonal tactic which officers often overlooked. The tactic is that of presenting expectations in the form of at least two specific alternatives. At times, officers presented ultimata which served to create further resistance to the officers' actions. Attempts by officers to reduce the threatening nature of their requests by pointing to more serious or damaging consequences that would follow, if their original requests were not honored often made the citizen feel that the situation was hopeless. This feeling of despair in turn gave rise to desperate attempts to escape from the situation, such as assaults on the officer. On the other hand, officers who managed to convince citizens that a few alternatives were available to them were also often successful in turning the attention of a potentially hostile citizen to the matter of choosing among the alternatives. This process of choosing among alternatives offered further advantages to the officer, since once a citizen had chosen an alternative acceptable to him and to the officer, the citizen became more likely to be committed to the alternative because he had made the choice.

Exploiting or Utilizing the Values of Citizens

Once a patrolman has accurately assessed the citizen's values operative in his interaction with the officer, the officer improves his chances of properly handling the citizen. Knowing what the citizen both negatively and positively values greatly reduces the possible range of decisions that the officer must consider with regard to his gaining the compliance of the citizen. Nevertheless, there still exists the problem of translating this knowledge into specific action that will produce compliance. The problem is how to act in such a way that a citizen feels that his values are enhanced or at least not threatened if he complies with an officer's request.

An interesting example of success in utilizing the values of a citizen occurred in one incident in which a patrolman was faced with a sixteen-year-old boy who was threatening his family and the officer with an axe. The officer knew the boy had been committed to a state mental hospital and dreaded returning to the hospital. The officer was able to avoid the use of force and got the boy to hand over the axe quietly by announcing the following: "You damned punk. You aren't going to get off easy. You're not going to a hospital, you're going to jail." The boy's resistance, primarily perhaps to the label of "psycho," was overcome through use of a label less pejorative to the boy.

The problems of resistance to an officer stemming from his failure to take into consideration the values of a citizen can be seen in those instances where male motorists assault patrolmen engaged in the process of "warning and admonishing" or issuing a traffic ticket to them. An examination of these incidents revealed that these motorists were frequently accompanied by their families. The officers in these situations failed to consider that their handling of the motorist tended to threaten his position of authority in the family and thus gave rise to hostile attempts to reestablish his position in the family or to reduce the amount of threat. Had an officer recognized he was unnecessarily threatening the man's perceived valued position as an authority figure (however fictional in fact) before his family, he might have resolved the problem by interacting with the citizen out of hearing of the family.

A broad range of types of incidents could be conceptualized as involving the utilization or exploitation of values. The possible types of relevant values that a New York City patrolman might encounter seem infinite, and the variations in utilizing these values are many. Perhaps critical for the police officer in this regard was first, his recognition of the citizen's values as legitimately meaningful even if they were not so for the patrolman personally, and second, some degree of awareness on the officer's part of the manner in which the citizen ranked his values. The task then remained for the officer to devise an approach consistent with this knowledge. Many obstacles to utilizing this knowledge were identified as stemming from both legal and departmental sources. The task of balancing off the immediate requirements of the situation and the legal and departmental requirements seemed often to be insuperable.

Presentation of Self

The last set of problems for officers in face-to-face interaction with citizens involved their failure to communicate an impersonal or decisive demeanor to the citizens. The failure to appear impersonally concerned with a citizen was especially problematic in cases involving some punitive action: the threat of using force, the use of force to gain compliance, an arrest, or the issuance of a summons (a ticket). The officer's failure to appear impersonally interested in such cases increased the probability of a citizen's feeling he was not treated impartially before the law. Such a failure also often seemed to give rise to a competitive feeling on the part of the citizen, who saw the officer as simply another person with no more authority than the citizen. In general, the department did not approve of the actions of those officers who came to share this competitiveness and complied with a citizen's suggestion that the officer ". . . take off his badge and gun and fight like a man."

Generally less serious were the incidents in which officers explained or justified their actions as being required by their immediate supervisors. Such officers apparently were perceived by the citizen involved as taking the actions they did purely because the officers were personally afraid of negative sanctions from their supervisors. Nevertheless some citizens were presumably more interested in their own personal welfare and thus responded negatively to the officers' requests for compliance. Citizens' awareness of, or belief in the existence of, "quotas" regarding the number of tickets to be issued in a given place or time period often seemed to underly a particularly hostile reaction to an officer who justified issuing a traffic ticket by indicating that he was being pressured by his supervisors. In this regard, the enforcement of traffic laws is greatly complicated interpersonally because of its probabilistic nature. The citizen who receives a ticket has generally seen many more serious violations of traffic law by others who were not stopped. They are much more likely to feel that the officer's action in serving a ticket is arbitrary and based on some other criterion than the traffic violation itself. Anything an officer says to such a citizen is far more likely to be seen as reflecting some personal interest or need of the officer.[11]

The department was aware of this problem of officers becoming or seeming to become overly personal in their approach to citizens and frequently admonished officers to "be firm, but courteous." Being courteous to someone who has just indicated that the officer is both illegitimate and doomed by a deity to perdition seemed somewhat inappropriate to officers, who frequently interpret such abuse as reflecting a criminal orientation on the part of the citizen. Being courteous was to many officers the equivalent of being deferential—and deference to criminals was unconscionable. Thus, they resolved the seeming contradiction between being firm and being courteous by favoring firmness over courtesy. A more appropriate resolution of this contradiction would be to conceptualize the task for the officer as one of being impersonally firm. The advantage to the officer in so doing is that he can appear to be simply a mechanism in the impartial administration of justice.

Similarly if an officer is decisive in his actions or communications, a citizen is more likely to view him as part of an efficient apparatus for the enforcement of laws or for meeting the "public service" function of police departments. The appearance of decisiveness serves one need common to many situations encountered by police, that of structuring a relatively unstructured situation. The advantages of a decisive manner are particularly apparent in the handling of "psychos" and their families. For police officers it seems that many, if not most, of the problematic aspects of dealing with the mentally disordered stem from the families of these persons. When police enter into a home in order to cope with such a problem, they encounter a great deal of disturbed behavior on the part of all concerned. The advantages of appearing decisive are clear in incidents where officers indicate to the family that this sort of problem is an everyday matter for them and that they will use the "usual approach," which, incidentally, requires that the family leave the area where the officers are dealing with the patient.

It is equally important for an officer to appear to be decisive in

[11] For a discussion of the relevance of impersonality for control, see the discussion of impersonal mechanisms of control by managers in P. M. Blau and W. R. Scott, *Formal Organizations* (San Francisco, Calif., Chandler Publishing Co., 1962).

threatening the use of force. In this respect many officers were apparently unaware of the nonverbal communication that occurred between themselves and citizens. In the role-playing exercises for police recruits, the manner in which a patrolman held his nightstick (a club 22 inches long) or moved it about while talking to the citizen became obviously important as a factor in determining the extent and kind of compliance given to the recruits in the role of police officer. Those who waved the nightstick about, hit it against the palm of one hand, or gesticulated with it were less likely to gain the compliance given to recruits who held the stick firmly in the combat position (diagonally, in front of the chest). Because some recruits had learned to designate this position as one of combat, they felt it appeared too threatening to citizens. In contrast, the observers of the exercises felt that the position not only communicated a willingness and competence to use the stick but also seemed less threatening than other positions from which an officer could readily use it.

Similarly, recruit officers in the role-playing exercises who shouted out their requests far louder than necessary for clarity communicated a lack of decisiveness in that a raised voice implies some expectation that requests will not be honored. It also implies a degree of excitement inappropriate to an officer's presentation of himself as competent and decisively engaged in routine police action. Hence, recruits who so shouted were less likely to obtain the compliance they sought. These findings lend strong support to the prescription of Theodore Roosevelt regarding a soft voice and a big stick.

ORGANIZATIONAL SOURCES OF UNCERTAINTY

The final set of uncertainties for police officers to be discussed in this paper is departmental policies and practices. The discussion is based on the research conducted on the New York City Police Department. The extent to which this particular department is representative of the population of metropolitan police departments is not clear. There are regional variations regarding the existence and significance of these organizational factors. There are also a great many variations within the New York Police Department itself, but the description below characterizes at least a majority of the units and patrolmen within the patrol force. The significance of this set of uncertainties appears to be at least equal to that of any of the other sources. The main thesis is that the department, for the most part, has the characteristics of a "punishment-centered bureaucracy" as delineated by Gouldner.[12] Many of the correlates of such a type of organization that were suggested in Gouldner's study also exist in the New York City department. The specific areas to be discussed are (1) the commitment of the administration of the department to a semimilitary organizational model with a relatively well-defined formal hierarchy of authority based on position in the bureaucratic structure, (2) the regulations of the department as these are incorporated into *Rules and Procedures*, the departmental handbook, and (3) the careers of the members of the department.

The Semimilitary Model[13]

Most police departments have structured themselves after the military under the assumption that in order to cope with the problems of controlling crime and maintaining order, a closely coordinated and disciplined body of personnel with clear-cut lines of authority is necessary. The police assume that their ability to respond to crises depends on the speed with which a variable number of police officers can be assigned to a given task and the speed with which orders are communicated to the assigned group of officers. It is further assumed that departments must also maintain a constant state of readiness for the eventualities an unruly citizenry will present to them. Among the main strategies employed in the patrol force of the New York City Police Department to maintain the capacity to cope with the city's crises, both major and minor, are the use of negative sanctions in the cases of patrolmen found guilty of violating the expectations of their supervisors and the attempt to create an appearance of "close supervision" exerted by the immediate unit (the precinct) to which the patrolman is assigned as well as by supervisors from division, borough, and headquarters offices.

The use of negative sanctions as motivators apparently has strong historical roots in the department. Officially, a patrolman may be charged with a wide range of violations of departmental rules; he may further be tried in a hearing conducted by superior officers of the department, and if found guilty, he may be subject to having his pay fined, his vacation time reduced, or to being demoted or dropped from the department. That the patrolmen feel this to be

[12] A. W. Gouldner, *Patterns of Industrial Bureaucracy* (Glencoe, Ill., The Free Press, 1954), pp. 207–14.

[13] For another critique of the semimilitary model in police work see R. A. Myren, "A Crisis in Police Management," *Journal of Criminal Law, Criminology and Police Science,* Vol. 50 (1960), pp. 600–4.

somewhat harsh is clear from a quarter-page advertisement placed in a major New York paper by the Patrolman's Benevolent Association in which the punishment imposed on a "moonlighting" patrolman was described as a form of "involuntary servitude." Unofficially, an officer is also subject to sanctions that are equally meaningful or painful, for example, being transferred from mechanized patrol in an automobile to foot patrol within a given precinct, being transferred from one area to another within a precinct or to a different precinct seen as less desirable, not being given a day off or the vacation period desired, being transferred from a detail (an assignment that differs from the usual patrol assignment) to patrol precincts, or not being recommended for a departmental award for an act of heroism or bravery.

In general, the use of negative sanctions and the threat or fear of their use pervades the day-to-day operation of the department. Perhaps of more importance is the strong consensus among patrolmen in particular but also among supervisors and detectives that punishment is the dominant mode of response to an officer's failure to meet the expectations of his supervisors or of the administration of the department. There is a strong moralistic quality in the relationships between supervisors and subordinates in which nonconformity is seen as stemming not from inability to conform nor from errors of judgment but from willful disobedience or negligence. In this regard, the organization has taken over with a vengeance the legal assumption of individual responsibility or accountability. Although the courts have generally been moving toward a more deterministic view of deviance, the department has retained a somewhat strict voluntaristic view of officers' violations or organizational norms. There is some evidence that the extent to which disciplinary problems are handled by official departmental hearings at headquarters is even increasing in recent years. A survey of departmental records concerning disciplinary actions during an eleven-year period from 1950 to 1960 revealed that when the charges are expressed as a rate per 1000 officers on the force as of the first of January in the indicated year, proportionately more charges were preferred against officers in the later half of the period than in the earlier half. The number of officers on the force in January in the years during the above time period varied from 18,500 to 24,000.

There are two points of interest in Table 1 regarding the variations in the number of charges preferred relative to the number of officers and the variations in the disposition of cases. First, the number of charges per 1000 personnel seems to be related to the appointment

Table 1 *Disciplinary Actions in the New York City Police Department from 1950 to 1960*

Year	Total Number of Charges Preferred	Number of Charges Per 1000 Personnel	Percentage of Charges Filed or Dismissed	Number of Fines[a] and Vacation Time Lost
1950	628	33.9	7.3	423
1951	491	25.8	18.4	258
1952	569	30.8	9.8	337
1953	558	29.7	10.1	392
1954	742	37.4	14.2	419
1955	1025	49.4	12.8	680
1956	975	43.4	15.9	412/242
1957	949	41.0	17.4	238/430
1958	973	40.4	11.0	151/596
1959	974	39.5	14.6	106/574
1960	962	40.4	15.8	172/443

[a] The fines up until 1955 involved only salary. From 1956 to 1960 the fines are presented as ratio of salary fines to vacation time fines.

of new police commissioners. During the above period four new commissioners were appointed, and the rate of charges increased with each new appointment.[14] The last commissioner appointed during the period was appointed in August 1955 and served through to the end of the period. We note an upsurge in the rate of charges preferred in 1955 and a subsequent leveling off and stabilizing of the rate. Nevertheless, over the eleven-year period the rate of charges increased.

This increase, it will be noted, is somewhat ameliorated by the reduced severity of sentences and by the tendency of the police department to dismiss or file (not prosecute) charges. The ratio of salary fines to vacation fines has reversed itself from the first year (1956) in which the option appeared. One possible interpretation of the two seemingly conflicting trends is that fewer field commanders are handling marginal disciplinary problems in their commands but are referring these to headquarters for disposition. This interpretation is consistent with the feeling expressed by a number of field commanders that authority is increasingly being located in police central headquarters. This bureaucratization of the disciplinary process is

[14] See W. S. Sayre and H. Kaufman, *Governing New York City*, Russell Sage Foundation (New York, 1960), p. 286 for a listing of commissioners.

further evidence for the assumption that the department is similar to the punishment-oriented bureaucracy studied by Gouldner.

In addition to the above disciplinary system, the department in 1955 instituted a unit for the processing of civilian complaints: the Civilian Complaint Review Board. In general, members of the force felt that this unit allows almost any citizen to lodge a complaint against an officer and that the processing of complaints is extremely biased against patrolmen in particular. A report on the first five years of this unit's existence does not support the feelings of the members of the force. During the first year 196 officers had complaints lodged against them alleging either an "abuse of authority" or the "unnecessary use of force." In that same year only 13 officers were convicted of the charges stemming from these complaints. Similarly, in 1959 there were 106 complaints recorded as officially lodged and only in seven cases were the officers charged by the department with abuse of authority or unnecessary use of force. At the end of the year only two officers had been found guilty of the charges. In general, the total number of complaints received, the percentage of these leading to the formal preferring of charges, and the percentage of officers found guilty were gradually reduced over the five-year period.

In view of these data, the fact that many, if not most, officers felt very strongly that they were at the mercy of the public because of the manner in which these complaints were processed by the department implied the existence of strong affective components regarding the use of sanctions by the administration of the department. In view of the discrepancy between the actual processing of these complaints and the feelings of patrolmen regarding this processing, a great deal of anxiety underlies the thinking of officers concerning the matter of negative sanctions.

The second component of the semimilitary model of maintaining a state of readiness for the crises of the city is the attempt to create an appearance of close supervision. Much of this apparently takes a ritualistic form such as the "see" in which a patrolman exchanges salutes with a sergeant riding by in a car. Patrolmen on foot patrol must also "ring in" once an hour to the precinct station house through the call-box system. They must also ring in to report that they intend to relieve themselves or that they are beginning or ending a meal and where they are eating. When patrolmen ring in they may be directed to a location where police attention is needed, but for the most part, ringing in is a matter of form. Patrolmen regard ringing in as somewhat incompatible with the authority associated with the role of police officer, particularly the requirement that officers notify the precinct of their habits of elimination. Of course, many officers do not follow the regulations concerning the appropriate times at which they should ring in. For the most part their actions do not result in their being punished, but occasionally a patrolman will be charged with such a violation of regulations and will be required to appear at a hearing at headquarters. The fact that this rule is enforced irregularly causes patrolmen to feel that its enforcement constitutes the arbitrary use of supervisory power. In general, many of the rules have as a primary function the "punishment-legitimating" function described by Gouldner.[15] If there is a choice of rules to use as a basis for punishment, the more expedient one is chosen. The less expedient rules are those whose violation is likely to lead to a punishment which will hurt a patrolman's family as well as himself or whose violation reflected too much on the supervisor or the department as a whole.

Even though rules such as those concerning ringing the station house were widely violated, many patrolmen felt it likely that the rules would be enforced if it suited some supervisor, particularly if he was looking for a patrolman to serve as a scapegoat for his errors. They also felt that this action was common and thus experienced some anxiety about many of the rules they violated even when the rules struck them as irrelevant or dysfunctional for the purposes of law enforcement.

Another source of tension for patrolmen was the departmental practice of using as field supervisors captains who had recently passed the civil service examination and had been appointed to that rank. These captains were known as "shoo-flies" (a term not used affectionately) and patrolled the field commands from offices at the division, borough, and headquarters levels. Patrolmen believed the shoo-flies were required in a given time period to file a minimum number of complaints against patrolmen. The captains often patrolled in civilian clothing and were sometimes not known to the patrolmen of a given precinct. Because of this, some patrolmen felt that these supervisors were constantly keeping the patrolmen under surveillance and any moment would find some minor violation of rules upon which to base a complaint. The patrolmen further believed that under this system of using supervisors unfamiliar with the past record of any given patrolmen, the patrolmen who were most deserving of a complaint were not likely to receive them. There was some consensus that because of their visibility while carrying out their duties, the

[15] A Gouldner, *op. cit.*, p. 238.

officers who least deserved complaints were most likely to receive them.

Whether or not these feelings could be supported by fact, it is easy to see how the procedures of supervision and disciplinary action described above would probably lead to a marked degree of ambivalence and anxiety on the part of patrolmen. It is important to note that patrolmen generally handled the work requiring their attention alone or with the assistance of another patrolman. The point at which they might have most needed some assistance from the supervisors—that is, in crises or emergencies—was not the usual point at which they received the attention of supervisors. Patrolmen often had to handle difficult situations without the assistance of supervisors in the early and often the most critical phases. They also often entered into situations that were repugnant or threatening to them personally without benefit of immediate directions or incentives that might be supplied by a supervisor.

This evaluation of the supervisory system has pointed up the need for development of a feeling of discretionary power, for well-developed skills, and for a strong self-directedness on the part of patrolmen assigned to the field units. We can argue that the anxiety shared by many patrolmen about disciplinary action and the supervisors' attempt to maintain an appearance of close supervision are inappropriate for the development and maintenance of the needed autonomy on the part of the patrolman. The semimilitary model, while attempting to generate confidence in the ability of the department to cope with the uncertainties of the police task, generates another set of uncertainties that are strongly experienced by the members of the field units.

Rules and Procedures

Since the New York City Police Department began as a metropolitan force in 1898, the department has had ample opportunity to codify and recodify its rules many times over. At the time when the author began his research on the department, a 400-page, 8½ by 11 inch handbook was much in evidence. The handbook, entitled simply *Rules and Procedures,* was accompanied by a number of pages of amendments which grew prodigiously over the research period.

An examination of the handbook revealed a number of brief paragraphs in a Foreword printed over the signature of the commissioner in office in 1956. The significance of these paragraphs for this discussion of uncertainties stemming from organizational sources is apparent.

> *The Rules and Procedures are designed to guide members of the force* and department in carrying out the duties imposed upon them by law. *Any violation of these Rules and Procedures shall be made the subject of disciplinary charges against all members of the department responsible for such violation as may be directed by the Police Commissioner.*
>
> These Rules and Procedures do not purport to be exhaustive. Periodic orders and directives of the Police Commissioner and commanding officers provide a constant supplementary guide to meet changing conditions. In this respect, suggestions of members of the force are welcome.
>
> *Above all, the Rules and Procedures must be considered as a means to an end, not as an end in themselves.* [My emphasis throughout.]

The question arose as to which characterization of the *Rules and Procedures* took precedence in the shared perspective of the members of the force—the "means to an end" or "guide" characterization versus any violation of the rules as the "subject of disciplinary charges against all members of the department responsible" characterization. It was hypothesized to be the latter in view of the occupational survival value of this characterization. The hypothesis still is viable.

One other specific feature of the handbook bears mentioning: a prescription found on page 31: "General regulation" 2/35.0. It reads, "A member of the force shall report to his commanding officer any violation of the *Rules and Procedures* which he observes or of which he has knowledge" (known succinctly and informally as the "rat rule"). This rule, combined with the knowledge that any violation of any rule may be the basis of disciplinary charges (note the plural usage), would seem at face value to provide a sufficient condition for anxiety for any but the finest of "The Finest."

The *Rules and Procedures* have an added significance, since much of the supervision takes either the form of a review of an officer's past performance by a supervisor or the form of observation of officers engaged in the routine of patrol rather than of officers engaged in handling specific police problems. Although supervisors at a scene in which specific police problems are being handled by patrolmen may tacitly approve of, or even order, an action seemingly in violation of the rules, in retrospect, they are less likely to endorse officially such actions of patrolmen, particularly if the actions ultimately led to further problems or failed to solve the immediate problem faced by the patrolmen. Thus, supervisors function analogously to judges in that they attempt to match up patrolmen's actions with departmental rules rather than with the consequences anticipated by the patrolmen at the time of their performance. This legalistic orientation influences some supervisors to stress the violation of rules even when the rules themselves are likely, if followed, to lead to ineffective job performance. In this way the supervisors avoid a confrontation with the administration of the department. It should be noted that many supervisors felt they had insufficient authority to question overtly and formally the validity of the rules. Furthermore, many supervisors hesitated to interpret rules in any way other than that which was clearly acceptable to the administration.

The rules of the department, in summary, are many and detailed as well as extremely comprehensive, particularly the rules concerning violations of other rules. Although the rules do cover many contingencies and thus reduce large areas of uncertainty to routine procedures, they also thereby create other areas of uncertainty. It would seem that there is an optimal point beyond which the number of rules and their degree of specificity become dysfunctional for effective performance of police duties. This proposition is valid to the extent that police work does not consist of a standardized product or service but consists rather of the application of general principles to the specific problems of the citizens served by the department. In this sense, police work is akin to the work done by professionals.[16] Given that the individual problems presented to officers are unique and given the existence of a bureaucratic structure within which these problems must be solved by individual officers, then one should expect to find that officers face many of the problems generally faced by professionals who are employed by large organizations.[17] Added to this set of problems is the tendency of the department to consider ineffective performance as willful negligence rather than as a technical or judgmental problem. This organizational orientation is particularly inimical to the development and maintenance of individual autonomy, a characteristic of critical importance for police personnel assigned to the field commands.

The extent to which other metropolitan police departments are subject to the problems generated by an elaborate system of rules

[16] For a discussion of some of the police discretionary areas see J. Goldstein, "Police Discretion not to Invoke the Criminal Process: Low-visibility Decisions in the Administration of Justice," *The Yale Law Journal,* Vol. 69, No. 543 (1960).

[17] See P. M. Blau and W. R. Scott, *op. cit.*, pp. 60–74, for a discussion of the problems generated by the admixture of the professional and the bureaucracy.

and procedures is not clear. One might hypothesize, however, that police departments or law enforcement agencies in general are particularly prone to the development of systems of rules that are highly articulated in terms of legal criteria because of the legal implications of police functions, particularly those relating to criminal law.

Careers in Police Work

The third set of uncertainties stemming from organizational factors revolves around the organizational careers of police officers, particularly the promotion and job assignment policies as they are seen by patrolmen. At the beginning of his career in the department a patrolman has three general alternatives regarding his career over the minimal twenty years of duty before he can retire. He can elect to remain a patrolman and hope for assignments that he finds desirable, he can try to improve his status in the hierarchy of authority by passing civil service examinations up to and including the position of captain (after which his promotions are through appointment by the police commissioner), or he can try for appointment to the detective division. The appointment as a detective involves an immediate increase in pay and the possibility of increasing the pay grade eventually to a salary approximately equivalent to that of lieutenant.

In any discussion of career possibilities which one might overhear in the department, some mention will sooner or later be made of the material in the individual officer's personnel file maintained by the police department and the bearing of this material on the assignments, promotions, or appointments that an officer is seeking. Concern focuses on letters of complaint or formal complaints registered by either citizens or police supervisors. (Few letters in the file are flattering.) Officers allege that any complaints, whether or not they have been dismissed, "filed," or found to be false, are placed in their personnel files and are used by supervisors in deciding upon the candidacy of an officer for a new position. Most officers state that supervisors are likely to consider an officer guilty of the charges in the complaint, even though the officer was not officially so judged. Officers also feel even when they have been officially found guilty of minor or trivial charges, supervisors reviewing the records are likely to consider the officer to have been charged with a less serious violation than actually occurred. (The practice of reducing certain charges against officers is not unusual.)

When a file contains unfounded or minor complaints or charges against officers, it is not likely to be used to block a promotion based on passing a civil service test, since these promotions are rather well circumscribed by laws and by standard, codified procedures. However, in the case of an assignment to the detective division ("The Bureau") or in the case of an assignment to a detail (work not of a routine patrol nature) the materials in this file are considered critically damaging by most officers. Therefore, many officers feel that they have little control over their future careers in the department. They eventually come to believe that regardless of what they do in the way of effective police work they are not likely to be rewarded for the work but are foreordained to remain in assignments they find undesirable. This feeling of having one's goals in life blocked underlies much ineffective performance.[18]

One other feature of the promotional system deserves mention. Few would insist that the civil service system of examinations has been a worse evil than the systems of patronage and nepotism that existed prior to the development of a comprehensive civil service. At the same time, many of the features of this system are problematic. With regard to the manner in which the police department has been served by the New York City Personnel Department, Rinck wrote some years ago that although the personnel department has the authority to supply candidates to the police department and recommend them for promotion on the basis of their written examinations, the personnel department does not have to live day-in and day-out with them.[19] Although this does not mean that the personnel department is ineffective, per se, it does clearly state one aspect of the difficulties inherent in such a system. In preparing examinations for police personnel any civil service agency is likely to find that there is little in the way of systematic or rigorous data available on which to base their examinations. For the above reasons and others, it is not surprising to find that many patrolmen have little regard for the validity of the process that provides them with their supervisors.

Many patrolmen go far beyond questioning the validity of the promotional procedures to the point where they consider that these procedures are dysfunctional with respect to producing the appropriate type of supervisor. Much of this feeling can be traced to the fact that the tests, for the most part, test the amount of knowledge derived from a program of study which is independent of effectiveness as a patrolman. One other reason offered as justification for the position that the tests are dysfunctional is the observation made by many patrolmen that those who are likely to be successful on the tests

[18] See D. L. Meier and W. Bell, "Anomia and Differential Access to the Achievement of Life Goals," *American Sociological Review*, Vol. 24 (1959), pp. 189–202, for a general discussion of the consequences of blocked achievement.

[19] Jane Rinck, *Career and Salary Feature of the Police and Fire Services*, Institute of Public Administration (New York, 1952).

are those who avoid their duties in order to find some place and time in which to study. Regardless of their accuracy, these assertions strongly support the feeling that the "bosses" (the superior officers) of the department do not deserve the respect which the organization requires or demands.

According to patrolmen the majority of supervisors lack the necessary detachment from the hierarchy of authority in the department and thus are afraid to stand up for patrolmen who are erroneously charged with inappropriate conduct.[20] Patrolmen who share this attitude seemed also inclined to explain what they regard as inadequate performance on the part of supervisors as a matter of personal cowardice or hostility rather than as an organizational characteristic. This interpretation provides the basis for a punitive orientation (the "grievance pattern") toward supervisors as shown in Gouldner's study of an industrial plant.[21] Interrelated with this negative orientation toward supervisors and toward the career and promotion patterns is a belief system that is both a product of this orientation as well as a supportive factor in maintaining it.

Among the components of this belief system are slogans and phrases about the futility of aspiring to mobility, the informal means that must often be invoked in police work, and the justification of ineffective and deviant performance. Perhaps the best expression concerning the futility of mobility aspirations is the following prescription the author heard a few times: "Don't look for trouble. It will find you." This and similar phrases abounded in the department and were used to justify inactivity and avoidance of potentially dangerous or difficult tasks, particularly those which might create some unfavorable publicity, for example, handling Negroes or demonstrators of one persuasion or another. This sort of slogan also often justified not trying to learn the materials covered on the civil service examinations, since change of any sort was seen as threatening.

Another slogan heard quite often from nonsupervisors in the department was, "The job is good for two things: time and money." The slogan served as justification for taking time off improperly and for taking graft that ranged from "clean money" to "dirty money."[22] It

[20] See P. M. Blau and W. R. Scott, *op. cit.*, esp. Chap. 6, "The Role of the Supervisor," for a discussion of the value of hierarchical detachment.

[21] A. W. Gouldner, *op. cit.*, pp. 207 ff.

[22] This distinction between approved and disapproved graft was explored in research conducted by A. Niederhoffer on a group of experienced police in the department. The results appear in A. N. Niederhoffer, *A Study of Police Cynicism.* Unpublished Ph.D. thesis, Department of Sociology, New York University, 1963.

also expressed the feeling that there were few intrinsic satisfactions to be found in a career in the department. Since money is easily translated into a wide variety of satisfying experiences, it is not difficult to see how officers failing to find intrinsic satisfactions in police work might turn to graft as a source of these satisfactions.

As an indicator of the extent to which patrolmen felt that mobility through appointment to the detective division was based on effective performance, there exists one of the more dramatic expressions of cynicism, "If you want to get 'out of the bag' and into the 'bureau,' *shoot somebody*." (The "bag" refers to the uniform.) Although it seems unlikely that many officers follow this advice literally, many of those who had chosen this mobility pattern were likely to make a bit more out of situations they encountered than did officers who chose other mobility patterns or chose to remain in the position of patrolman. For example, some officers deliberately antagonized citizens in the hope that the citizens would assault them and that the officer would then have some grounds for making a felony arrest or for using the "necessary force in order to effect the arrest."

The final component of the belief system concerning promotions and assignments had to do with the existence of patrons within the department who exerted their influence on behalf of officers lower in the hierarchy than the patrons. For reasons unclear to the author, in view of the fact that the hierarchy was dominated by men with Irish-Catholic backgrounds, an individual officer's patron was known as his "rabbi." Whatever its etymology this term occupied a psychologically significant role in the thinking of many members of the force whether they had a "rabbi" with influence or not. As Becker and Strauss have pointed out, a "good sponsor" can manipulate in many ways the customary universalistic criteria in favor of his client in order to promote his client's career.[23] Not only did those officers with patrons utilize them in this and other ways, but also others assumed that influential patrons played a part in many assignments to the detective division or to the desirable "details." In addition, many officers felt that requisite personal background for any of the more desirable assignments was less important than the influence of the sponsor. This assertion served both as an explanation for mobility and as a justification for failure to satisfy job requirements.

The above discussion has attempted to show the variety of types and sources of uncertainty that face police officers, particularly those engaged in field work in the patrol force. Although few rigorous

[23] H. S. Becker and A. L. Strauss, "Careers, Personality and Adult Socialization," *American Journal of Sociology*, Vol. LXII (1956), pp. 253–63.

data have been introduced to support the discussion, the author has been able to draw upon three years of daily and direct personal contact with a large number of officers with varying work experiences and statuses in the New York City Police Department and upon a variety of unstructured data gathered from these officers.

The major emphasis in the foregoing description of uncertainties facing patrolmen has been on the interrelationship of the different components of the authority associated with the role. The discussion identified inconsistencies and conflicts within and between the legal basis for police authority, the public recognition of police authority, one major type of technical competence (the interpersonal skills underlying gaining of compliance) supporting the implementation of police authority, and the delegation of authority to individual officers by the administration of the police department. These inconsistencies and conflicts strongly affect the job performance of patrolmen. In brief, the daily functioning of police officers is circumscribed by legalistic, moralistic, and punitive orientations that are inappropriate to the development and maintenance of truly professional police officers. The manner in which the New York City Police Academy served to prepare recruits for these uncertainties will constitute the focus of the next section.

RECRUIT TRAINING AS PREPARATION FOR UNCERTAINTIES IN THE FIELD

During 1964 the New York City Police Academy graduated 1543 recruit police officers who were then assigned to field commands in the five boroughs of New York City. The four months of formal training given in the academy is primarily aimed at preparing the recruits for patrol duty in the precincts. It is to the precincts that the majority will be assigned, and most of the recruits will be assigned within the precincts to patrol on foot. Less than 10% of one group of 140 patrolmen from a number of precincts questioned in 1963 after they had been assigned to the field for one year had as their "most frequent duties" some duties other than foot patrol. Patrolmen on foot patrol almost invariably patrol alone; thus, the importance of their acquiring a good working knowledge of their duties as well as some ability function autonomously is clear.

Other considerations of the nature of police work also support the contention that the patrolmen graduated from the academy should be self-directing. Their work frequently has potential extreme consequences in terms of human life that are probably only surpassed in frequency by those on the medical or military professions.[24] Much of the work, moreover, is extremely distasteful to members of American culture, for example, handling dead bodies or seriously risking one's life for strangers or for persons whom one may personally dislike. Finally, since much of the work that officers handle requires prompt action, patrolmen cannot wait for assistance from their supervisors or from other patrolmen. These considerations and the fact that most of the recent academy graduates were assigned to foot patrol emphasize the need for academy graduates who are capable of performing police duties, are aware of the appropriate specific measures to be taken in an infinite variety of stituations, and are appropriately motivated to take these measures. In view of the demands placed on the individual officer it would seem unlikely that four months of formal training is sufficient to develop the above characteristics to the appropriate degree. In evaluating the following discussion, however, it should be remembered that many smaller police departments have training programs of only a few weeks duration and that some have almost no formal training. Germann reports that many police administrators considered an initial training period to be superfluous. The discussion is based on a preliminary analysis of data gathered over a three-year period from 1960 to 1963.[25]

BACKGROUND CHARACTERISTICS OF RECRUIT POLICE OFFICERS

Many of the attitudes and past experiences of newly appointed recruit police officers are relevant to a discussion of the functions of recruit training for the uncertainties of police work. Immediately after a patrolman was first appointed to the department he, along with a number of other recruits, began his formal training. Prior to his appointment he had been subjected to a number of examinations and investigations. He must have passed a written civil service exami-

[24] The decision to shoot at a person is tantamount to a decision to kill, since police aim at the abdomens of their adversaries. The only persons other than police officers who are required to decide whether to kill or not are judges, whose decisions are strongly governed by legal criteria as well as other considerations, and military personnel, whose individual decisions are usually rather simple—shoot at the people who are wearing a different uniform. Military personnel individually are far more likely to be following rather specific orders and to be under the direct control of their supervisors. Police thus occupy a unique position with regard to the continuance of human life.

[25] A. C. Germann, *Police Personnel Management* (Springfield, Ill., Charles C Thomas, 1958), p. 126.

nation which was considered by the personnel department to serve not only as an intelligence test, but also as a test of knowledge concerning police work.[26]

Following the civil service written test, the candidate is required to pass qualifying medical and physical tests. Finally, the candidate had to be approved by the unit conducting his "character investigation." The character investigation was an attempt to assess the degree to which a candidate would be likely to withstand the ethical and psychological risks involved in police work. The investigation was somewhat comprehensive in that the investigation of each candidate required approximately twenty-five man-hours of the investigators. They attempted to construct a pattern of each candidate's character from such data as his occupational history, financial status, conduct in school or in the military, sexual habits, and criminal or delinquent experiences of the candidate, his friends, and his relatives. Interviews conducted by an investigator with a candidate were considered valuable because the investigator could personally assess the degree to which the candidate was cooperative and truthful. These interviews often approximated a stress interview in which the reaction of the candidate to the authority of the investigator (usually a police sergeant) was recorded. Thus, a candidate was given a foretaste of the semimilitary model governing interaction between superordinate and subordinate even before he was appointed to the force.

The recommendation of the investigator that the candidate be approved or disapproved or that a "hearing board" pass on the suitability of the candidate was governed by the phrase, "All doubts about a candidate should be resolved in favor of the department." In effect this meant that any candidate about whom there was doubt should not be approved. In each of two groups of patrolmen in the study, only two-thirds of the candidates were approved by the character investigation unit. Of a combined total of 272 patrolmen in the two groups, 27% were referred to the hearing board and the remaining 7% were disapproved of but later hired as a result of a hearing board's recommendation or as a result of civil service limitations on the police commissioner's discretion regarding appointments. Although the candidate's first encounter with the department may seem somewhat harsh, the selection procedures in departments which employ the polygraph or lie detector routinely are equally, if not more, harsh.

[26] See L. R. Eilbert, J. H. McNamara and V. L. Hanson, *op. cit.*, p. 4, for a brief discussion of the relationship between scores on one civil service examination and scores on the Otis intelligence test. The product-moment correlation between the two sets of scores was .54.

Table 2 *Occupational Levels of Police Recruits' Fathers*

Occupational Level	Percent of Recruits' Fathers	Percent, Work Force, New York S.M.S.A.
Professional, technical, managers, officials, proprietors	10.8	22.2
Clerical, sales	9.4	27.2
Craftsmen, foremen	19.3	11.3
Operatives	16.6	17.3
Service, household workers	28.1[a]	11.8
Laborers	5.7	3.4
Not reported	10.1	6.7

[a] One-third of the recruits' fathers in this category were recorded as having the occupation of police officer or an occupation involving police-type duties, for example, private detective or watchman.

As a result of recruiting, the selection program, and the self-selection of candidates, newly appointed patrolmen tended to be primarily from the lower-middle-class segments of the population. If we use the measure of their fathers' eleven major occupations for three combined groups of 574 recruit patrolmen relative to the distribution of the labor force for the New York "S.M.S.A." as reported in the 1960 U.S. census, it is clear that the recruits are not drawn from families in the "higher skill" segments of the population (Table 2).

The recruits themselves, as a group, had held at least one full-time job treated by the census classification as being a "higher skill" occupation than their fathers. Table 3 presents the percentages of the

Table 3 *Prior Full-Time "Highest Skill" Occupation of Recruits*

Occupational Level	Percentage of Recruits
Professional managers, etc.	7
Clerical, sales	44
Skilled, foremen, craftsmen	22
Operatives, kindred	12
Service, household	8
Unskilled, laborer	3
Not reported	4

"highest skill" full-time occupations prior to entrance into the police force. Generational and age differences between the recruits and their fathers as well as the shifting nature of work are relevant to a comparison of the percentages of recruits and their fathers classified as having clerical or sale occupations. The mean age of the recruits at the time they listed their occupations was 24.3 years of age. Two-thirds of the group were between the ages of 21 and 24 inclusive. The increasing need for personnel in the "tertiary" areas of work also accounts in part for the generational differences.

The recruits further tend not to be from the more educated segments of the population. In order to be appointed to the force, a recruit was required to have a high school degree. Of one combined group of 574 recruits, however, 21% had not earned a diploma but had "equivalency degrees," given upon passing an examination. In this same group, less than 2% had earned their Bachelor of Arts degree and 28% had had some college at the time they were tested.

Given the socio-economic level of the recruits, we hypothesized that they would be somewhat more authoritarian than the general population and thus would score somewhat higher on the F-scale, but not as high as many sociologists posit.[27] One group of 166 recruits was tested prior to their entrance into the police academy, and another group of 294 recruits was tested in their third month of training in the academy. Both groups had a mean of 4.15 and a standard deviation of .65 on the F-scale. Adorno *et al.*[28] report mean scores of 4.19 and 4.06 respectively for 61 "working-class men" and 343 "maritime school men." The authors also report a mean of 3.84 and a standard deviation of 1.10 for a group of 1518 subjects of varying background characteristics.

For sociologists who propose that recruits are attracted to police work by the power residing in the role these mean scores may be surprisingly low. The main attraction of the work for recruits, however, seemed more to be found in the civil service security coupled with the relatively high economic benefits associated with the job. In support of this it was found that a large proportion of each incoming group of recruits had taken entrance examinations for both the police department and the fire department. The latter had similar job security conditions and economic benefits but fewer openings and more stringent physical requirements. A number of police recruits,

[27] The F-scale is an instrument for measuring the authoritarian personality syndrome.

[28] T. W. Adorno, *et al., The Authoritarian Personality* New York, Harper and Brothers, (1950), esp. pp. 255–8.

Table 4 *Percentage Distributions of Scale Types: Punitiveness Scale (in Per Cent)*

Scale Types	Community Leaders[a]	Police Recruits
IV (punitive)	17	2
III	20	12
II	10	17
I	40	39
0 (nonpunitive)	13	31

[a] See Nettler, *loc. cit.*

moreover, expressed their preference for the fire department primarily because of their dislike of dealing with the public in police work. Further, although a number of men who resigned from the police department to join the fire department, the police department gained almost no personnel who resigned from the fire department.

Additionally, the recruits' responses to a "punitiveness" scale constructed by Nettler from responses of a sample of 939 community leaders in a metropolitan area seem relatively nonpuntive.[29] (See Table 4.) The scale scores of 157 recruits in their first week of training at the police academy were markedly lower than those of the community leaders. (The scale requires the respondent to indicate which societal response—treatment or punishment—is appropriate for different types of juvenile deviants.) This comparison may be inappropriate, since there is a large age difference as well as a regional difference between the two samples, and recruits might identify more closely with juvenile deviants. Since the questionnaires were not anonymous, the recruits' responses may have been subjected to a "social desirability" influence and hence lower than they might have been. Recruits are probably somewhat sensitive to any imputations of tendencies toward "police brutality." It would seem that recruits were less interested in "disinterested punishment"[30] than in avoiding some harm to themselves or to certain other prople.

Relevance of Recruits' Backgrounds for Legal Uncertainties

From the above discussion we see that the recruits are likely to be drawn from different segments of the population than those from

[29] G. Nettler, "Cruelty, Dignity and Determinism," *American Sociological Review*, Vol. 24, No. 3 (1959), esp. p. 380.

[30] See Nettler, *op. cit.*, p. 377, in which he cites Ranulf's thesis that disinterested punishment is characteristically a middle-class phenomenon.

which legislators and jurists are drawn. Thus, there exists a potential set of tensions between police and law-makers' definitions of crime and ranking of seriousness of different crimes. For example, the courts tend to treat violations of vice laws as minor offenses, but police departments traditionally expend a great deal of time and manpower in the search for marijuana users, prostitutes, homosexuals, etc. In this connection, the author heard the chief magistrate of New York City, at a meeting of a police officers' association, request that fewer arrests of narcotics addicts be made in view of the lack of both court and treatment facilities.

Although the recruits score on the F-scale within the limits expected on the basis of their socio-economic origins, their group mean score still exceeds the overall mean of a "purposive" sample (intended to test a cross-section) presented in the original study by Adorno *et al.*[31] Therefore it could be predicted that the recruits would be less likely than the general public to appreciate the subtleties and qualifying conditions that are associated with both substantive and procedural criminal law. Moreover, the academy relied mainly on classroom presentation and study in order to transmit some understanding of the laws police enforce. We also hypothesized that this reliance on the classroom for teaching law to the recruits would be problematic in view of the limited formal academic backgrounds of the recruits.

Similarly, given the socio-economic backgrounds of the recruits, one could predict that their view of the effects of a less punitive court orientation would be quite different from that of court personnel. We examined the responses to an item asked of 294 recruits in their third month of training to indicate whether they agree with a number of reasons offered to explain ". . . why some citizens assault police." A statistically significant difference existed between recruits dichotomized into two groups on the basis of their fathers' occupations. Recruits with fathers in the higher skill classification were less likely to feel that the leniency of courts and laws accounts for assaults on the police (Table 5).

This difference in attitudes regarding the determinants of assaultive behavior implies not only a difference in attitudes toward the courts and laws but also a difference in their attempts later to reduce the frequency of intensity of these assaults. It might be hypothesized that recruits who see the responsibility for these assaults as that of the courts and laws do not see it as that of the police department or the individual officer. The recruits, however, still dichotomized

[31] T. W. Adorno *et al.*, *op. cit.*, p. 258.

Table 5 *Responses to "Courts and the Laws Are too Lenient" as One Reason Why Citizens Assault Police (Recruits Differentiated by Fathers' Occupations)*

Fathers' occupation	Actually Is a Reason	Do Not Know, Uncertain	Not Actually a Reason
Higher skill[a]	74	15	41
Lower skill	97	33	34
$p < .05$ (Chi-square = 6.58; $df = 2$)			

[a] Higher-skill occupations are professional, managerial, technical, clerical, sales, skilled, craftsmen, and foremen. Lower-skill occupations are all others.

by their fathers' occupational skill level, do not respond differently to three other possible reasons why citizens assault police: "Some arrests are unlawful," "Some people are handled poorly," and "Police aren't firm enough." The differentiated responses to the item concerning the leniency of courts and law seem to reflect a belief concerning the existence of this leniency as much as a belief in the effects of leniency.

Relevance of Recruits' Backgrounds for Uncertainties Regarding Police Prestige

When recruits were asked to indicate the prestige that the general public might assign to police work relative to other career possibilities they had entertained or to other jobs they had prior to coming into the police department, they were likely to consider police work as more socially *prestigious* (Table 6). Further, as recruits moved from considering remote (career possibilities) to more proximate (prior) jobs, they tended to indicate that police work increased its level of relative prestige in the eyes of the general public. Thus, although 34% considered past career possibilities more prestigious than police work, only 14% considered jobs they had actually had to be more prestigious than police work. The recruits clearly considered their new employment in the department as a step for themselves at the time they joined the force.

Even though approximately two-thirds of the recruits considered police work to be equally or more prestigious than other career possibilities they had seriously considered, the recruits were not so convinced that police work as a career fared so well in the relative

Table 6 *Percentages of Recruits' Estimates of Relative Prestige Assigned by the "General Public" to Recruits' Past Job or Career Possibilities and to Past Jobs*

	Prestige of Other Jobs Relative to Police Work					
Careers or Jobs	Much Higher (1–1.9)[a]	Somewhat Higher (2–2.9)	About the Same (3–3.9)	Somewhat Lower (4–4.9)	Much Lower (5)	*N*
Past career possibilities of greatest interest	8	26	40	22	5	257[b]
Jobs recruits had "good chance of getting" when they joined police department	7	18	37	28	10	166
Prior full-time, "nontemporary" jobs of recruits	4	10	26	46	13	268

[a] Mean ranks were computed for each respondent, with a value of 1 assigned to "much higher," 2 to "somewhat higher," etc.

[b] Only recruits ranking the jobs in each of the above categories were considered in computing the percentages. The total number of respondents was 279. (Two groups were combined.)

prestige assigned to it by the general public. In general and similar to more experienced patrolmen, police recruits do not see the position of patrolman as possessing much prestige. For example, only 12% of one sample of 171 recruits agreed or strongly agreed with the statement "The respect that citizens have for a patrolman and his position has been steadily increasing over the years," whereas 72% disagreed or strongly disagreed with the statement. Thus, although the recruits consider police work to be more prestigious for themselves, they do not consider the position as one which is increasing its share of respect. There may be some difficulty in treating "respect" as synonymous with "prestige." The notion of respect accorded police often was equated with fear of police. Whether this latter component predominated in the responses to the item cannot be determined from the data. Perhaps the distinction made by recruits is one between a descriptive statement (prestige) and a normative statement (respect). That is, although the job involves an increase in the personal mana of the recruits, they believe there is not presently enough mana imputed to the role of the patrolman.[32]

It might be predicted that this feeling of insufficient respect for the role of the patrolman might become more salient for the recruits after they leave the academy and begin their work in the field units. But in a follow-up of the group of 171 recruits it was found that the percentage disagreeing or strongly disagreeing with the statement "Respect . . . for a patrolman and his position has been steadily increasing over the years" changed only 1% after they had been working in the field for one year. Nevertheless, the underlying attitude that patrolmen are not bettering their degree of respect may come to have a different meaning for an individual patrolman who, as one consequence of this attitude, feels he cannot rely on a high degree of public respect in carrying out his duties.

Relevance of Recruits' Backgrounds for Uncertainties Regarding Effective Interpersonal Tactics

As indicated above, the recruits tend to be relatively homogeneous with respect to socio-economic background, educational level, and scores on the F-scale. (The standard deviation was lower than that of any of the groups reported by Adorno, *et al.*)[33] They are also homogeneous in religion (in one combined group of 567 recruits, 80% were Catholic, 15% Protestant, and 4% Jewish), ethnicity (in a combined group of 565 recruits, 5% were Negro and 95% white, and it is the author's impression that less than 1% of the recruits were of Puerto Rican background), and age (two-thirds of the group of 574 were between the ages of 21 and 24 inclusive).

The homogeneity of police recruits, while perhaps desirable in some regards, particularly for ease of administrative practice, implies an immediate problem in terms of their ability to do veridical role-taking with the many different types of citizens that make up the heterogeneous urban population of New York. Given the recruits' homogeneity, the department was not able to select each man carefully for his optimal first assignment. Instead, the primary consideration in assigning men to precinct duty was the ease of commuting from their residence precinct to their assigned precinct. (Police officers could not be assigned to precincts in which they lived primarily be-

[32] See E. Goffman, "The Nature of Deference and Demeanor," *American Anthropologist*, Vol. 58 (1956), pp. 473–502, for an application of the concept of mana to interaction in urban society.

[33] T. W. Adorno *et al.*, *op. cit.*, p. 258.

cause they would find it difficult to make impartial judgments in their interactions with the public.)

Equally important from the standpoint of the recruits' role-taking skills, is that the recruits are homogeneous in specific dimensions. For example, their somewhat high average score on the F-scale implies some difficulty in veridical role-taking.[34] Similarly, the fact that only 5% of the recruits were Negroes and less than 1% were of Puerto Rican background implies immediately some role-taking problems because of a lack of common experience or shared perspective in dealing with Negroes and Puerto Ricans who together comprise 22% of the population of New York City. This is, of course, particularly problematic, since members of these groups are predominantly in the lowest socio-economic strata, and these strata are over-represented in interactions with police, whether in regard to crimes or to the personal "service functions" served by police officers.

The socio-economic level of recruits similarly implies certain difficulties regarding veridical role-taking. Schatzman and Strauss found a significant difference between middle-class and lower-class patterns of role-taking in which lower-class interviewees were characterized by a "relative insensitivity to disparities in perspective" between themselves and the interviewers as well as by a "notable assumption of correspondence in imagery."[35] In general, the lower-class subjects were far less able to perceive others as being members of different classes with different types of roles; that is, they were less able to impose a more impersonal or abstract frame of reference on others divorced from the others' unique identities. As Newcomb *et al.* point out, accurate perception of others requires that the perceiver have available to him some general principles or concepts with which to account for his observations of others.[36] Although the recruits do not come from the lowest socio-economic segments, they do come from the segments in which the high skill occupations are underrepresented. Thus, their ability to do "interpersonal testing" was perhaps less marked than if the department had been able to recruit from the economically more favored segments of the population.

Of course, the characteristics of the citizen with whom a police

[34] See T. M. Newcomb, R. H. Turner and P. E. Converse, *Social Psychology* (New York, Holt, Rinehart and Winston, 1965), pp. 172–9, for a discussion of the negative relationships found between scores on the F-scale and veridical role-taking.

[35] L. Schatzman and A. Strauss, "Social Class and Modes of Communication," *American Journal of Sociology*, Vol. 60 (1955), pp. 329–38.

[36] T. M. Newcomb *et al.*, *op. cit.*, p. 177.

officer is interacting must be taken into consideration in any discussion of the determinants of his effective interpersonal testing. For the most part, the more problematic or potentially problematic situations were those involving members of the lower socio-economic strata and police officers in interaction. And even though middle-class persons may be generally more successful in role-taking, it is also a commonplace finding that similarity of background between two persons increases the accuracy of any role-taking between the two. Hence, the increase in role-taking skills that would follow upon the selection of a larger proportion of recruits from among the middle socio-economic strata might be offset by the decrease in similarity of backgrounds between the more problematic citizens from the lower strata and such police officers.

At least one other consideration is relevant to this discussion of socio-economic background and role-taking skills. Increased empathy between two persons may also be associated with increased sympathy between the two. As Turner has pointed out, role-taking may or may not involve taking the "standpoint of the other," that is, accepting the other's point of view as one's own.[37] The inappropriateness of a police officer's accepting the point of view of a prisoner who is resisting arrest while threatening the officer with a knife seems clear enough. If similarity of background were the primary basis for veridical role-taking, then it would be more likely that a role-taker would also take over the standpoint of the other for his own than if some other basis were primary, for example, low scores on the F-scale, whatever the identity of the relevant variable being measured by the F-scale.

Some of the characteristics of the recruits are also relevant to their ability to bring about effective *clarifications of their expectations* for citizens with whom they are interacting. Schatzman and Strauss have identified communication differences between lower- and middle-class subjects as involving the middle-class practice of using many ". . . devices to supply context and clarify meaning" and of being especially sensitive to communication problems with persons who fail to share their individual viewpoints or frames of reference.[38] It is relevant to note that the "decoders" in this study were middle-class interviewers. Even if all police were from the middle classes or above, their

[37] R. H. Turner, "Role-Taking, Role Standpoint, and Reference-Group Behavior," *American Journal of Sociology*, Vol. 61 (1956), pp. 316–28. Reprinted in *Approaches, Contexts and Problems of Social Psychology*, E. E. Sampson, (ed.) (Englewood Cliffs, N.J., Prentice-Hall, 1964), pp. 219–31.)

[38] L. Schatzman and A. Strauss, *op. cit.*

communication "devices" and sensitivity to communication problems would perhaps be more appropriate for other members of the middle classes than for members of the lower classes. Nevertheless, the skills involved in specifying expectations would be of great value to a police officer in view of the high degree of stress and consequent "narrowing of perception" which many of his interactants are experiencing at the time he is with them.

Recruits also tend not to have had much experience as supervisors prior to their coming into the department. In one group of 295 recruits the percentage having had any supervisory experience was 30.1. In the same group of 295 only 17% had had more than six months' experience as supervisors. This is not an unexpected finding in view of the usual age structure of the recruit groups. In another group of 279 recruits, 181 had been in the military for a mean period of 3.3 years. Of the 181 with service experience, 57% had had three or more years in the service and 54% had held the rank of E-4 or above. Of course, some of these latter ranks were specialist rather than line ranks; the recruits had approximately the same distribution of ranks relative to their length of service as do service personnel in general.

In view of the relatively little supervisory experience that recruits have had, it should be expected that they would have had little experience in clarifying expectations to persons in a subordinate or lower status position. This experience would undoubtedly aid them in being able to find and present desirable alternative modes of compliance with their expectations to citizens with whom they must interact. The extent to which past supervisory experience would aid in this regard, however, is also a function of a number of other conditions such as the specific nature of the task, the degree to which the lower-status person subscribes to the norms underlying the expectations of the higher status person, the specificity of the role relationship between the two, and so on. Thus, supervisory experience alone is not a sufficient condition for the recruit's ability to clarify expectations.

There seems to be little in the recruits' backgrounds that would point to their being unusually adept at *exploiting or utilizing the values of citizens* in attempting to gain their compliance. Since the recruits are homogeneous with respect to a number of social and psychological factors, it could be hypothesized that they might support one anothers' values to the point where it becomes difficult for them to see many citizens' values as anything but wrong or at least not legitimate. Such an orientation makes it unlikely that a police officer would do much veridical role-taking or have much awareness of the existence of different citizens' values.

Furthermore, the problem for police officers in suspending their own values in order to consider a citizen's values different from their own would be more a problem for recruits with high F-scale scores and for those from the lower socio-economic segments. We can hypothesize that recruits with these characteristics have a relatively ethnocentric orientation, and therefore they would be more likely to rely on the use or threat of force to gain compliance.

Similarly, the recruits' backgrounds do not particularly indicate an ability to effect a *presentation of self* as decisive or as impersonally concerned with a citizen and his problems. The recruits' relatively young ages and their lack of supervisory experience imply little opportunity to develop the skill of dissembling their uncertainties regarding an appropriate line of action.

In addition, since they are not recruited from the middle classes in which tension-binding and the cultivation of "manners" are more likely to predominate, the recruits would be relatively less able to effect an impersonal presentation of self. "Acting out" of problems is to some extent valued behavior in lower-middle and lower classes, especially when their members are confronted with status challenges of the sort that police officers constantly face. The notion of "disinterested punishment" is characteristically a middle-class orientation, and members of lower socioeconomic strata are far more likely to inject themselves more directly into the punishment of deviants.

Relevance of Recruits' Backgrounds for Organizational Uncertainties

Since a large proportion of the recruits have had some experience in the military services, the use of negative sanctions and the appearance of close supervision that together constitute the *semimilitary model* would not be unfamiliar to many of them. In addition, the majority of recruits have not been employed before in jobs where they were loosely supervised or where the use of negative sanctions was likely to be considered highly inappropriate by their supervisors. Therefore, the newly appointed recruits should not experience much of a "culture shock" with regard to the police department's expressed policy of supervision. The specific actual practices of supervisors may later concern them, but in general the recruits seem to feel that close and strict supervision is common and is appropriate for patrolmen.

The responses of one group of 171 recruits in their first week of training support the above assertion. Their responses to items A and B in Table 7 approximately two-thirds either agree or strongly agree

Table 7 *Recruits' Perception of Semimilitary Aspects of Department (in Per Cent)*

Item	No Answer	Strongly Agree	Agree	Uncertain	Disagree	Strongly Disagree
A	1	11	56	17	15	0
B	1	19	44	14	20	2
C	1	3	6	39	46	5
D	2	2	17	31	38	10

Item A: "Generally, police supervisors manage to observe patrolmen at work very closely."
Item B: "The department expects supervisors to deal with their patrolmen in a very strict manner."
Item C: "One of the major problems with law enforcement is that each patrolman is not given enough latitude by his supervisors to handle the police problems in his area of responsibility."
Item D: "Patrolmen often fail to take necessary police action due to a feeling that supervisors will disapprove of their actions."

with the items—indicate that the recruits expect supervision to be close and strict. Their responses to items C and D further indicate they do not consider such supervision as negatively affecting the performance of patrolmen.

Not only are the recruits prepared for the general orientation of close and strict supervision, but they also regard this type of supervision favorably. After recruits complete their training and have been assigned to the field for some time, they maintain approximately the same point of view regarding the existence of close and strict supervision. A combined group, which includes the group just discussed, was tested at a point when 137 had had one year and 83 patrolmen had had two years of work in the field. The percentage of the combined experienced group in agreement with item A (Table 7) was again 67%. These in agreement with item B changed only six points from 63% to 57%.

There was, however, a different degree of change with regard to the evaluation of this sort of supervision. Those patrolmen in agreement with item C as recruits constituted only 9% of the group, but after some field experience those of the combined group in agreement increased to 25% of the group. Similarly, 19% of the patrolmen as recruits were in agreement with item B, but 32% of the combined group were in agreement after their field experience. Although it is difficult to tell whether this reflected specific experiences of the patrolmen or a more general change in their evaluation of the dominant supervisory style in the department, there is little doubt that the patrolmen shifted toward a more negative evaluation of that style. In the discussion of the organizational sources of uncertainty, we explored the implications of such an evaluation and hypothesized the primary difficulty to be that patrolmen need to feel some sense of autonomy in order to make appropriate decisions in stressful situations.

The more negative evaluation of supervision made by officers after their field experience seemed to be related, to some extent, to an increased perception of the sanctions used by supervisors as being of a punitive nature. The responses to the following item are relevant: "Patrolmen are frequently found guilty of violating departmental rules and procedures and are consequently penalized severely." Twenty per cent of the group of 171 were in agreement with this statement at the outset of their recruit training; after some field experience, 33% of the combined group were in agreement. Further, within the group of experienced patrolmen, those with two years' as contrasted with those with one year's experience tended more to be in agreement with the statement. Thirty-eight per cent of the group with two years' experience agreed with the statement.

Recruits at the outset of their careers in the department seemed to be well aware that any violation of the rules and regulations of the department could be the basis for disciplinary action against patrolmen. Of the group of 171 recruits 91% agreed and only 4% disagreed with this paraphrased passage from the preface to the *Rules and Procedures.* It is interesting to note that although there was little change in the distribution of responses to this statement after the training and field experience, there was some increase in the amount of disagreement—from 4% to 5% at the end of training to 8% after one year of field experience. A comparable group of patrolmen with two years' field experience had 13% of its responses in disagreement with the statement. It appears that experience tends somewhat to meliorate the rather strict or literal interpretation of this part of the preface to the *Rules and Procedures* but only slightly, since 83% of the patrolmen with one year's field experience still were in agreement with the item.

The degree of awareness of the "rat rule," as so designated, is quite different. In a group of 107 recruits tested at the beginning and at the end of their training, both times only five correctly identified the meaning of "rat rule" presented along with other words and phrases associated with police work. Since the recruits were scheduled to be familiarized with the "rat rule" during their fourteenth hour of instruction at the academy, we must assume that the instructors at the academy probably did not refer to the rule by the above designation. Although the group was not asked again to define the phrase when they were tested after two years in the field, we may be sure that the phrase was familiar then to more than five of the group.

The same group of 107 recruits was questioned about their *career aspirations* during their first week of training. The modal choice for the assignment the recruits "would most like to have after ten years on the job" was the detective division. Thirty-eight per cent indicated this assignment as their most desired career pattern. In another group of 296 recruits tested during their third month of training, 58% chose the detective division as their most desired assignment after ten years.

The recruits not only considered an assignment to the detective division to be the ideal assignment but they also *expected* to be given this assignment after their first ten years on the force. Thirty-two per cent (the modal response) of the group of 107 recruits so indicated in response to an item asking "What assignment do you think you will have ten years from now?" (Forty-one per cent failed to indicate any assignment in response to this item.)

It was hypothesized that the recruits' socio-economic backgrounds might account for their interest in and expectations about an assignment to the detective division. But there was no significant difference between recruits whose fathers' occupations were characterized as in the top three skill levels of the census classification and other recruits with regard to both their expected and desired assignments in the tenth year on the force. The choice of the detective career pattern is more akin to the modal choice of airline pilot made by high school male students in that the work of a detective is strongly glamorized in the mass media. It is also considered to be a high status appointment by officers. Further, assignment to the detective division for many obviates the long hours of study that seem necessary for patrolmen to pass the civil service examinations for promotion to sergeant and above.

Eventually the goal of becoming a detective apparently changed for many of the recruits. In a group of officers tested after they completed either one or two years' experience in the field, the percentage *still* desiring appointment to the detective division "after ten years on the job" shifted to 28%. The percentage that still *expected* to be detectives "after ten years on the job" shifted even more markedly to only 16%. (As recruits, those *expecting* to be detective in ten years constituted anywhere from 32% to 55% in different samples.)

This shift away from the detective career pattern was accompanied by an increased acceptance of the civil service promotional pattern as well as an increased acceptance of both the desirability and likelihood of being assigned to the patrol force after ten years. Those *desiring* an assignment to the patrol force after ten years shifted from 6% of the group of 107 new recruits to 20% in the group of experienced patrolmen. Those *expecting* to be assigned at the end of ten years to patrol duties also shifted—from 12% among the recruits to 33% among the experienced officers. It would seem then that the career aspirations of police were tempered by a more realistic appraisal of the available opportunities.

In this section dealing with background characteristics of the recruits we have attempted to show how the recruits are prepared to cope with the uncertainties of police work as well as with the requirements of the police academy. We noted that the recuits are better prepared to cope with uncertaintites stemming from organizational sources and from the perceived low prestige attached to the role of police officer by the general public. On the other hand, their background characteristics and atitudes at the outset of their careers in police work do not prepare the recruits as well for the uncertanties regarding the use of effective interpersonal skills and the uncertainties stemming from considerations of the legality of police actions.

One major task for the recruit training school of the police academy would then seem clear: a systematic attempt to give the recruit the appropriate knowledge and attitudes that would reduce the uncertainties regarding the legality of his actions as well as a systematic attempt to move the recruits toward an acquisition of interpersonal skills. In the following section we consider the experiences of the recruits in their socialization into police work as related to the problem of managing the uncertainties of police work.

RECRUIT TRAINING AND UNCERTAINTIES REGARDING LEGALITY OF POLICE ACTIONS

The difficulties for any recruit training program in transmitting a working knowledge of both procedural and substantive laws are many and complex. Earlier it was pointed out that American federal, state, and local legislative laws combined with the judical decisions making up the common law system do not constitute a well constructed axiomatic system. That is, one cannot discern general principles consistent with one another that would allow a police officer to make decisions regarding the legality of his actions with any marked degree of confidence in the correctness of his decision.

The system of laws with which a police officer must operate is thus not one that can easily or succinctly be presented. Further, police departments, with some justification, feel strongly that errors made by police personnel regarding the legality of their actions are likely to have severe consequences for the individual officer as well as for the department as a whole. It is not surprising, therefore, to find the academic curriculum of the New York City Police Academy heavily loaded with detailed presentations of procedural and substantive laws from a variety of sources: New York State Penal Law, New York State Code of Criminal Procedure, New York City Administrative and Health Codes, the Federal Constitution and its amendments, etc. Although some instructors tried to present the general history and political philosophy underlying this system of laws, both class presentation and the recruits' program of study largely consisted of stating or memorizing page after page of laws and the conditions associated with different laws.

One indicator of the extent to which recruits failed to derive any general sense of the legality of police actions was found in the responses of 250 recruits to the following item: "*According to my instructors* the following are the most important *principles of law as* far as patrolmen on patrol are concerned." (The item was followed by space for written descriptions of three separate principles.) We were unable to find a manageable number of categories that adequately summarized the range of responses and thus could not code the responses. The responses ranged from "patrol on the left (side of the street)" to "protection of life, limb, and property." The same item was given again to some of the same group after they had completed two years in field assignments; the results were the same.

Along with a lack of consensus among the recruits regarding basic principles of law, there developed an increased support for the belief that police lack the basic legal authority appropriate to their position. Responses of recruits tested at the beginning and end of their training to questionnaire items concerning such authority were found to move in the direction of belief that police have insufficient legal authority. The movement of beliefs further continued in the same direction during the first year of assignment to field work. A second group, tested after two years in the field, showed a general tendency to be slightly more convinced of the insufficiency of police authority

Table 8 *Changes over Time in Recruits' Beliefs in the Sufficiency of Police Legal Authority (in Per Cent)*

Item	Time[a]	No Answer	Strongly Agree	Agree	Uncertain	Disagree	Strongly Disagree
A	T_1	1	5	19	29	35	11
	T_2	0	14	30	16	35	5
	T_3	1	24	39	17	13	6
	T_4	1	27	36	18	18	0
B	T_1	1	6	13	46	25	9
	T_2	0	12	33	30	21	5
	T_3	1	14	41	18	22	4
	T_4	1	17	43	19	17	3
C	T_1	1	10	29	36	21	3
	T_2	0	13	40	26	20	1
	T_3	1	27	43	21	7	1
	T_4	1	30	48	15	6	0
D	T_1	1	12	64	8	14	1
	T_2	1	5	57	8	24	5
	T_3	1	1	38	13	39	8
	T_4	1	1	34	17	31	16

Item A: "The present system of state and local laws has undermined the patrolman's authority to a dangerous extent."
Item B: "The courts have tended in recent years to discount the testimony of patrolmen where there are no other witnesses or there is no other proof regarding an alleged crime, offense, or violation."
Item C: "A number of pressure groups have been successful in getting legislation and court decisions that severely restrict the police actions that patrolmen can take."
Item D: "Generally speaking, patrolmen today have enough legal authority to get their jobs done efficiently."

[a] The symbols T_1, T_2, and T_3 refer to one group tested at the beginning of its recruit training (T_1), at the end of its recruit training (T_2), and after one year in field assignments (T_3). The N's are, respectively, 171, 164, and 137. The symbol T_4 refers to another group of eighty-three patrolmen with two years' experience in the field.

than the group with one year in the field (Table 8). The largest proportionate increase in the belief that police have insufficient legal authority, however, took place between the beginning (T_1) and the end (T_2) of the recruit training.

There is also a large change in the recruits' attitudes regarding the sufficiency of police legal authority after they have had one year of field experience. This finding is consistent with our hypotheses that a "cultural discontinuity" existed between the police academy curriculum and the later requirements of the field assignments.[39] We had sufficient reason to believe that the curriculum would not include discussion of many of the informal practices that were widespread in the department, particularly those in violation of the *Rules and Procedures.* Police academy personnel were reluctant to discuss these practices because they feared their discussion would be interpreted as a form of endorsement or legitimation of the patterned evasion of rules.

We believe one consequence of the failure of the academy personnel to discuss the informal practices would be that the patrolmen would later be required by social pressures from other officers in the field to follow the informal practices. In order to justify following these practices the recruits would eventually come to believe that there is insufficient authority granted the police officer by the courts and legislatures. One of Westley's findings concerning the use of unnecessary force by police officers on sex offenders is similar in that police believed that the force was justified because the courts were seen as failing to punish sex offenders adequately.[40]

It is interesting to note that the recruits do not change much in any consistent direction either during their training or during the first two years in the field with regard to the amount of legal discretion they believe is accorded to them by the supervisors and administration of the department. (See Table 9.) One reason why the recruits did not perceive the departmental hierarchy of authority to be as responsible for the insufficiency of police authority as the courts and legislatures may be that an officer's negative evaluation would hurt his career. Also many of the respondents may have remained unconvinced that the research was being conducted by an agency other than the department. A number of recruits expressed such a belief to the author and to one another. Although every effort was made to convince

[39] See R. Benedict, "Continuities and Discontinuities in Cultural Conditioning," *Psychiatry*, Vol. 1 (1938), pp. 161–7.

[40] W. A. Westley, "Violence and the Police," *American Journal of Sociology* Vol. 59 (1953), pp. 34–41.

Table 9 *Changes in Recruits' Beliefs Concerning Discretion Allowed by Supervisors and Administration (in Per Cent)*

Item	Time[a]	No Answer	Strongly Agree	Agree	Uncertain	Disagree	Strongly Disagree
A	T_1	1	2	16	25	46	10
	T_2	1	1	20	14	57	7
	T_3	1	4	15	18	52	10
	T_4	1	6	23	11	52	7
B	T_1	1	3	6	39	46	5
	T_2	0	1	11	30	51	7
	T_3	1	1	22	22	50	4
	T_4	1	8	21	25	45	0
C	T_1	2	2	17	31	38	10
	T_2	0	2	15	27	51	5
	T_3	1	8	25	12	50	4
	T_4	1	7	23	15	47	7
D	T_1	1	6	32	44	15	2
	T_2	0	5	45	33	16	1
	T_3	1	5	52	20	18	4
	T_4	1	7	55	16	20	0

Item A: "The department does not seem to allow patrolmen enough discretion regarding the arrests they might make or summons they might serve."
Item B: "One of the major problems with law enforcement is that each patrolman is not given enough latitude by his supervisors to handle the police problems in his area of responsibility."
Item C: "Patrolmen often fail to take necessary police action due to a feeling that supervisors will disapprove of their actions."
Item D: "Police supervisors almost never instruct a patrolman to reverse his plans when he has planned to make an arrest or to issue a summons."

[a] See Table 8, footnote [a].

the respondents that their replies were to remain anonymous and that their responses would not affect their careers, some believed that they had been singled out by a unit at headquarters for investigation.

Along with the change toward a decreased belief in the sufficiency of police legal authority there was an accompanying increase in the authoritarianism of patrolmen as measured by the mean scores on the

F-scale. The scores increased from a mean of 4.15 for a group of recruits tested just before they began training to a mean of 4.18 at the end of training to a mean of 4.31 at the end of the first year in the field. Another group of 83 patrolmen with two years' experience had a mean score of 4.46. Assuming the comparability of the above groups and a continued increase in the F-scale scores with more experience, we can hypothesize that in time the discrepancy between the police officers' attitude and the courts' thinking regarding criminal law will increase, since the authoritarian orientation is probably negatively related to an emphasis on personal rights as against property rights. We cannot explore the implications of this change rigorously at this point, but it seems likely that it is related to the police's feeling that their authority has been subverted by forces outside the department.

Table 10 indicates the officers' attitude toward the use of force in a somewhat ambiguous situation. The percentage of recruits endorsing the use of force increased between the beginning of their training (T_1) and the end of their stay in the police academy (T_2). We should note that the recruits reported informally that some differences existed among the instructors as to their orders regarding the conditions under which force should be used and the conditions determining the degree of force to be used. The major difference apparently existed between the "academic" instructors and the instructors in firearms and physical training. The latter group of instructors, primarily patrolmen, were more likely to endorse the more frequent use of force and the use of more serious force than the academic instructors, who generally were either sergeants or lieutenants. Thus

Table 10 *Responses to: "If a Patrolman Thinks He May Have to Use Force in a Situation He Should Use It Right after His Entrance into the Situation in Order to Gain the Advantage of Surprise"* (*in Per Cent*)

Time[a]	No Answer	Strongly Agree	Agree	Uncertain	Disagree	Strongly Disagree
T_1	0	6	33	22	36	3
T_2	0	8	38	13	37	4
T_3	1	8	40	10	38	3
T_4	0	6	26	18	46	4

[a] See footnote Table 8, footnote [a].

Table 11 *Responses to: "Most Officers Agree That Some Force Is Necessary and Justified When a Citizen Unjustly Insults and Curses a Police Officer."* (*in Per Cent*)

Year in Academy	Time when Tested	Strongly Agree	Agree	Uncertain	Disagree	Strongly Disagree	*N*
1961	End of training	5	33	28	28	6	(107)
	Two years in field	4	44	10	39	3	(83)
	Start of training	2	25	15	50	8	(171)
1962	End of training	3	23	18	49	7	(164)
	One year in field	1	34	16	45	4	(137)
1963	Third month of training	2	30	15	46	7	(296)
	Fourth month of training	4	31	19	43	3	(266)

some inconsistencies in the recruits' training were related to the hierarchical position of their instructors. The academic instructors adhered more closely to the expectations of the administration of the department.

We previously hypothesized that a major rationale underlying the use of force was the attempt to cope with disrespect shown to police. Westley found that disrespect for police was the most frequently mentioned justification by police for the use of force.[41] Piliavin and Briar similarly found that disrespect shown by juveniles to police often was grounds for taking juveniles into custody.[42] The patrolmen tested in the New York City Police Department do not strongly concur that disrespect shown to police provides a sufficient condition for the use of force. The responses to an item intended to measure their perception of the degree of consensus among police officers concerning the use of force against abusive citizens (Table 11) indicate that the majority of patrolmen tested at different time periods during their first two years on the force do not agree that such consensus exist. The table does indicate, however, that their field experience somewhat influenced the patrolmens' perception, the change being that more officers agreed that the group supported the use of force in the case of disrespect shown to officers.

[41] *Ibid.*

[42] I. Piliavin and S. Briar, *loc. cit.*

The faith in the use of force was also based upon considerations other than those we have just discussed. As indicated in Table 12, the majority of the patrolmen entered the department with the view that police need "more leeway and fewer restrictions on the use of force" in order to reduce the serious police problems of "tough neighborhoods." This view of the recruits was little changed at the end of their training but incraased after one year of field work to the point where 74% endoresed this view.

Another means by which force frequently is legitimated by police is the view that a patrolman's failure to accept "challenges to fight" will cause the more aggressive residents in an area to feel that they can "get away with anything" or feel they can "push the police around." The degree of agreement with this sentiment is indicated in the responses to item B in Table 11. As shown, the degree of agreement was slight at the outset of training (T_1); it increased during the training and then increased more during the first year of field experience (T_3), at the end of which the modal response was agreement with the item.

As we can see from the three tables concerning the officers' attitudes toward the use of force in situations that are legally marginal, by no means does a consensus exist among the more experienced patrol-

Table 12 *Justifications for the Use of Force (in Per Cent)*

Item	Time[a]	No Answer	Strongly Agree	Agree	Uncertain	Disagree	Strongly Disagree
A	T_1	0	14	43	23	17	3
	T_2	1	16	42	17	23	1
	T_3	0	30	44	14	12	0
	T_4	0	39	39	13	8	0
B	T_1	0	3	18	31	44	4
	T_2	0	4	26	15	47	8
	T_3	1	7	39	12	36	4
	T_4	0	12	30	14	40	4

Item A: "If patrolmen working in the tough neighborhoods had more leeway and fewer restrictions on the use of force many of the serious police problems in those neighborhoods would be greatly reduced."
Item B: "A patrolman who frequently ignores challenges to fight from citizens will probably make it harder for other patrolmen to work his post or sector."

[a] See Table 8, footnote [a].

men. The attitudes favorable to the use of force in such situations, however, are more likely to form following the academy training rather than during the training. It is apparent that the academy does not immunize the recruits against the sort of changes that academy personnel would find undesirable. The author's impression is that this is probably a consequence of the academy's failure to provide properly controlled counterarguments endorsing the opposite view from the desired one. In turn, this failure seems to be caused by a fear that discussion of beliefs or practices at variance with the position of the administration will be taken by all relevant parties as endorsement of these beliefs or practices. Whether or not this fear was justified, it seemed to have the opposite effect from that intended, in as much as the recruits later moved closer to positions seen as inappropriate by the administration of the department.[43]

RECRUIT TRAINING AND UNCERTAINTIES REGARDING POLICE PRESTIGE

As we indicated in the discussion of the recruits' backgrounds, the recruits' perception of the prestige accorded the role of the police officer by the general public was that the appointment to the force was seen as upwardly mobile. The element of prestige assigned to the role has special personal significance for each officer in that the role has what may be termed a "transcendental" character. That is, both while on duty or off, the nature of the officer's interaction with any other person is likely to be affected by his and by the other person's knowledge that he is a police officer. When recruits are told that it is a "twenty-four-hour a day job," they are unlikely to realize the full significance of the statement. Although they may know that they will be required to wear their revolvers at all times they are away from their homes, they are not likely to realize that, as happened to one recruit, their girl friend's father may not allow them to enter his house.

Nor are they likely to be aware of the number of times they will be told of the ineffective or corrupt action of other police officers by persons anxious to seek some psychological redress. They also may not realize that any purchase made by themselves or by their family members may be scrutinized by neighbors or by some investi-

[43] See P. F. Secord and C. W. Backman, *Social Psychology* (New York McGraw-Hill Book Co., 1964), for a recent review of research on the consequences of presenting counter-arguments for attitude change.

gating unit in the department as a sign that they have become corrupt and have decided to "be on the take" or to begin "shaking down" motorists, bar owners, or grocery store operators that violate the sabbath laws.

In the academy a good deal of effort was made to instill some "pride in the job." The recruits were told that the department was "over a hundred years old and proud of its tradition." Moreover, some handout material entitled *Recruit Issue Material,* which described the contemporary department as the "finest" informed the recruit that he must keep it 'the finest'." In order to do so the recruit "must be dedicated, disciplined, courageous, patient, and forebearing." Further, he "may not achieve the material rewards of other professions, but he has the greatest opportunities for spiritual satisfaction." (One wag, after reading the last quoted statement, indicated his disagreement by pointing out that the department does not have a particularly high rate of deaths in the line of duty.)

During recruit training the professionalization of police work was stressed as a realistic objective for all members of the force. Academy personnel also stressed the technology of police work and encouraged the recruits to take extra courses in police science. (Recruits received ten semester hours credit for the academy training toward a Bachelor's degree at New York City College Baruch School.)

During the training period in the academy recruits were also exposed to some work experiences both of a police nature and of a clerical and janitorial nature. The types of police work one group was exposed to were primarily traffic control, parade duty (in which officers stand alongside the parade route and maintain order among spectators), and patrol car duty with an experienced patrolmen for one eight-hour period. By far the most interesting experience for the recruits was the opportunity to observe closely the patrolmen in the patrol car. The clerical work was primarily filing of forms and work in the various offices of the academy. The other work was transporting police barriers (similar to a sawhorse) to various areas of the city and setting them up.

In general, the recruits thought that the clerical and janitorial work was somewhat inconsistent with their newly acquired status. Ninety-eight per cent of one group of 164 recruits at the end of their training indicated they felt they should have had more patrol car experience, whereas only 15% felt they should have been given more clerical work and only 7% felt they should have had more assignments involving the transportation of police barriers. Interestingly enough, only 12% felt they should have had more parade duty. Since the duty usually consists of standing in one spot and observing the spectators, they considered it boring. The reluctance of the academy personnel to have the recruits patrol with experienced patrolmen because of their fear that the recruits would be exposed to officially improper performance of duties was somewhat borne out by the experience of the above group of 164 recruits. When the recruits were asked to indicate whether the experiences they had in the field "coincided or conflicted with academy teaching," 4% indicated that their experience with traffic control conflicted, 6% indicated that parade duty conflicted, and 14% indicated that their assignment to a patrol car conflicted with what they had been taught at the academy. The last assignment, of course, was one in which the patrolmen were not so closely supervised and one in which a much broader range of types of police duties were likely to be encountered.

We indicated earlier that recruits at the beginning of their training are not likely to agree that the prestige attached to the position of patrolman has been increasing (Table 13). At the end of their training there was little change in their feeling, or much change after their first year in the field (T_3). The group of patrolmen with two years of field experience (T_4) had a slight tendency to disagree more with the statement in Table 13, than the other group but did not differ markedly. The four months of training did little to increase the officers' faith that their work was becoming more recognized by the public as having much prestige.

In this regard, two different groups of officers who had had some field experience were asked to "indicate how you think the general public feels the prestige of jobs you had before coming on to the force compares with police work." Their responses (Table 14) were

Table 13 *Changes in Responses to: "The Respect that Citizens Have for a Patrolman and His Position Has Been Steadily Increasing Over the Years (in Per Cent)*

Time[a]	No Answer	Strongly Agree	Agree	Uncertain	Disagree	Strongly Disagree
T_1	0	3	9	16	45	27
T_2	1	5	13	11	54	16
T_3	0	3	13	13	56	15
T_4	0	2	6	11	59	22

[a] See Table 8, footnote [a].

Table 14 *Prestige Seen as Assigned by the "General Public" to Jobs Police Officers Had Prior to Entering Police Work (Prestige of Past Jobs Relative to Police Work in Per Cent)*

Year in Academy	When Tested	Much Higher	Somewhat Higher	About the Same	Somewhat Lower	Much Lower	(N)[c]
1961	Start of training[a]	7	11	24	49	9	(105)
	Two years in field[b]	13	20	21	39	7	(83)
1962	Start of training[a]	2	10	27	45	16	(163)
	One year in field[b]	8	19	21	45	7	(164)

[a] See Table 6, footnote [a] for item and coding. (Some differences exist between the items given before training and after field experience.)
[b] This item is presented in the above paragraph. (The response categories in the table were presented to officers.)
The "no answer" respondents are excluded from this table.

compared with what they had indicated at the start of their training (Table 6). It seems that there was a shift toward reevaluation of their past jobs as having more prestige than indicated at the time they entered the department. Of course, the influence of the academy training cannot be inferred rigorously from this table, but it would appear that the patrolmen were again not immunized against the pressures of police work which serve to convince officers that their position does not have sufficient prestige assigned to it to facilitate their carrying out police duties. That police have somewhat high aspirations for the prestige level of police work is clear from the responses of the patrolmen with one or two years' field experience to the following: "Police work should be ranked alongside that of doctors or lawyers." Seventy-five per cent of the experienced men agreed with the statement and only 15% disagreed. Thus the problem of living with the discrepancy between the desired status and the perceived actual status of patrolman exists for the majority of officers. One manner in which the problem is resolved has been investigated by Niederhoffer in his study of the development of cynicism among police.[44]

[44] See A. Niederhoffer, *loc. cit.*

RECRUIT TRAINING AND UNCERTAINTIES REGARDING INTERPERSONAL SKILLS

The curriculum of the recruit training school in the academy has a number of class hours scheduled during which recruits were exposed to such topics as "the personal element in police work," "groups of people," "courtesy," "racial prejudice and common sense," "child development and psychology," and "the adolescent gang." These topics were covered primarily by lectures given by the academic instructors in formal class meetings. In addition, instructors often used examples drawn from their own experience with the public that dealt with interpersonal problems in the police officer's relations with the public. For the most part, any principles regarding interpersonal skills were presented either in the form of rather general prescriptions, for example, "be firm but courteous," or in the form of rules of thumb which individual instructors had evolved from their own experience in patrol work. Many of these latter prescriptions were quite ingenious, such as the recommendation that a patrolman when issuing a traffic ticket to a motorist find out whether the motorist is from the neighborhood. If the motorist was from the neighborhood, the patrolman was to indicate that he would not cite the motorist for any additional violation the officer noticed, since the motorist was from the area. If the motorist was not from the area, this fact also ostensibly served to keep the officer from issuing more than one citation. Presumably, motorists found either justification plausible because it was consonant with their desire to avoid additional citations.

The major difficulty in any attempt to transmit knowledge concerning interpersonal skills or in any attempt to improve these skills is that little exists in the way of such knowledge. This lack of knowledge is matched by the inadequacy of most measures used to improve such skills. Although laboratory studies of social interaction may yield some knowledge about a limited number of variables and relationships, the utility of such knowledge is restricted, since it must be applied in noncontrolled settings. Furthermore, there are few clear-cut and reliable methods by which one can proceed from experimental findings to the application of these findings in everyday life.

For police, the range of situations in which they must interact with citizens is at least as broad as that for any other occupation. Recruits had few, if any, opportunities to test their interpersonal skills, to develop them or to integrate them with the skills and knowledge acquired during their stay in the academy. Their first opportunity to do so was in the field after they had left the academy. In the field, unfortunately, errors were frequently irreversible and lessons learned "the hard way" were quite costly to both the officers and citizens involved.

Since the task of developing and maintaining these skills is an extremely difficult one, many academy personnel involved in the selection and training of recruits tended to treat the matter as one of having common sense or not having it. They assumed that common sense is something you have or you do not, that is, an ability that cannot be developed or taught. Common sense was also a characteristic highly valued by the patrolmen tested both in the academy and in the field. The groups at the different time periods indicated in Table 11 never had more than 7% in agreement with the statement "Well developed skills of selfdefense are more useful than common sense to a patrolman." Similarly, only 10% or less of each of the same groups tested at different times agreed that "One of the least important problems for patrolmen is that of gaining the cooperation of the public." The recruits were aware, at a general level of discourse, that their task involves some interpersonal skills in order that it be accomplished. But their judgment of the difficulty of this task varies greatly at different stages in their early careers.

The responses to the items in Table 15 show that the recruits entered the department somewhat skeptical of the degree to which patrolmen received the needed cooperation from the public (item A). Thirty-two per cent agreed, at that point, that "Patrolmen almost never receive the cooperation from the public that is needed . . ." At the end of the training period (T_2) the per cent agreeing with the statement decreased to only 18%. At the latter point, we might consider that the academy training had prepared the recruits effectively, since it is useful for patrolmen to believe that at least some of the general public will assist police in their duties. As pointed out earlier, police can be greatly assisted in a variety of ways by the general public, but it is important for them to believe in at least the possibility they can and will receive this cooperation in order for them to seek it out. After the patrolmen had completed one year in the field, however, their responses moved closer to those they gave as beginning recruits, with the per cent in agreement about the lack of cooperation even higher (46%).

A similar trend can be observed in the remaining items in Table 15. The recruits became more convinced during their training that public cooperation and assistance are not extremely rare commodities, but then shifted during their first year's field experience toward

Table 15 *Recruits' Estimates of Cooperation from Public (in Per Cent)*

Item	Time[a]	No Answer	Strongly Agree	Agree	Uncertain	Disagree	Strongly Disagree
A	T_1	0	7	25	25	39	4
	T_2	1	2	16	18	62	1
	T_3	1	9	37	12	41	1
	T_4	0	10	40	14	34	2
B	T_1	1	3	36	34	26	1
	T_2	0	3	33	24	39	1
	T_3	0	6	46	17	30	2
	T_4	0	10	51	10	30	0
C	T_1	1	2	40	33	22	2
	T_2	1	3	62	19	15	0
	T_3	1	2	42	15	37	2
	T_4	0	2	40	18	39	1
D	T_1	1	1	34	34	26	4
	T_2	0	4	41	27	21	7
	T_3	0	2	42	21	29	6
	T_4	0	1	38	22	34	5

Item A: "Patrolmen almost never receive the cooperation from the public that is needed to handle police work properly."
Item B: "It is usually quite difficult to persuade people to give patrolmen the information they need."
Item C: "The public in general is usually quite helpful to a patrolman who can use the public's help."
Item D: "Most people will try in some way to help a patrolman who is being attacked on the street."

[a] Table 8, footnote [a].

a skepticism regarding the availability of such commodities. A second group of patrolmen with two years in the field either was similar in their responses to the group with one year in the field or was even more convinced that they could not rely on much help from the public. This trend seems to be opposite to that observed in medical students by Becker and Geer, in which the students became more cynical about humanitarian values during their training in medical schools but regained their former idealism after they completed their

Table 16 *Responses to: "Respect for the Police in a Tough Neighborhood Depends on the Willingness of Patrolmen to Use Force Frequently and Effectively"* (*in Per Cent*)

Time[a]	No Answer	Strongly Agree	Agree	Uncertain	Disagree	Strongly Disagree
T_1	0	6	26	31	34	3
T_2	0	5	21	19	49	5
T_3	1	7	44	14	28	5
T_4	0	13	42	20	24	1

[a] See Table 8, footnote [a].

training.[45] As were the changes in medical students, the changes in the police recruits' attitudes can probably be seen as a function of the kinds of social support for them. Much of the support in the academy for the recruits' attitudes comes from the instructors, whereas in the field it is more likely to stem from other patrolmen and additionally from the recruits' experiences with citizens. Which of the two sources of support in the field contributed more to the change toward an increased lack of faith in public cooperation is not clear, but probably both were operative.

A related process of change occurred with regard to the belief that respect in tough neighborhoods for police is dependent on the extent to which police are willing to use force. (See Table 16.) At the end of their training (T_2), the recruits are more likely to disagree with the position that force serves as a solution to the problem of respect for police than they were at the beginning of their training (T_1). However, following their first year in the field, they moved in the opposite direction to a point where twice as large a percentage of patrolmen (51%) agreed with the statement as the percentage (26%) at the end of the recruit training. The group of patrolmen with two years in the field tended slightly to be in even more agreement with the statement.

The implications of the changes shown in Tables 15 and 16 for the interpersonal tactic of *information gathering* would seem to be in the negative direction. That is, an increased reliance on the use of force and a lack of trust in the public's cooperation and assistance would create difficulties for patrolmen in acquiring the necessary in-

[45] H. S. Becker and B. Geer, "The Fate of Idealism in Medical School," *American Sociological Review*, Vol. 23 (1958), pp. 50–6.

formation on which to base a decision concerning the handling of individuals or groups of citizens. If patrolmen believe they are not likely to receive help, they would presumably be less likely to seek help in gathering information. Similarly, if they rely heavily on force, they may be able to gather information, but its reliability is that much more suspect than information received without the use of force.

The increases in the F-Scale scores mentioned earlier should also be negatively related to the ability of the patrolmen to do interpersonal testing, since one distinguishing characteristic of the authoritarian personality is the tendency to ignore or not perceive a wide range of differences among people. This would be particularly true in the case where the differences may be related to status or to such perceived attributes as respect for law and order. Patrolmen must interact with many persons from the lower socio-economic levels whose orientation toward the legal system is seen by the patrolmen as at variance with the proper level of respect due the law. These perceived disparities between their own and the citizens' status levels and orientations toward the legal system would create some difficulty for patrolmen who score high on the F-Scale with regard to their perception of the unique values or needs of such individual citizens. For such patrolmen, the salience of the above differences between themselves and citizens would probably obviate the necessity for information gathering prior to their making a decision about how to gain the citizen's compliance.

Even though new patrolmen may face some difficulties in taking the role of citizens with whom they will interact, they seem to be quite aware of the general necessity for their *clarification of expectations*. A group of 266 recruits at the end of their training were similar to 221 patrolmen with one or two years in the field in their distribution of responses to the following: "Generally, police make things much easier to handle if they immediately make clear to people why they were called to the scene." Only 10% of each group disagreed with the statement. The two groups similarly agreed that "A patrolman's authority is not weakened by his giving citizens a few alternative ways in which they can cooperate with the patrolman." (Only 8% in each group disagreed with the statement.)

A slight difference existed between the recruit and experienced groups with regard to the public's understanding of laws which patrolmen enforce. The experienced patrolmen, with one and two years in the field, were somewhat more likely to feel that the public understands the laws patrolmen enforce than were the recruits tested at the end of their training. This difference follows from the experienced patrolmen's increased familiarity with laws, if we assume that they project their own familiarity onto the general public and that recruits are more likely to be aware of the difference between a police officer's understanding and the public's understanding of legal matters because of their recent status as part of the public. (See Table 17.)

There are few differences between the experienced group and the group of recruits tested at the end of their training in regard to some hypothesized correlates of the interpersonal tactic of *exploiting or* utilizing the values of citizens. As seen in Table 18, the majority in each group indicated agreement with the prescription that police should not altercast citizens into a criminal role (item A). This attitude would obviate some of the many difficulties for police officers in handling violators that result from the officers' failure to create or reestablish the conditions in which a citizen's normal values are operative and can hence be utilized by the officers in gaining compliance.

Both groups are also similar in their disagreement with the proposition that citizens' resentment of police causes them to withold needed information (item B). The attitude that citizens resent police in general is probably one that causes individual officers to interact in a defensive manner with citizens. Such interaction would make it difficult for the officer to devise an approach which recognizes the values of citizens and utilizes them. Thus, in at least the respects measured

Table 17 *Patrolmen's View of Public Understanding of Laws* (*in Per Cent*)

Item	Group	No Answer	Strongly Agree	Agree	Uncertain	Disagree	Strongly Disagree
A	Recruits	0	6	50	18	25	1
	Experienced patrolmen	1	5	40	11	41	2
B	Recruits	1	4	48	19	27	3
	Experienced patrolmen	0	4	67	8	20	1

Item A: "Few people really understand the laws that police must enforce."
Item B: "Most citizens seem to have a pretty good working knowledge of their legal rights and obligations."

Table 18 *Correlates of Exploiting or Utilizing Values: Facilitators (in Per Cent)*

Item	Group	No Answer	Strongly Agree	Agree	Uncertain	Disagree	Strongly Disagree
A	Recruits	0	5	62	17	16	0
	Experienced patrolmen	1	2	55	15	26	1
B	Recruits	0	1	12	31	55	1
	Experienced patrolmen	0	0	16	17	65	2

Item A: "A patrolman generally should not try to make a person who has violated some law feel like a criminal."
Item B: "Complainants or witnesses don't like to give all the necessary information to police chiefly because they resent police in general."

by the items in Table 18, police are prepared to deal with the problem of utilizing the values of citizens.

In other respects the attitudes of the officers do not seem so well prepare for the task of utilizing the values of citizens. Again, the groups of experienced and recruit patrolmen were similar in their responses to the items in Table 19. There was a marked agreement with the statement that police expectations are "only natural" (item A). One of the more striking features of the police officer's role, however, is that not only are many of his own actions such that if he were not a policeman his actions would be met by a strong societal reaction, but also his requests for compliance from citizens often involve punitive consequences for the citizens, who generally do not see themselves as deserving of these consequences, particularly at the time the officer makes the request. A police officer's failure to recognize the extraordinary nature of his expectations would present certain problems for him in attempting to work with or through the values of citizens with whom he interacts.

Similarly, a patrolman who fails to see the utility of manifestly treating an offender as law-abiding probably experiences some difficulty in attemping to utilize the values of an offender in gaining compliance. The responses to item B in Table 19 would seem to contradict the responses to item A in Table 18 in that the responses in Table 19 indicate a lack of agreement that officers should generally make

Table 19 *Correlates of Exploiting or Utilizing Values: Inhibitors (in Per Cent)*

Item	Group	No Answer	Strongly Agree	Agree	Uncertain	Disagree	Strongly Disagree
A	Recruits	0	5	70	14	11	0
	Experienced patrolmen	0	3	80	11	6	0
B	Recruits	0	3	36	30	30	1
	Experienced patrolmen	0	2	33	20	42	3
C	Recruits	0	1	38	31	28	2
	Experienced patrolmen	0	2	38	28	31	1

Item A: "The things that patrolmen want citizens to do in accordance with the law are only natural."
Item B: "A patrolman should generally try to make offenders feel as though they were really law-abiding but had just made this one mistake."
Item C: "A patrolman can be pretty sure he will gain compliance from a person who appears to be somewhat frightened of the patrolman."

the effort to induce this sense of being law-abiding. The two items differ, of course, regarding the degree to which officers should take steps to avoid giving citizens the impression the officers consider them to be criminals. Hence, item B in Table 19 may not be an adequate measure of beliefs concerning the utility of the tactic of attempting to "normalize" the situation of the citizen in order that his usual values be operative. Further, the tactic requires that the values of the citizen be congruent in some sense with the values implicit in the relevant law being enforced. As Miller points out, the values of members of the lower classes conflict in a number of dimensions with middle-class values and particularly in a way that would create problems for police officers.[46]

The final problem for officers in using the values of citizens stems from their failure to reject the notion that fear of an officer implies compliance on a citizen's part (item C in Table 19). Again, both

[46] W. B. Miller, "Lower Class Culture as a Generating Milieu of Gang Delinquency," *Journal of Social Issues*, Vol. 14 (1958).

groups showed a similar tendency to be slightly more in agreement with the statement that a citizen's frightened appearance implies his compliance. That fear is an unstable solution to the problem of gaining compliance has been shown in a number of research settings. Strict reliance on fear, although not necessarily implied by agreement with item C, should then create a rather unstable set of relations between police and public. Nevertheless, some police conceive of the police officer's role as requiring behavior aimed at inducing fear in citizens. The police objection to abolition of the death penalty rests to a great extent on this conception of the role. Similarly, it seems that the failure to develop a nonlethal alternative to the police revolver can be traced to the reluctance of police to give up what they perceive as an essential role component as well as a necessary deterrent. The legal basis on which the use of revolvers rests, however, is that of simply stopping someone from committing a serious crime or escaping from apprehension. Again, reliance on fear is a tactic that obviates the utilization of values because of the stress level induced in the citizen. The relationship between stress levels and rationality (taken here to refer to behavior consistent with the individual citizen's values) has clearly been shown to become negative with increases in stress beyond a critical point.[47]

The interpersonal skills characterized as involving both a decisive and impersonal *presentation of self* apparently are affected to some extent by the academy training program. As shown in Table 12, during training recruits increased their degree of agreement with the proposition (item B) that a patrolman's ignoring of challenges from citizens to fight creates a problem for other patrolmen in the area. The same group further increased its agreement with the statement during the first year of field experience. This attitude would not serve to assist patrolmen in maintaining the appearance of emotional distance that is particularly important in situations in which officers take punitive action. That is, by responding to challenges of this sort the officer is likely to appear to be acting on his own and not as a representative of the law. Hence, his requests for compliance may be rejected by a citizen on the grounds that no personal obligations exist between himself and the officer.

A similar change can be discerned in Table 11, in which the agreement slightly increased over time for three groups of patrolmen that "Most officers agree that some force is necessary and justified when

[47] See C. E. Osgood, *An Alternative to War or Surrender*, (Urbana, Illini Books, 1962), for an excellent and succinct discussion of this relationship applied to military and political relations among hostile nations.

a citizen unjustly insults the curses a police officer." Patrolmen apparently come to perceive more support from their fellow officers for actions which are not consistent with the need for police impersonality. As indicated earlier, the changes primarily take place during assignment to the field. There was little change during recruit training in regard to the recruits' perception of consensus regarding the use of force under such conditions. The later increases probably reflect, to some extent, the increasing identification of the patrolman with his role as well as an increasing familiarity with a wider range of types of officers and police behavior.

The patrolmen tested after some field experience indicate a marked awareness of the value of an impersonal demeanor when attempting to handle a noncriminal dispute. As shown in Table 20 there is an unusually high degree of agreement with item A regarding the value of not appearing to take sides in such disputes. It would appear that the power problems of coalition formation in the triad are well known to police, who are required to handle disputes between husband and wife, landlord and tenant, merchant and customer, etc.

The patrolmen show less consensus on the matter of maintaining

Table 20 *Correlates of Impersonal Presentation of Self (in Per Cent)*

Item	Time[a]	No Answer	Strongly Agree	Agree	Uncertain	Disagree	Strongly Disagree
A	T_3	0	26	69	0	4	0
	T_4	0	20	71	1	7	0
B	T_3	0	0	28	19	52	2
	T_4	0	0	37	8	54	1
C	T_3	0	2	39	12	47	1
	T_4	0	0	44	17	36	3

Item A: "A patrolman should invariably avoid appearing to take any side in a dispute where no crime has been committed."
Item B: "Patrolmen generally will appear less authoritative if they tell a citizen that a court has the final say about the citizen's case."
Item C: "When patrolmen indicate they will use the force necessary to gain compliance from a citizen, they are helped considerably if the citizen thinks they are getting angry."

[a] See Table 8, footnote [a].

an impersonal appearance through pointing to the courts as having "the final say" and hence indirectly pointing to their function as delimited or delineated and somewhat independent of their personal convictions regarding a "citizen's case," (item B). Although a majority in each group indicated disagreement that a patrolman loses some authority by such a tactic, the majorities are slim. Patrolmen in agreement with this item presumably are less likely to use the alternative, for example, in interaction with a motorist who disagrees with the patrolman that any traffic violation occurred, of indicating that the citizen can contest the officer's decision and that the officer considers it proper for the citizen to do so. This action need not be supported by a lecture on the virtues of the democratic state or the adversary system in American courts. Nor would the well-worn "tell it to the judge" seem appropriate. If appropriately used, the tactic can help prevent a citizen from thinking that the patrolman has a personal interest in "getting" the citizen.

The third item (item C) in Table 20 was constructed as a measure of the extent to which patrolmen feel that the appearance of emotional involvement on their part assists them in situations in which some punitive action has been presented as likely. The patrolmen in each group were fairly evenly split between agreement and disagreement that patrolmen "are helped considerably" by an appearance of anger in such situations. A significant number of patrolmen assumed that the credibility of the threat of force depended on their appearing angry. The difficulty with this assumption is that anger reduces the perceived impersonality of the officer and consequently places him in a position where he is likely to be seen as personally competing with a citizen. This perceived personal competition, in turn, implies a different set of rules governing the patrolman-citizen interaction. These rules allow for the exchange of punitive actions.

The appearance of anger has the further potential disadvantage of reducing the decisive appearance of the officer, inasmuch as emotion often implies an ambivalent state. Hence, the risks of using an angry appearance to support the credibility of a threat are great enough so that the tactic can be considered useful only under carefully defined conditions. Data are not available on the degree of agreement that the patrolmen might have given this item at the start or at the completion of their training. Personal observation of interaction between some academy personnel and the recruits, however, indicated that the recruits were not without police role models in which the association between an appearance of anger and punitive action occurred.

RECRUIT TRAINING AND UNCERTAINTIES FROM ORGANIZATIONAL SOURCES

As indicated in the section concerned with background characteristics of police officers, recruits were exposed to some of the *semimilitary aspects of police work* in the selection process. Prior to their appointment they had undergone a character investigation, in which the sincerity of their motives or the truth of information they had given may have been openly questioned by an investigator. It is in the selection process that the potential recruit also learns that "all doubts are to be resolved in favor of the department"; that is, unless the appropriate police personnel are completely satisfied, the applicant is to be disapproved as a candidate for the position of patrolman.

Once the candidate enters the department, he is immediately presented with information that supports the ascendancy of the organization over the individual. On the first page of the first lesson plan used by academy instructors, the introduction to the hour lecture, "Note Taking and Study," ends with the following: "What you dont' learn, or principles which you fail to accept may result in improper performance of police duty and possibly may also lead to your appearance as a defendant in a department trial."

The second hour of academic lectures reviewed a number of rules of the police academy and of the department in general. The introduction to the hour ends with the following: "Your compliance with these rules will go a long way in helping your first steps toward a successful career in this department." In the second hour the recruit is referred to the handout material entitled *Recruit Issue Material.* This material covers a number of areas in the training program and also contains nine pages of 117 rules and regulations of the Police Academy Recruit Training School. The rules and regulations vary greatly with regard to their specificity, from using a specific entrance to the building to one rather comprehensive rule: "Conduct, disorder or neglect prejudicial to good order, efficiency or discipline, whether or not specifically mentioned in the Rules and Procedures, including cowardice or making a false statement is prohibited."

The recruit, on or off duty, is further explicitly enjoined from drinking "intoxicants at any time to an extent making him unfit for duty," from entering "at any time, any premises licensed for 'on-premises consumption of alcoholic beverages except when necessary in the performance of police duty'," and while on the street in uniform, from eating, smoking, chewing gum or tobacco, reading newspapers or other material, running, loitering, using vile or indecent language, and "expectorating." While at home ("the official residence") the recruit is expected not to be absent "between midnight and 6:00 A.M. except when necessary in the performance of police duty or while expeditiously traveling to or from an assigned duty, or with permission of the Commanding Officer, Police Academy."

The Introduction to the *Recruit Issue Material* ends with a paragraph containing the following:

> . . . Of necessity, our discipline is severe and our program is rigorous. You will be confronted with many regulations. You may not understand the purpose of each rule or requirement, but each is designed with a purpose and tested by time. . . . There is no easy way. . . . The man who cooperates, works with the Academy, will find his training period most rewarding. The shirkers will be eliminated.

The comprehensive nature of his commitent to the police force and the potentially punitive consequences of his failure to fulfill any aspect of that commitment are thus made clear early in his training to the incoming recruit. He may find, for example, that his failure to report immediately a sickness that keeps him from attending classes in the morning results in a police patrol car calling on his home in the afternoon. He may also find that the character investigation continues on during his stay in the academy and that his sexual behavior as a bachelor has become a matter of departmental concern.

For the most part, recruits do not appear to evaluate negatively the rather close supervision and rather large number of rules and regulations in the academy. As might be predicted on the basis of their past work experiences and on the basis of their F-scale scores, they tend not to find the atmosphere repressive or overly restrictive. As was indicated earlier in Table 7, one group of 171 recruits in their first week of training perceived supervision throughout the department as close and, further, did not evaluate this as problematic. The recruits' perception of supervision throughout the department as close or strict probably assists them in their adjustment to the semimilitary conditions of the academy.

One other factor that may account for the recruits' positive evaluation of the dominant supervisory style is the belief that supervisors are obligated not only to observe patrolmen closely but also to give patrolmen whatever assistance they can. The responses in Table 21 are indicative of the extent to which patrolmen see their supervisors as obligated to exchange assistance for the patrolmen's positive evaluation of close supervision and the patrolmen's complaint behavior implied by this evaluation. The recruits also did not disagree that the assistance is forthcoming from supervisors, as indicated by their responses to item C in Table 21. After some experience in the field, however, the patrolmen were less likely to agree that their supervisors "are extremely helpful toward patrolmen." By far the larger number still agreed (T_3 and T_4) with the statement, but a trend away from endorsement of this item can be discerned.

As shown in Table 21 the patrolmen changed little with respect to their agreement that supervisors carry heavy obligations to patrolmen (items A and B). We can hypothesize that an imbalance between the perceived obligations of supervisors to patrolmen and the perceived extent to which supervisors fulfill these obligations exists for the experienced patrolmen. The manner in which this imbalance is

Table 21 *Patrolmen's View of Their Supervisors' Obligations (in Per Cent)*

Item	Time[a]	No Answer	Strongly Agree	Agree	Uncertain	Disagree	Strongly Disagree
A	T_1	0	23	60	16	1	0
	T_2	0	24	62	11	2	1
	T_3	1	26	63	5	4	1
	T_4	0	25	63	6	6	0
B	T_1	0	17	56	22	4	1
	T_2	0	17	65	11	6	1
	T_3	0	17	63	16	4	0
	T_4	0	18	63	11	7	1
C	T_1	0	12	54	31	3	0
	T_2	1	8	56	29	5	1
	T_3	2	6	47	23	18	4
	T_4	0	4	40	35	19	2

Item A: "A patrolman is officially entitled to all the help he needs from his supervisors."
Item B: "Supervisors are expected to give help without any reservations to patrolmen who need help with police problems."
Item C: "Supervisors in the police department are extremely helpful toward patrolmen."

[a] See Table 8, footnote [a].

resolved cannot be rigorously identified, but it seems to consist, in part, of a restructuring of the patrolmen's view of supervisors. The restructuring often takes the form of viewing supervisors as somehow personally lacking in courage or as failing to be hierarchically independent of higher ranking supervisors. This latter view probably underlies the small degree of disagreement (17%) on part of the experienced patrolmen with a statement that "Police supervisors usually go along with each other when one wants to take disciplinary action against a patrolman."

The changes in the general views of patrolmen regarding the disciplinary or punitive practices and policies of the department are somewhat more marked than their view of the closeness of supervision. The patrolmen, as recruits, tended to see the discipline to which they were exposed in the academy as fair, impartially administered, effective, and necessary for the organization. In a combined group of 271 recruits tested at the end of their training, 49 (18%) had received one or more "delinquencies" during their stay at the academy. The delinquencies were officially recorded violations of academy and department rules and regulations. Recruits were given a hearing or trial, with academy personnel presiding, and if found guilty were usually given extra work assignments as punishment. The separate responses of the two combined groups are listed in Table 22 and show the extent to which the recruits endorsed the general policy of discipline.

Their endorsement of the general policy is not quite matched, however, by their endorsement of the administration of delinquencies nor by their belief in the effectiveness of the delinquencies. Although more than three-fourths of the recruits agree that the rules and regulations are worthwhile (item D) and that delinquencies are necessary for organizational order (item E), only one-half or less agreed that the delinquencies were fair, deserved, and effective (items A, B, and C respectively.) It is the author's impression that the discrepancy between the level of agreement with the general policy and the level of agreement concerning the propriety of implementing the policy of discipline was associated with a process of "personalizing" the disciplinary system similar to the process previously mentioned. That is, as the recruits progressed through their training they became more likely to account for the delinquencies given to recruits by pointing to personal characteristics of the police superior officer who charged a recruit with a violation of rules and regulations. Some instructors, for example, came to be known as "petty" and others as "hairy" (punitive). Still, the majority of the recruits did not come to see

Table 22 *Recruits' Perception of Academy Disciplinary System (in Per Cent)*

Item	Group	No Answer	Strongly Agree	Agree	Uncertain	Disagree	Strongly Disagree	(*N*)
A	1960	16	9	41	22	5	7	(107)
B	1961	4	10	35	26	20	6	(164)
C	1961	4	3	43	34	15	4	(164)
D	1961	2	9	68	12	8	1	(164)
E	1961	2	12	64	7	13	2	(164)

Item A: "Do you agree that the delinquencies and complaints given to your company were fair?"
Item B: "Do you agree that only the recruits who most deserved delinquencies were the ones who received them?"
Item C: "Do you agree that the delinquencies had the effect the instructors wanted on those who received them?"
Item D: "Do you agree that the rules and regulations which serve as a basis for delinquencies are worthwhile?"
Item E: "Do you agree that delinquencies are necessary in order to keep recruits behavior in line with the rules and regulations?"

the administration of discipline in these personalized terms during their training.

During the training period the recruits apparently also changed their view of the extent to which punitive techniques are utilized by supervisors in the field. A slight trend can be discerned in Table 23 toward a view of supervision as less punitive than the view expressed at the beginning of the recruit training. At the end of the training period, the percentage of recruits in disagreement with the statement that police supervisors use punishment as their main method of ensuring effective performance (item A) rose to 53% from an initial 35% at the outset of training. Similarly, more recruits disagreed at the end of their training that patrolmen frequently are found guilty of rule violations and severely punished (item B) than at the beginning of their training. After one year in the field, however, (T_3), the group returned to a view closer to their view at the beginning of training. A second group of patrolmen (T_4) with two years in the field tended to perceive their supervisors as even more punitive.

The 221 patrolmen with field experience whose responses are listed in Table 23 actually received a reported total of eight complaints (officially recorded violations of rules), four of which were given

Table 23 *Perception of Field Supervisors' Punitive Tactics (in Per Cent)*

Item	Time[a]	No Answer	Strongly Agree	Agree	Uncertain	Disagree	Strongly Disagree
A	T_1	1	8	30	25	29	6
	T_2	1	5	25	16	46	7
	T_3	0	10	29	14	44	3
	T_4	0	12	42	11	31	4
B	T_1	0	7	13	26	43	11
	T_2	0	3	15	18	53	12
	T_3	1	9	21	18	41	10
	T_4	1	11	27	18	35	8

Item A: "The main method used by supervisors to keep their men working properly is that of punishment for ineffective performance."
Item B: "Patrolmen frequently are found guilty of violating departmental rules and procedures and are consequently penalized severely."

[a] See Table 8, footnote [a].

to the group of 83 patrolmen with two years in the field. No individual patrolman in either experienced group received more than one complaint. On the other hand, there are twenty-two reported instances in which patrolmen in these two groups were given departmental recognition (medals officially given for acts of heorism and bravery as well as for "good collars," that is, worthwhile arrests of persons who have committed serious crimes where the arrest may have required some ingenuity on the part of the patrolman).

Additionally, six patrolman in the two groups reported they had received civilian complaints. These were primarily complaints from citizens alleging police brutality and abusiveness. None of the complaints were reported as leading to a verdict of guilty by the Civilian Complaint Review Board, a hearing board made up of civilian and uniformed personnel in the department. It is interesting to note that the experienced patrolmen generally considered the departmental handling of the civilian complaints less fair than the handling of complaints issued by police supervisors. In Table 24 we can see the relative degree to which the handling of civilian complaints (item A) and the administration of departmental complaints (item B) met the standards of fairness held by patrolmen. The handling of civilian

Table 24 *Perceived Fairness of Departmental Handling of "Complaints" and Departmental Awards (in Per Cent)*

Item	Group[a]	No Answer	Very Fair	Somewhat Fair	Don't Know	Somewhat Unfair	Very Unfair
A	1961	2	8	6	21	38	25
	1962	0	6	8	36	25	24
B	1961	0	5	18	33	31	13
	1962	0	7	17	31	27	18
C	1961	1	8	39	30	15	6
	1962	1	11	25	50	12	1

Item A: "In general, how do you feel about the fairness of the department's handling of civilian complaints?"
Item B: "In general, how do you feel about the fairness of disciplinary action in the department?"
Item C: "In general, how do you feel about the fairness of departmental recognition?"

[a] The groups are identified by year of graduation from the academy. The 1961 group had two years in the field (N = 84) and the 1962 group had one year in the field (N = 137).

complaints was seen as fair by only 14% in each group, whereas departmental complaints were seen as fair by a slightly larger percentage. The responses of the two groups are almost identical regarding departmental complaints, but the more experienced group held somewhat stronger negative attitudes than did the less experienced group concerning civilian complaints. In general, both groups justified their stand by indicating that the investigation by the department of civilian complaints was either biased in favor of the civilian's position or inadequate.

In contrast, both groups were more favorably inclined toward the fairness of the system of departmental awards (item C). The less experienced group, however, seems to have witheld judgment more so than the group with two years in the field, since 50% of the former group indicated they did not know how to rank the system. This would appear to follow from the nature of their field experience relative to that of the group with two years. The less experienced men were less likely to find themselves in situations in which they would be required to show bravery or heroism, as they were less likely to patrol in cars. Foot patrolman were less likely to be summoned in an emergency because of the ease and rapidity of establishing communications with the patrolmen in radio cars. Therefore, they were less often considered for an award.

The patrolmens' evaluations of more specific aspects of the disciplinary system in the field may help to clarify their feelings. The experienced patrolmen were asked to evaluate the practice of having outside supervisors or "shoe-flies" observe the men. These supervisors were police captains not assigned to a specific precinct who were perceived by patrolmen primarily as punitive agents. The practice seemed potentially quite useful in that it relieved the supervisors of a given unit somewhat from having to take punitive action against patrolmen with whom they worked. It was felt that in this way the supervisors and patrolmen in a given unit would function more effectively as a team.

As indicated by their responses to items A and B in Table 25, the patrolmen show little sympathy with this solution. Only 7% of each group agreed that the system of outside supervision serves effectively as such a solution. Among the reasons indicated earlier for their dislike of such a system was the feeling on the part of patrolmen that these outside supervisors were rated on the basis of the number of complaints they issued to patrolmen (something akin to the "quota system" citizens see as operative in the issuance of traffic tickets). A related reason for the objections by patrolmen to the system of outside supervision was their belief that complaints given by these supervisors were based on isolated instances of violations of departmental rules rather than on a patrolman's total performance. The responses to item B in Table 25, in which only 5% of each group disagreed with this sentiment, indicate the extent to which patrolmen shared this view of the outside supervisors' administration of discipline.

The patrolmen further saw the general system of departmental discipline as dysfunctional in the sense that being given a complaint often leads to a withdrawal on the part of a patrolman from his duties (items C and D). In each group a slightly larger percentage of patrolmen agree than disagree with the belief that patrolmen become "too cautious" after receiving a complaint, and in both groups there is marked agreement that disciplining a patrolman usually results in his becoming a "less active cop." This shared feeling regarding the dysfunctional results of punishment is somewhat substantiated elsewhere, where it has been shown to be a common consequence

Table 25 *Evaluation by Experienced Patrolmen of Discipline in the Field (in Per Cent)*

Item	Group[a]	No Answer	Strongly Agree	Agree	Uncertain	Disagree	Strongly Disagree
A	1961	1	0	7	11	35	46
	1962	0	0	7	11	35	47
B	1961	0	35	45	15	1	4
	1962	0	29	47	18	5	0
C	1961	0	6	32	25	30	7
	1962	0	6	34	29	26	5
D	1961	0	27	35	26	10	2
	1962	0	12	38	29	19	2
E	1961	0	11	21	7	54	7
	1962	0	7	21	7	54	11

Item A: "The system of outside supervision (shoo-flies) seems to be a good solution to the problem of discipline."
Item B: "Outside supervisors rarely take into consideration the past record of a patrolman."
Item C: "More often than not, a patrolman becomes too cautious after getting a complaint."
Item D: "Disciplining a patrolman usually has the effect of making him a less active cop."
Item E: "Most patrolmen spend the major part of their tours watching for supervisors."

[a] See Table 24, footnote [a].

in laboratory studies involving the use of punishment.[48] The nature of the patrolman's role is such that if he is not appropriately motivated, his actions may become quite ineffective because he must of necessity often handle threatening and distasteful situations often without assistance from either supervisors or other patrolmen.

One further point may be made about the disciplinary system. It appeared to the author that the system often engendered more concern on the part of patrolmen with what their supervisors were up

[48] See E. R. Hilgard, *Theories of Learning,* (New York, Appleton-Century, Crofts, 1956), esp. pp. 112–3.

to than concern with the problems of the citizenry. A strongly worded item (item E) was presented to the patrolmen and produced a disagreement on the part of approximately two-thirds of the respondents. Twenty-nine per cent of the group showed some agreement that "*most* patrolmen spend the *major* part of their tours watching for supervisors." In view of the strong wording of the item, this percentage of agreement is somewhat high. Whether or not the patrolmen were accurately reporting the practices of most patrolmen, their perception of the disciplinary system and its effects on the patrolman rather clearly indicates an unfavorable view. We might interpret this attitude as a function of a perceived discrepancy between the patrolmen's "investment" (in terms of experience in the field) and a form of supervision seen as inappropriate or as appropriate only for "rookies."[49] The phenomenon of police inactivity thus is not only a fear of punishment but also a result of a perceived failure of the department to honor its end of the exchange. At the same time, supervisors probably impute a more voluntaristic set of motives to more experienced patrolmen who violate rules and regulations, since experience implies an increased awareness or knowledge of these rules. This voluntaristic view of behavior, by the same token, is probably used by patrolmen in viewing their supervisors. Given the liklihood of behavior being viewed as voluntaristic, we can expect that much of the interaction between supervisors and patrolmen will conform to the characteristics of a "punishment-centered bureaucracy."[50]

As pointed out previously, the recruits felt that both the rules of the academy and the rules and regulations of the department contained in the departmental handbook, ***Rules and Procedures,*** are necessary and proper. In Table 22, recruits at the end of their training indicated their support of the rules and regulations as a basis for punitive action against recruits. Similarly, they believed that conformity to the rules and regulations required the system of delinquencies.

In response to an item asking the same sample of recruits to rank their study materials with regard to "how useful they will be in the field," the *Rules and Procedures* was ranked the most useful over lecture notes, the penal code, the code of criminal procedures, and

[49] See G. C. Homans, *Social Behavior* (New York, Harcourt, Brace and World, 1961), esp. pp. 75–8 and Chap. 12, "Justice," for a discussion of the manner in which a person's investments in an interaction or organization influences the manner in which he perceives his "costs" of interaction or membership in an organization.

[50] See A. W. Gouldner, *loc. cit.*, and also G. Nettler, *loc. cit.*, regarding the relationship between punitiveness and a voluntaristic view of deviance.

other publications having to do with traffic law and the administrative and health codes. The question of the particular utility of the handbook is interesting, since there was a high level of *disagreement* (69%) with the statement that "patrolmen who rely entirely on the *Rules and Procedures* of the department are probably excellent police officers." Another group of 107 recruits earlier tested at the end of their training responded similarly to the following: "If a patrolman relied entirely on the *Rules and Procedures* of the department to do his work, he probably would be: a terrible police officer (36%); an average police officer (19%); a good police officer (33%); an excellent police officer (12%)."

The importance of the *Rules and Procedures* to the patrolmen apparently then did not stem from their belief that conformity to its provisions ensured adequate or outstanding performance—more likely from its punishment—legitimating function, as delineated by Gouldner.[51] Although there are no data directly bearing on this point, the recruits were probably quite concerned with knowing the rules and regulations, since 90% of the 1962 graduates agreed that "any violation of the rules and regulations of the department can be the basis for disciplinary action against patrolmen." Knowledge of the rules and regulations, if the above interpretation is accurate, would then protect a patrolman in two ways. He would be more likely to avoid violating a rule (when the violation was detectible, at least), and he would also be better prepared to defend himself against what he might perceive as the arbitrary use of authority by a supervisor. Nevertheless, the patrolmen did not see many situations in which they could or should refuse to obey an order from a superior. Only 10% of the same group agreed that "there are quite a few situations in which patrolmen are not officially required to obey orders from superior officers." Similarly, only 10% disagreed that "generally, it is a wise policy for a patrolman to do almost anything a superior officer orders."

After the recruits have had some field experience they appear still to remember the phrase in the introduction to the *Rules and Procedures*, since approximately three-quarters of each experienced group agreed that any violation of rules may provide a supervisor with a basis for some punitive action (item A in Table 26). In this connection increasing experience had inclined the patrolmen with two years in the field to agree less that the *Rules and Procedures* is meant as a "guide" for patrolmen (item B). Sixty-seven per cent of the patrolmen with only one year in the field (the 1962 group) agreed

[51] A. W. Gouldner, *op. cit.*, pp. 168–72.

Table 26 *Rules and Procedures as Seen by Experienced Patrolmen (in Per Cent)*

Item	Group[a]	No Answer	Strongly Agree	Agree	Uncertain	Disagree	Strongly Disagree
A	1961	1	23	54	9	12	1
	1962	2	21	55	4	7	1
B	1961	0	8	43	13	25	11
	1962	0	8	59	7	21	5
C	1961	0	21	60	7	12	0
	1962	0	22	58	9	10	1
D	1961	0	10	45	8	35	2
	1962	1	4	36	15	42	2
E	1961	0	2	53	14	29	2
	1962	0	3	64	15	16	2

Item A: "Any violation of the rules and regulations of the department can be the basis for disciplinary action against patrolmen."
Item B: "The *Rules and Procedures* is meant to be a guide for patrolmen and not something to be followed to the letter."
Item C: "It is impossible to always follow the *Rules and Procedures* to the letter and still do an efficient job in police work."
Item D: "A patrolman, for his own good, should never deviate from the provisions contained in the *Rules and Procedures*."
Item E: "Most supervisors are careful to fit the *Rules and Procedures* to the situation rather than insisting the *Rules and Procedures* have to be followed regardless of the situation."

[a] See Table 24, footnote [a].

with the item, whereas 51% of the men with two years showed agreement. Both groups, however, show the same rather high level of agreement that efficient police work would be impossible if an officer were to follow the *Rules and Procedures* to the letter (item C).

It is interesting to note, in view of the agreement that efficient police work cannot be accomplished by adhering to the letter of the *Rules and Procedures,* that the majority (55%) of the men with two years in the field agree that a patrolman, "for his own good," should adhere closely to the *Rules and Procedures* (item D). A smaller percentage (40%) of the men with one year in the field agreed with this item. A smaller percentage (18%) of this last group also showed disagreement with the statement that supervisors do, in fact, use the *Rules and Procedures* as something more akin to a guide (item E). Thirty-one per cent of the more experienced group indicated disagreement with this item.

Thus, adherance to the *Rules and Procedures* is probably a function of the extent to which patrolmen believe this adherance serves to protect their careers as well as a function of their perception that the supervisors are rule-bound. Since this adherance conflicts with the patrolmen's feelings about what is effective police work, we might expect that the patrolmen who experience this conflict will find few intrinsic satisfactions in their work.

The responses to items intended to measure the officers' perception of the intrinsic satisfactions of a *career* in police work are presented in Table 27 and indicate the extent to which the experienced patrolmen perceive their work as intrinsically satisfying. Both groups of patrolmen are split almost equally with regard to whether the intrinsic satisfactions balance off the dissatisfactions associated with police work (item A). There is more agreement within both groups that a recruit's expectations that the work will be intrinsically satisfying are unrealistic (item B) and even more agreement that the economic

Table 27 *Perceived Intrinsic Satisfactions in Police Work (in Per Cent)*

Item	Group[a]	No Answer	Strongly Agree	Agree	Uncertain	Disagree	Strongly Disagree
A	1961	1	2	47	6	34	10
	1962	0	4	40	16	35	5
B	1961	0	12	41	18	29	0
	1962	0	7	48	20	24	1
C	1961	0	20	53	9	17	1
	1962	0	18	44	17	20	1

Item A: "All in all, there are enough satisfactions just in performing police duties to make up for the headaches of the job."
Item B: "A recruit who thinks he is going to get much personal satisfaction just from performing police duties is due for a rude awakening."
Item C: "It would be difficult to keep most patrolmen on the job if it weren't for the salary and other benefits connected with the job."

[a] See Table 24, footnote [a].

benefits of the work are necessary to keep patrolmen "on the job" (item C).

Another indication of the extent to which the patrolmen are satisfied with the work is the anticipated length of time they expect to remain in the department. Two groups of respondents were asked in 1961 and 1962 at the outset of their training how long they expected to stay on the force. They were asked the same question again in 1963 after one group completed two years and the other one year in the field. Their responses in Table 28 show a tendency for both groups to foreshorten their anticipated stay in the department after completing their training and some experience in the field.

Similarly, the level of aspiration of the patrolmen both with regard to promotion to higher ranks and with regard to assignment to the detective division or to other desired assignments (the "details") changed. The patrolmen in the 1961 group in Table 28 appreciably changed their reported expectations regarding where they would be assigned after ten years on the job. Twenty-five per cent of the group at the beginning of their training indicated they expected to be in the patrol force or in the safety (traffic) division, but after two years in the field 56% of the group indicated they expected to be in one of these assignments when they have completed ten years on the job. Those expecting to still be a patrolman after ten years on the job increased from 3% at the outset of their training to 20% after two years in the field. Finally, although 62% of the group with two years in the field indicated they were studying for the next examination for promotion to sergeant, only 20% reported they were studying more than eight hours a week, on the average, for the next test.

It is not the case that the patrolmen failed to see the advantages

Table 28 *Responses of Patrolmen to: "Approximately how many years do you expect to stay on the force?"* (*in Per Cent*)

Group[a]	When Tested	Less than 20	20 to 25	25 to 30	30 to 35	35 or More
1961	1961	8	67	16	4	5
	1963	14	73	8	4	1
1962	1962	9	65	19	5	2
	1963	8	79	9	2	2

[a] See Table 24, footnote [a].

Table 29 *Patrolmen's View of Their Privileges Relative to Those of Police Superior Officers (in Per Cent)*

Item	Group[a]	No Answer	Strongly Agree	Agree	Uncertain	Disagree	Strongly Disagree
A	1961	0	20	36	17	27	0
	1962	2	13	41	15	29	0
B	1961	0	33	42	14	11	0
	1962	1	25	44	9	13	0

Item A: "Patrolmen have almost no privileges compared with what their supervisors have."
Item B: "It's a bosses' job."

[a] See Table 24, footnote [a].

of rank. On the contrary, they tend to see the relative advantages as marked for superior officers in the department. The experienced patrolmen indicated a high level of agreement that privileges are quite different for superior officers. In Table 29 the two groups of patrolmen with experience agreed pretty much that patrolmen have few privileges relative to their supervisors (item A). They show even more agreement with the frequently heard statement that "It's a bosses' job."

The patrolmen apparently changed their view of the extent to which patrolmen could rely on a "rabbi" or "hook" (a patron) to help them get the transfers or assignments they wanted (Table 30). In only 8% of the 1962 group at the end of their training agreed that patrolmen often got jobs they wanted as a personal favor, but after one year in the field 33% agreed (item A). The 1961 graduates after two years in the field were even more in agreement; 54% of this latter group agreed with item A.

The distribution of responses to an evaluative statement regarding this practice changed little for both the 1961 and 1962 graduates between their graduation and the time they were tested after some field experience. The modal response—to a statement that this practice is in the interests of the department as a whole—was that of "uncertain" for both groups at both points in time. From an individual patrolman's personal point of view the practice was both desirable and potentially undesirable, since he was not likely to be the only patrolman with a "rabbi." Thus, although the "rabbi" system may have given some sense of confidence about one's future in the department when an individual faced problems with the formal organization, the system did not guarantee that any one individual patrolman could better his lot relative to other patrolmen. Of course, sponsors varied in the degree they were "hung heavy," (that is, influential or powerful in the organization), and those with an influential sponsor could anticipate some ease in getting the sort of duty they desired.

This informal solution to the problem of getting a desired assignment is of course not the only solution to an individual patrolman's career problems in the organization. The high degree of perceived cohesiveness among patrolmen at the beginning of their training does not seem to be appreciably affected by their field experiences. As shown in Table 31, patrolmen tested at a number of different points

Table 30 *Attitudes Toward the "Rabbi" System (in Per Cent)*

Item	Group[a]	When Tested	No Answer	Strongly Agree	Agree	Uncertain	Disagree	Strongly Disagree
A	1962	End of training[b]	1	1	7	28	47	16
		One year in field	2	12	21	29	29	7
	1961	Two years in field	0	16	38	18	22	6
B	1962	End of training	0	1	19	45	27	8
		One year in field	2	2	22	44	25	5
	1961	End of training	3	7	28	40	14	8
		Two years in field	0	10	24	42	22	2

Item A: "Transfers or assignments are quite often made as a personal favor to a patrolman."
Item B: "Transfers or assignments made in this way usually work out all right for the department as a whole."

[a] See Table 24, footnote [a].
[b] The *N*'s at the end of training for the 1961 and 1962 academy graduates were, respectively, 108 and 164.

Table 31 *Perceived Cohesiveness among Patrolmen (in Per Cent)*

Item	Group[a]	No Answer	Strongly Agree	Agree	Uncertain	Disagree	Strongly Disagree
A	T_1	0	29	43	14	13	1
	T_2	1	25	47	11	14	2
	T_3	0	20	49	11	17	3
	T_4	0	17	52	6	20	5
B	T_1	1	42	40	8	8	1
	T_2	0	57	31	4	8	6
	T_3	1	61	26	4	7	1
	T_4	1	47	34	5	12	1
C	T_1	1	54	42	2	1	0
	T_2	5	58	34	2	1	0
	T_3	0	69	28	1	0	2
	T_4	0	64	33	2	0	1
D	T_1	0	4	20	26	39	11
	T_2	0	2	20	17	43	18
	T_3	0	3	19	11	46	21
	T_4	0	2	28	16	42	12

Item A: "The police department is really a large brotherhood in which each patrolman does his best to help all other patrolmen."
Item B: "A patrolman can always count on getting assistance from other patrolmen whenever he needs it."
Item C: "Patrolmen will quite automatically join in to help other patrolmen when it is apparent that help is needed."
Item D: "There is a significant number of patrolmen who will try to get out of doing anything to help other patrolmen."

[a] See Table 8, footnote [a].

in the early phase of their careers tend to be in strong agreement that the patrolmen constitute a "brotherhood" (item A) and that assistance from other patrolmen is not a rare commodity (items B and C). They further concur with one another in disagreeing that a significant number of patrolmen will avoid helping other patrolmen (item D). This cohesiveness is not only related to difficulties associated with handling citizens or police problems but also extends to the difficulties associated with a patrolman's relations with other officers, particularly with his supervisors.

The experienced patrolmen tested after one and two years in the field were more likely than not to agree that they should try on their own to participate informally in the education of police recruits. In Table 32 the majority of the experienced patrolmen in both groups endorsed statements to the effect that experienced patrolmen should familiarize recruits on field training exercises with practices and conditions at variance with academy training (items A and B).

The experienced men also concurred strongly with one another that experienced patrolmen do, in fact, contribute more to the job socialization of new patrolmen than do their supervisors (item C and D). The informal organization is probably maintained in this manner. Moreover, the experienced patrolmen are likely to feel that their sharing of knowledge is required behavior. Probably the individual novice patrolman quite often welcomes their help. He may often

Table 32 *Perceived Role of Experienced Patrolmen Vis-à-Vis Police Recruits (in Per Cent)*

Item	Group[a]	No Answer	Strongly Agree	Agree	Uncertain	Disagree	Strongly Disagree
A	1961	0	4	47	13	33	3
	1962	0	8	48	16	24	4
B	1961	0	2	51	18	28	1
	1962	0	4	52	15	27	2
C	1961	0	26	61	8	5	0
	1962	0	21	67	7	4	1
D	1961	0	17	72	5	5	1
	1962	1	18	66	7	7	1

Item A: "When experienced patrolmen have the chance they should let recruits who are on field training exercises know about the things the academy instructors won't talk about."
Item B: "Experienced patrolmen should let recruits in field training exercises know just how actual police work differs from the ideals taught at the academy."
Item C: "A new patrolman learns more from the older patrolmen than from his supervisors."
Item D: "The more experienced patrolmen generally do more to help a newer patrolman adjust to the job than do his supervisors."

[a] See Table 24, footnote [a].

Table 33 *Evaluation of Academy Training by Recent Graduates (in Per Cent)*

Item	Group[a]	No Answer	Strongly Agree	Agree	Uncertain	Disagree	Strongly Disagree
A	1961	0	6	39	25	29	1
	1962	0	10	35	23	32	0
B	1961	0	0	22	19	52	7
	1962	0	1	16	17	62	4

Item A: "The academy should change its training program a great deal in order to make it more useful for newer patrolmen."
Item B: "There is some truth to the statement that a new patrolman may be hurt more than helped by the training he gets in the academy."

[a] See Table 24, footnote [a].

find himself embroiled in a number of difficulties both with other patrolmen and with supervisors, since the academy training generally avoids discussion of many common practices which, to a greater or lesser degree, violate the rules of the department. Many experienced patrolmen and supervisors thought the academy had an "unrealistic" or "impractical" orientation. In attempting to present the "ideals" of police work, academy personnel were considered by many older officers to be overlooking critical aspects of police work. It was thus a common feeling among older officers that academy personnel must have never actually worked in the field units. For such officers in the field units this view of instructors served to explain the fact that the typical recruit was unaware of what experienced officers considered as important practices in the field.

The samples of patrolmen who received their academy training in 1961 and 1962 were not so negative in their evaluation of the training they received in the academy. Their responses (in 1963) to two items are somewhat but not not markedly unfavorable relative to the attitudes of "old-timers" (Table 33). Although the patrolmen in both groups are more likely to agree than disagree that the training would provide a more useful basis for the work (item A), approximately two-thirds of them disagreed that the training is more dysfunctional than functional (item B). Nevertheless, their overall response would not be encouraging to academy personnel.

Perhaps even less encouraging are the responses to the set of items

Table 34 *Patrolmen's Evaluation of Level of Job Activity (in Per Cent)*

Item	Group[a]	No Answer	Strongly Agree	Agree	Uncertain	Disagree	Strongly Disagree
A	1961	0	5	60	13	22	0
	1962	0	5	54	17	22	2
B	1961	0	4	51	15	28	2
	1962	0	6	29	24	39	2

Item A: "A patrolman will usually get along better on the job if he doesn't go looking for situations requiring police attention but handles them as the situations arise."
Item B: "Patrolmen who are always out looking for situations requiring police attention are the ones who usually get into trouble with their supervisors."

[a] See Table 24, footnote [a].

in Table 34. It has been stressed throughout this report that the problems of uncertainty for police create a large variety of difficulties for them. Although social scientists are familiar with police misconduct in regard to their use of force and other more visible areas of job performance, for the most part there has been almost no discussion of police inactivity. The responses in Table 34 bear on this problem rather directly and support the earlier thesis that inactivity becomes an informal prescription for patrolmen in the context of the uncertainties they face. The patrolmen are in some agreement that patrolmen should not "go looking for situations requiring police attention" (item A). Furthermore, the more experienced patrolmen (the 1961 group) strongly supported the statement that active patrolmen are those who "usually get into trouble with their supervisors" (item B). It would appear that the less experienced group had not yet attained the level of disenchantment of the more experienced group, which had a majority in agreement with this statement. Whether the 1962 graduates were moving in the same direction of the 1961 group is not clear, but almost one-quarter of the later graduates indicated they were uncertain concerning these particular costs to them of being an "active cop."

SUMMARY

We have presented some aspects of the training of police recruits and their first field experiences as these bear on the uncertainties experienced by police officers. Particular attention has been given to problems of adjustment to the role experienced by new patrolmen in the New York City Police Department.

The difficulties in organizing knowledge about the legal basis of police authority and in transmitting it to recruits are many. These difficulties are partly a function of the complexities of law and partly a function of a departmental concern that police officers be prepared to defend themselves from criticism through knowledge of the letter of the law rather than its spirit. Although not mentioned in our discussion, these difficulties may account in part for some officers' view of the law as fixed and immutable. Such a view of the law can create difficulties because it predisposes police to seek out quasi-legal or illegal solutions to their perceived problems.

In attempting to develop an *esprit de corps,* the academy seems not to have been successful in immunizing patrolmen against experiencing a strong feeling that their work is one that rates quite low in prestige in the eyes of their public. At the same time, the emphasis on police professionalization in recruit training probably increases the patrolmen's perception of the discrepancy between the socio-economic status that officers should have and the status they actually have.

We have seen that the academy's attempt to prepare recruits for the problems associated with face-to-face interaction with the public was problematic with respect to the appropriateness of content, for example, the admonitions to "be firm but courteous" and to "use your common sense," and with respect to the pedagogical methods used to transmit this knowledge, that is, the classroom lecture. Further, the reluctance of the academy to develop a comprehensive series of field training exercises was particularly problematic in regard to the development of interpersonal skills of the recruits.

This same reluctance to expose recruits to the field conditions associated with patrol presented problems for their adjustment to uncertainties stemming from the department, particularly the policies and beliefs about patrolman-supervisor interaction. Although it is difficult to conceive of a training program that would prepare recruits effectively for immersion in the belief system about supervision and use of punitive tactics by supervisors and the administration, the academy experiences of the recruits were likely to create a receptivity to the belief that supervisors often took punitive actions. Another problem was that of the recruits' receptivity to beliefs questioning the appropriateness of the administration of negative sanctions and to a belief in the damaging effects of such sanctions on the careers of patrolmen.

We consider that the training received by the recruits did not immunize them against other central attitudes that underlie ineffective performance. A case in point is the development, following the end of recruit training, of increased support for the use of force in situations where the legal basis is unclear. The development of attitudes supporting inactivity or apathy toward police problems encountered in the field, as related to the fear of punishment, was also discussed and presented as having severe consequences in view of the fact that the job performance of patrolmen is not supervised at the time a problem occurs and the fact that the nature of the work is often distasteful and threatening.

Perhaps our most significant inference from the analysis of the data on the New York Police Department is that a training program for police recruits faces two major dilemmas in preparing recruits for their later duties in the field. The first involves the question of whether to emphasize training strategies aimed at the development of self-directed and autonomous personnel or to emphasize strategies aimed at developing personnel over whom the organization can easily exercise control. It appears that the second strategy is the one most often emphasized.

The second dilemma is that involving the inconsistencies between what the academy considers ideal practices in police work and what the majority of men in the field consider to be the customary and perhaps more practical procedures in the field. The training program appeared to emphasize the former approach.

The costs to the department, as a whole, of choosing these alternatives have been described. Whether the costs might have been greater if the opposite strategies were chosen is not clear. Further, it is not even clear, that the dilemmas are as they appear to be; the conflict between control and autonomy and the conflict between ideal and actual may be more apparent than real. For example, the longer period of training undergone by professionals increases the control by the profession of the individual professional through the process of socialization rather than through direct control. In this manner social control and self control become synonymous.

Similarly, a better strategy to resolve the perceived conflict between ideal and actual practices might be to conceive of the conflict as a problem of adapting innovations in police work to the context of traditional practices in the field. That is, rather than conceive of ideal police work as being irreconcilable with many aspects of actual police work, training personnel perhaps should make every effort to introduce what they consider ideal practice into the training in such a way that it does not call for a major scrapping of what the men in the field units consider to be "tried and true." In this way, the ideal practices would be less likely to call forth a defensive reaction from personnel who see their own position or their advantages as threatened by innovations. The net effect of such a strategy should then be less subversion of academy training by experienced men in the field.

Under most circumstances one can expect that a change of any sort will have a number of costs for an organization. For police departments, which will always be strongly affected by social change in the larger society, an orientation that accepts change and its costs as a condition of organizational existence is far more functional than either the "reformer" or the conservative orientations that call for total change or none at all. The costs of the battle between reformers and the entrenched interests in police departments are not few. The conflict has often caused both factions to expend enormous amounts of time and energy conducting the battle on terrain not worth winning. The consequence for the "rookie" in police work is that he must choose between one faction or the other and his choice of one precludes conforming to the expectations of the other. From his point of view, withdrawal from the conflict may be the only possible solution to a conflict that he may see as irrelevant to the major objectives of law enforcement.

Selected Bibliography

Scholarly and applied interests in the police are so diverse and the potentially relevant literature so vast that no brief bibliography can suffice. The titles below were selected with emphasis on more recent works and those of a more sociological cast but also with an eye to introducing the reader to the range of material. No effort was made to cover the technical and administrative police literature; however, the items marked with a single asterisk(*) are important standard works which should serve as an introduction to that area.

A few books and articles have appeared in recent years which are especially significant for an appreciation of sociological perspectives on the police and law enforcement, though not all have been produced by sociologists. These titles are indicated by a double asterisk (**). The reader for whom a limited number of works must suffice would do well to start with these. Within this more limited list three books can be especially recommended, *The Policeman in the Community* by Michael Banton, *Arrest: The Decision to Take a Suspect into Custody* by Wayne R. LaFave, and *Justice without Trial: Law Enforcement in Democratic Society* by Jerome H. Skolnick.

GENERAL: POLICE FUNCTIONS AND SOCIAL CONTROL

** Bordua, David J., and Reiss, Albert J., Jr., "Command, Control and Charisma: Reflections on Police Bureaucracy," *American Journal of Sociology*, Vol. 72 (July 1966), pp. 68–76.

Coatman, John, *Police*. New York, Oxford University Press, 1958.

* International City Managers Association, *Municipal Police Administration*, 5th ed. Chicago: I.C.M.A., 1961.

International Police Association, *International Bibliography of Selected Police Literature*. Geneva: I.P.A., 1936.

* Los Angeles Police Department, *Daily Training Bulletin* (consisting of Bulletins 1–173). Springfield, Ill.: Charles C Thomas, 1954.

* Los Angeles Police Department, *Daily Training Bulletin* (consisting of Bulletins from volumes II, III, IV). Springfield, Ill.: Charles C. Thomas, 1958.

Westley, William A., *The Police: A Sociological Study of Law, Custom and Morality.* Unpublished Ph.D. dissertation, Department of Sociology, University of Chicago, 1951.

** Westley, William A., "Violence and the Police," *American Journal of Sociology,* Vol. XLIX (August 1953), pp. 34–41 .

** Westley, William A., "Secrecy and the Police," *Social Forces,* Vol. XXXIV (March 1956), pp. 254–7.

Whitaker, Benjamin C., *The Police.* London: Eyre and Spottiswoode, 1964.

* Wilson, O. W., *Police Administration,* 2d ed. New York: McGraw-Hill Book Co., 1963.

** Wilson, James Q., "The Police and Their Problems: A Theory," *Public Policy,* Vol. XII (1963), pp. 189–216.

POLICE HISTORY AND COMPARATIVE PERSPECTIVES

Bacon, Selden D., *The Early Development of American Municipal Police.* Unpublished Ph.D. dissertation, Yale University, 1939.

Baker, Joseph, *The Law of Political Uniforms, Public Meetings and Private Armies.* London: H. H. Just, 1937.

Bornecque-Winandy, E., *Histoire de la Police.* Paris: Les Editiones Int., 1950.

Buisson, Henry, *La Police, Son Histoire.* Paris: Nouvelles Éditiones Latines, 1958.

Chapman, Samuel G., *The Police Heritage in England and America.* East Lansing, Mich.: Michigan State University Press, 1962.

Costello, Augustine, E., *Our Police Protectors.* New York: C. F. Roper, 1885.

Cramer, James, *The World's Police.* London: Cassell, 1964.

Faralicq, René, *The French Police from Within.* London: Cassel, 1933.

Fosdick, Raymond, *European Police Systems.* New York: Century, 1915.

Hart, J. M., *The British Police.* London: Allen and Unwin, 1951.

Jeffrey, (Sir) Charles, *The Colonial Police.* London: M. Parrish, 1952.

MacNamara, Donal E. J., "American Police Administration at Mid-Century," *Public Administration Review,* Vol. X (Summer 1950), pp. 181–9.

NaKahara, Hidenori, "The Japanese Police," *Journal of Criminal Law, Criminology and Police Science,* Vol. 46 (1955), pp. 583–93.

Reith, Charles, *The Blind Eye of History.* London: Faber and Faber, 1952.

Reith, Charles, *A New Study of Police History.* Edinburgh: Oliver and Boyd, 1956.

Smith, Bruce, *Police Systems in the United States,* 2d rev. ed. New York: Harper and Row, 1960.

Solmes, Alwyn, *The English Policeman, 1871–1935*. London: Allen and Unwin, 1935.

POLICE AND THE INSTITUTIONS OF MODERN SOCIETIES

Bell, Daniel, *The End of Ideology*. Glencoe, Ill.: The Free Press, 1960.

Hirsch, Julius, *Polizei und Wirtschaft*. Berlin: Gersbach, 1926.

Marshall, Geoffrey, *Police and Government*. London: Methuen, 1965.

** Stinchcombe, Arthur, "Institutions of Privacy in the Determination of Police Administrative Practice," *American Journal of Sociology*, Vol. LXIX (September 1963), pp. 150–60.

** Stinchcombe, Arthur, "Social Structure and Organizations," *Handbook of Organizations*. James March, ed., Chicago, Rand-McNally, 1965.

Vollmer, August, *The Police and Modern Society*. Berkeley: University of California Press, 1936.

TOTALITARIAN CONTROL AND POLICE STATES

Arendt, Hannah, *The Origins of Totalitarianism*. New York: Harcourt, Brace, 1951.

Bramsted, Ernest J., *Dictatorship and Political Police*. London: Routledge and Kegan Paul, 1945.

Byrnes, Asher, *Government Against the People*. New York: Dodd, Mead, 1946.

Halevy, Daniel, *Decadence de la Liberte*. Paris: B. Grasset, 1931.

Neumann, Franz, *Behemoth*. London: V. Gollancz, 1942.

Thompson, Craig, *The Police State*. New York: Dutton, 1950.

POLICE IN THE COMMUNITY: PATTERNS OF CIVIC RELATIONSHIP AND PUBLIC PERSPECTIVE

** Banton, Michael, *The Policeman in the Community*. New York: Basic Books, 1965.

** Clark, John P., "Isolation of the Police: A Comparison of the British and American Situations," *Journal of Criminal Law, Criminology and Police Science*, Vol. 56 (1965), pp. 307–19.

Commission on Civil Rights, *Law Enforcement: A Report on Equal Protection in the South*. Washington, D.C.: U.S. Government Printing Office, 1965.

Gourley, G. Douglas, *Public Relations and the Police*. Springfield, Ill.: Charles C. Thomas, 1953.

Hare, Nathan, "The Ambivalent Public and Crime," *Crime and Delinquency*, Vol. 9 (Apr. 1963), pp. 145–51.

Ingersoll, John E., "The Police Scandal Syndrome," *Crime and Delinquency*, Vol. 10 (July 1964), pp. 269–75.

International Association of Chiefs of Police, *Police-Community Relations, Policies and Practices: A National Survey*. Washington, D.C.: I.A.C.P., 1964.

** Janowitz, Morris, Wright, Deil, and Delany, William, *Public Administration and the Public—Perspectives toward Government in a Metropolitan Community*. Ann Arbor: Bureau of Government, Institute of Public Administration, University of Michigan, 1958.

** Kephart, William M., *Racial Factors and Urban Law Enforcement*. Philadelphia: University of Pennsylvania Press, 1957.

Lieberson, Stanley, and Silverman, Arnold R., "The Precipitants and Underlying Conditions of Race Riots," *American Sociological Review*, Vol. 30 (December 1965), pp. 887–98.

** McMillan, George, *Racial Violence and Law Enforcement*. Atlanta: Southern Regional Council, 1960.

** McMullen, M. "A Theory of Corruption," *Sociological Review*, Vol. 9 (July 1961), pp. 181–201.

Rolph, C. H., ed., *The Police and the Public*. London: Heinemann, 1962.

Royal Commission on the Police 1962, *Final Report*, Cmnd. 1728. London: Her Majesty's Stationary Office, 1962.

** Royal Commission on the Police, Morton-Williams, R., *Relations Between the Police and the Public*, Appendix IV to the Minutes of Evidence. London: Her Majesty's Stationary office, 1962.

Shafter, Albert J., "Numerical Strength of Small Police Departments," *Journal of Criminal Law, Criminology and Police Science*, Vol. 52 (1961), pp. 344–6.

Wade, Richard C., *Slavery in the Cities: The South 1820–1860*. New York: Oxford University Press, 1964.

THE POLICEMAN'S ROLE AND LAW ENFORCEMENT DECISIONS

Barrett, Edward, "Police Practices and the Law—From Arrest to Release or Charge," *California Law Review*, Vol. 50 (March 1962), pp. 11–55.

Blum, Richard H., "The Problems of Being a Police Officer," *Police* (November–December 1960), pp. 10–3.

Blum, Richard H., "The Problems of Being a Police Officer," *Police* (January–February 1961), pp. 33–7.

** Cumming, Elaine, Cumming, Ian M., and Edell, Laura, "Policeman as Philosopher, Guide and Friend," *Social Problems*, Vol. 12 (Winter 1965), pp. 276–86.

Deutsch, Albert, *The Trouble with Cops*. New York: Crown, 1955.

Goldstein, Herman, "Police Discretion: The Ideal versus the Real," *Public Administration Review*, Vol. 23 (September 1963), pp. 140–8.

Goldstein, Joseph, "Police Discretion Not to Invoke the Legal Process: Low Visibility Decisions in the Administration of Justice," *Yale Law Journal*, Vol. 69 (1960), pp. 543–94.

LaFave, Wayne R., "The Police and Non-Enforcement of the Law," Parts I and II, *Wisconsin Law Review*, (January and March 1962), pp. 104–37 and 179–239.

Niederhoffer, Arthur, *A Study of Police Cynicism.* Unpublished Ph.D. dissertation, New York University, 1964.

** Piliavin, Irving, and Briar, Scott, "Police Encounters with Juveniles," *American Journal of Sociology*, Vol. LXX (September 1964), pp. 206–14.

** Preiss, Jack J., and Ehrlich, Howard J., *An Examination of Role Theory: The Case of the State Police*, Lincoln: The University of Nebraska Press, 1966.

** Skolnick, Jerome H., *Justice Without Trial: Law Enforcement in Democratic Society*, New York: John Wiley and Sons, 1966.

** Wilson, James Q., "Generational and Ethnic Differences among Career Police Officers," *American Journal of Sociology*, Vol. LXIX (March 1964), pp. 522–8.

LAW ENFORCEMENT AND SOCIAL POLICY: THE LEGAL CONTEXT OF POLICE WORK

Allen, Francis, *The Borderline of Criminal Justice: Essays on Law and Criminology.* Chicago: University of Chicago Press, 1964.

Arnes, Richard, and Lasswell, Harold D., *In Defense of Public Order: The Emerging Field of Sanction Law.* New York: Columbia University Press, 1961.

Blumberg, Abraham, *The Criminal Court: An Organizational Analysis.* Unpublished Ph.D. dissertation, New School for Social Research, 1964.

Donnelly, Richard C., Goldstein, Joseph G., and Schwartz, Richard D., *Criminal Law*, New York: The Free Press of Glencoe, 1962.

Hart, H. L. A., *Law, Liberty and Morality.* Stanford: Stanford University Press, 1963.

Kamisar, Yale, Inbau, Fred, Arnold, Thurman, *Criminal Justice in Our Time.* Charlottesville: The University Press of Virginia, 1965.

** LaFave, Wayne R., *Arrest: The Decision to Take a Suspect into Custody.* Boston: Little, Brown, 1965.

LaFave, Wayne R., "Improving Police Performance through the Exclusionary Rule— Part I: Current Police and Local Court Practices," *Missouri Law Review*, Vol. 30 (1965), pp. 391–458.

LaFave, Wayne R., "Improving Police Performance through the Exclusionary Rule—Part II: Defining the Norms and Training the Police," *Missouri Law Review*, Vol. 30 (1965), pp. 566–610.

Newman, Donald J., *Conviction: The Determination of Guilt or Innocence without Trial.* Boston: Little, Brown, 1966.

Packer, Herbert L., "Two Models of the Criminal Process," *University of Pennsylvania Law Review*, Vol. 113 (November 1964), pp. 1–68.

Simon, Rita James, *The Jury and the Plea of Insanity*. Boston: Little, Brown, 1966.

Skolnick, Jerome H., "The Sociology of Law in America: Overview and trends," *Law and Society* (a supplement to *Social Problems*) Vol. 13 (Summer 1965), pp. 4–39.

Sowle, Claude R., ed., *Police Power and Individual Freedom*. Chicago: Aldine Publishing Co., 1962.

Trebach, A. S., *The Rationing of Justice*. New Brunswick: Rutgers University Press, 1964.

Mary Kay

4/5 849-3281